Gibbons v. Ogden

LANDMARK LAW CASES

AMERICAN SOCIETY

Peter Charles Hoffer
N. E. H. Hull
Series Editors

HERBERT A. JOHNSON

Gibbons v. Ogden

John Marshall, Steamboats, and

the Commerce Clause

UNIVERSITY PRESS OF KANSAS

Published by the University Press of Kansas (Lawrence, Kansas 66045), which was
organized by the Kansas Board of Regents and is operated and funded by Emporia
State University, Fort Hays State University, Kansas State University, Pittsburg State
University, the University of Kansas, and Wichita State University

Library of Congress Cataloging-in-Publication Data

Johnson, Herbert Alan.
Gibbons v. Ogden : John Marshall, steamboats, and the commerce clause /
Herbert A. Johnson.
p. cm. — (Landmark law cases & American society)
Includes bibliographical references and index.
ISBN 978-0-7006-1733-3 (cloth : alk. paper)
ISBN 978-0-7006-1734-0 (pbk. : alk. paper)
1. Gibbons, Thomas, 1757–1826 — Trials, litigation, etc. 2. Ogden, Aaron,
1756–1839 — Trials, litigation, etc. 3. Fulton, Robert, 1765–1815 — Trials, litigation, etc.
4. Interstate commerce — Law and legislation — United States — History — 19th
century. 5. Inland navigation — Law and legislation — United States — History — 19th
century. 6. Steamboats — Law and legislation — Hudson River (N.Y. and N.J.) —
History — 19th century. I. Title. II. Title: Gibbons versus Ogden.
KF228.G528J64 2010
343.730815 — dc22
2010017082

British Library Cataloguing-in-Publication Data is available.

Printed in the United States of America

10 9 8 7 6 5 4 3 2 1

In memory of Colonel Abraham S. Robinson,
member of the New York Bar and
my mentor in appellate advocacy

CONTENTS

EDITORS' PREFACE

Gibbons v. Ogden, the so-called Fulton Steamboat Case, was one of the most complex and significant cases of the Marshall Court. At stake was the future of the interstate commerce clause of the federal Constitution and under it federal regulation of the economy, relations among the states relating to management of the waterways, the law of patents, and free enterprise itself. To top this off, the tangle of parties to the suit, ensnaring the leading businessmen, lawyers, and financiers of the day in a series of state and federal cases, was itself important to the resolution of the dispute. The outcome of the case, a victory of sorts for competition and federal regulation, heralded the expansion of entrepreneurship and investment in technology characteristic of the next two hundred years of American life. The steamboat industry was to the economy of early national America what the automotive industry is to our modern economy. *Gibbons* is surely a landmark case in American history.

It is also a vital case for understanding the personal and intellectual relationships on the High Court. Chief Justice John Marshall was not only a forceful advocate of national government and the central role of the federal courts, he was also a superb manager of the people who served on the Court with him. By 1824, no longer surrounded by fellow Federalists, *Gibbons* required all of Marshall's managerial skills to achieve consensus, and his opinion for the Court reflected the concessions and agreements that Marshall engineered to achieve near unanimity.

Finally, in its elaboration of the exclusive powers of the federal government, Congress, and the federal courts to monitor the course of interstate commerce, *Gibbons* was the first of what would become a flood of commerce clause cases. Indeed, until the passage of the Civil War Amendments, the commerce clause was the centerpiece of the High Court's docket. Thus *Gibbons* was the linchpin of much of the pre–Civil War Court's constitutional adjudication. For a time after the passage of the Fourteenth Amendment, the Court curbed Congress's power to regulate interstate commerce, but at the height of the New Deal, the Court once again deferred to Congress in this vital area of regulatory activity.

Gibbons has in the pages below found the perfect expositor. For nearly four decades, law professor and historian Herbert Johnson has explored the intricacies of the Marshall Court, in the process writing the definitive account of the Court and its members. Here he not only untangles the issues and the arguments in *Gibbons*, but also brings the protagonists to life. The human element — subterfuge, greed, and ambition, added to a family tragedy and an untimely death — played vital roles in the outcome of the litigation. So too did the elaborate and passionate pleading of the Irish-born Thomas Emmet and New England's own Daniel Webster. As he parses their argument, Johnson reveals how Emmet won the battle of the briefs (despite Webster's later boast that he alone had won the case for his client). We are once more treated to Chief Justice John Marshall and William Johnson's learned and elegant opinions from the bench.

Although there are other book-length accounts of the case, none is so clear, so compelling, and so definitive as this. It will be a landmark in the Landmark series.

The hardest task that a historian faces is to answer the query, "Why?" After forty-six years of studying, writing, and teaching about *Gibbons v. Ogden*, the answer still evades me. In part that is due to the meager nature of the surviving documentary evidence, a situation common to most decisions announced by the early Supreme Court of the United States. And the paucity of official records is accentuated by the relatively small corpus of private manuscript material left by Chief Justice John Marshall and many of his associate justices. To a limited degree, this situation has been improved by extensive recent explorations into the ways in which the Court conducted its business and the relationships that existed among the justices. This groundbreaking effort has greatly affected the way we view the so-called Marshall Court and the degree to which the chief justice influenced his colleagues. Today, virtually every scholar in the field would agree that Senator Albert J. Beveridge laid undue stress upon Marshall being a strong and forceful leader. Instead, there gradually has developed a broad consensus that after 1812 (and certainly after 1819), the chief justice began to serve as a mediator of differences among his associates. By the end of his judicial career, his persuasive abilities became the primary source of his authority within the counsels of the Court.

Indeed, this alteration in Marshall's functions, coupled with jurisprudential changes in key fields of constitutional law, has been identified as a mark of his decline in influence and as a failure of his leadership. Such a judgment mistakes the place that he inevitably would take in American history. When he was nominated by President John Adams and confirmed by the Senate in the last months of federalist political control, John Marshall's mission was clear: he was to guide the efforts of elderly federalist justices. Because most of them stood in proximate danger of impeachment and conviction by the incoming Jeffersonian Congress, they were badly in need of the political skills of their new chief justice. Having assumed a low profile, they willingly accepted an expansion of the per curiam opinions of the Ellsworth Court into the unitary opinion of the Court. Yet even then, it was abundantly clear that time would clear the federalist bench by death, illness, or resignation, and that new appointees would be chosen by Thomas Jefferson and confirmed by a Jeffersonian majority in the new Senate.

At the time of Marshall's appointment, there was doubt about how long the Supreme Court would retain its pro-federalist bias. When the Federalist Party unwisely and untimely compromised its future at the secessionist Hartford Convention late in 1814, and when universal white manhood suffrage was adopted by most states after 1820, there was no question that John Marshall was fated to lead a Supreme Court that increasingly would differ from him both in jurisprudence and in its view of the federal system. By the 1819 term, considered by many to be the high point of Marshall's influence, *Sturges v. Crowninshield* evidenced diversity of opinion concerning the constitutionality of state insolvency and bankruptcy laws. And in 1827, the chief justice dissented from the views of the majority in *Ogden v. Saunders*, and the Court fractured into a series of separate opinions by the justices. Almost at the chronological midpoint between those two cases, the Steamboat Case came before the Supreme Court.

A major supposition of this volume is that *Gibbons* represents an important transitional point in Marshall's career — and it is also the most significant example of his ability to gain agreement despite the existence of extreme differences among his colleagues. This is, in fact, the primary skill required for the effective exercise of the chief justice's office today. But we have failed to recognize its introduction by Chief Justice Marshall, probably because of his historical identification by Senator Beveridge as a "strong" chief justice who dominated his colleagues throughout his presidency over the Court. *Gibbons*, as a mediated opinion and as a demonstration of the deft use of dicta coupled with a narrow holding, is entitled to much closer attention than it has hitherto received.

I hope that this book will begin to answer the "why" questions surrounding *Gibbons:* (1) Why is the Court opinion so ambiguous and even self-contradictory? (2) Why did Justice Johnson file a nationalist-oriented concurring opinion? (3) Why did Marshall avoid key issues, such as the role of the dormant commerce clause, or the relationship of foreign trade, interstate commerce, and diplomatic relations? (4) Why did the New York courts and both sets of trial counsel anticipate that the Court would deal with the federal patent versus state monopoly issue, and why didn't Marshall do so? Perhaps the most perplexing question of all is, "Why do we persist in claiming that the Webster–Wirt team won their case, and why do we accept the inaccurate perception that *Gibbons* established that the Constitution bestowed upon Congress an exclusive power to regulate interstate commerce?"

Scholarship may be a solitary occupation, but it is made enjoyable and enriched by contributions of others. At an early stage in the development of this project, I was asked to conduct a two-hour presentation on *Gibbons* for a group of high school teachers at a Teaching of American History conference. A short way into our time together, it became apparent that talking about the case also involved dealing with a vast body of material that we in higher education artificially divide into law and economics, sociology, Supreme Court history, constitutional law and theory, politics, and biography. It was a learning experience for me, and it has shaped the approach I have taken toward gaining a greater understanding of Chief Justice Marshall and the Steamboat Case. Similarly, some of the "why" questions I have asked, and the explanations I have tendered, are derived from those frequent times in the classroom when the questions and perceptions of students have jarred me away from preconceptions and inadequately considered judgments. Academic administrators tend to stress the fact that scholarly research and writing enriches teaching, but it is also true that in the classroom, our routine assumptions are challenged and new understandings are launched by the questions and requests for clarification raised by students. More than four decades of teaching, at the undergraduate, graduate, and law school levels, have done much to sharpen my analysis of *Gibbons* and the work of the Marshall Court.

This study would never have been undertaken had it not been for the persistent urging from Peter Hoffer, who flattered me with the assertion that I was the one who should write this book for the Landmark Law Cases series. After completing a first draft, I received a vigorous reading from Professor Hoffer as editor of the series. That review was invaluable in reorienting and simplifying the organization of the book. He graciously refrained from observing that his hard editorial work was payback for his earlier misplaced enthusiasm about my writing abilities.

It was my good fortune that Dr. Charles F. Hobson, the principal editor of *The Papers of John Marshall*, was asked by the University Press of Kansas to serve as an outside reader for the book. Predictably, his comments were exceptionally useful in identifying errors concerning Marshall's career and in correcting particular points involving *Gibbons v. Ogden*. More generally, Dr. Hobson has been generous in providing advice from, and facilitating access to, the reference files of the John Marshall Papers project; and with all students of the Marshall Court, I am most grateful to him for his outstanding editorial work on the recently completed *Papers of John Marshall*.

At an early stage in writing this book, I profited from an extensive discussion with Professor Thomas H. Cox of Sam Houston State University, who has recently published his doctoral dissertation on *Gibbons v. Ogden*. He kindly permitted me access to the text of the dissertation before its publication, and this was most helpful in allowing me to check various details concerning the case and the social and economic factors touching upon the development of the steamboat and the Livingston–Fulton monopoly.

Editors are the unsung heroes in the desperate battle to maintain the clarity and accurate use of the English language. My editors at the University Press of Kansas have been precise, painstaking, and long suffering; it has been a pleasure and privilege to work with them. They include Karen Hellekson, Larisa Martin, and Kelly Chrisman Jacques. I am deeply grateful for all that they have done to make this a better book.

Finally, it has been a pleasure to work with Michael J. Briggs. As editor in chief at the University Press of Kansas, he always has been available to provide help and support as the project moved forward. Despite our long and pleasant association through the years, this is my first experience of working on a book under his guidance, and I have been impressed with how, despite his many obligations, he can still find the time to make an author's manuscript seem to be of primary concern both to him and to the press's staff.

Families always play an important, but sometimes only intangible, role in the research and writing of a book. My family has sweat equity — or, more properly, eyestrain — in this volume. My daughter, Amanda

B. Johnson, carefully read the chapters as they emerged from my computer and made several useful corrections—typographical, grammatical, and substantive. As has always been the case since our marriage, my wife, Jane McCue Johnson, read the book in its completed state and made similar corrections. In humoring my persistence in writing history some seven years into retirement, Jane has been patient and tolerant as boxes of notes and cartons of books accompany us south to St. Simons Island every winter. For this family support, both tangible and intangible, I am deeply grateful.

Herbert A. Johnson
St. Simons Island, Georgia
December 2009

Gibbons v. Ogden

Introduction

Gibbons v. Ogden (1824) was a case heard by the U.S. Supreme Court on appeal from New York's court for the trial of impeachments and the correction of errors, the highest court in the New York court system. The New York legislature had granted a monopoly of steamboat navigation to Robert R. Livingston and Robert Fulton on the basis of their successful establishment of regular steamboat service between New York City and Albany. Colonel Aaron Ogden, a former governor of New Jersey, was licensed by the Livingston–Fulton syndicate to navigate by steam between Elizabeth, New Jersey, and New York City. In the New York chancery court, he sued for, and obtained, an injunction against Thomas Gibbons, a steamboat operator who carried passengers between the same two cities, contrary to the terms of the New York monopoly. Gibbons asserted that the federal Coasting Licensing Act of 1793 authorized him to operate his steamboats in all coastal waters of the United States. He also argued that the Livingston–Fulton monopoly under which Ogden sued violated the commerce clause of the federal Constitution and thus was illegal. The New York state courts upheld the monopoly and continued to enjoin Gibbons until their decision was reversed by the U.S. Supreme Court in *Gibbons v. Ogden.*

Also known as the Steamboat Case, *Gibbons* is undoubtedly one of the most important appellate cases ever decided by the Supreme Court of the United States, and yet thirty-seven years have elapsed since the publication of Maurice G. Baxter's excellent volume, *The Steamboat Monopoly*, Gibbons v. Ogden, *1824*. A component part of the Borzoi Series in United States Constitutional History, edited by Paul L. Murphy, this little and well-written volume has served its readers well and has been of great value to teachers and students of American constitutional history. Now out of print, Baxter's monograph continues to be a valuable store of factual information concerning *Gibbons*, but it is in need of supplementation by a brief volume that will draw on more recent scholarship in constitutional history as well as new understandings of the Marshall Court and the chief justice himself.

Since 1972, American legal and constitutional history has been involved in integrating this hitherto highly specialized field into the mainstream of American history. This "law and society" approach, initially developed by James Willard Hurst and his even more influential disciple, Lawrence M. Friedman, has definitely come of age since 1972. Among other interpretive innovations, it has called the legal history community to pay closer attention to the nondoctrinal and extrajudicial factors that shape the development of law; at the same time, it has called to the attention of nonlegal historians the rich treasure of social and cultural history that previously laid dormant in statutes, court records, and law office papers. Despite the sharp decline in American constitutional history offerings in undergraduate curricula, the law and society approach has greatly affected both teaching and research. Quite properly, it has insisted that what had once been an undue focus on U.S. Supreme Court opinions should be broadened to deal with political and legislative activity as primary factors in shaping an ever-evolving federal Constitution. Increasingly, the emphasis on economic determinism, originating in the work of Charles Beard and Max Lerner in the early twentieth century, has achieved greater credibility in the constitutional history field, and it also plays a role in current writing in and teaching of American constitutional history.

Recently, *Gibbons* has received the broad law and society coverage that it deserves: in 2009 Thomas H. Cox published his detailed and exhaustively researched monograph, Gibbons v. Ogden, *Law, and Society in the Early Republic*. As the Bibliographical Essay at the end of this book indicates, this monograph has provided me with valuable information; however, the conclusions in this volume do not necessarily duplicate those reached by Cox.

Less spectacular in a historiographic sense is the redirection, since 1972, of the older institutional approach to the history of the Supreme Court of the United States. Initially the institutional writing limited its inquiries primarily to discussing the jurisdiction, procedures, and personnel of courts and other judicial and quasi-judicial bodies. This nuts-

2 { *Introduction* }

and-bolts examination of judicial activity produced a vast expansion of knowledge concerning administrative details and the common-law method of adjudication. But when applied to the work of the U.S. Supreme Court, it ignored vital considerations of the degree to which the justices were influenced by factors quite remote from the arguments of counsel or the demands of precedent. As a consequence, there has been a change in historical approach to constitutional history, beginning in the late 1960s and drawing on the availability of data processing methods to handle Supreme Court documentation more efficiently.

Fortunately, this more expansive approach to understanding Supreme Court decision making coincided with the initial publication of the first volumes in the *Oliver Wendell Holmes Devise History of the Supreme Court of the United States*. Specifically, the second volume of that series, *Foundations of Power—John Marshall, 1801–1815*, written by George L. Haskins and Herbert A. Johnson, and the third and fourth volumes, *The Marshall Court and Cultural Change*, authored by G. Edward White, combine exhaustive coverage of the Court's case law with due attention to nonjudicial elements that impacted policy choices and decision making. In addition, there have been numerous monographs dealing with the institution of the chief justice of the Court, augmented by important biographical studies of individual justices. On the chief justiceship, the works of Peter G. Fish, *The Office of Chief Justice*, and Robert J. Steamer, *Chief Justice: Leadership and the Supreme Court*, are particularly notable, and the biographical contributions of R. Kent Newmyer, *John Marshall and the Heroic Age of the Supreme Court* and *Supreme Court Justice Joseph Story: Statesman of the Old Republic*, are exceptional examples of the new biographical approach to the Marshall Court. Finally, the praiseworthy national effort at editing of statesmen's papers dating to 1947 has produced two recent publications of valuable source materials useful for understanding the Supreme Court in the Marshall era: *The Documentary History of the Supreme Court of the United States, 1789–1800* (edited by Maeva Marcus et al.), and *The Papers of John Marshall* (edited by Charles F. Hobson et al.). These editorial projects have in turn generated important monographic studies, including a series of essays, *Origins of the Federal Judiciary: Essays on the Judiciary Act of 1789* (edited by Maeva Marcus), and a monograph by Charles F. Hobson, *The Great Chief Justice: John Marshall and the Rule of Law*.

With such an abundance of new materials and a broadening perspective on the history of the U.S. Supreme Court, there has occurred a modest revision in historical understanding both of Chief Justice John Marshall and of his Court. Senator Albert J. Beveridge's four-volume Pulitzer-winning biography of Marshall, *The Life of John Marshall* (published 1916–1919), cast a long shadow on studies of the chief justice and his Court. Consequently there was a tendency to view Marshall as the dominant figure on the highest court until his death in 1835, with only a slight decline in authority after 1830. More recent scholarship, following the 1954 lead of Donald G. Morgan in his biography of Justice William Johnson, *Justice William Johnson, the First Dissenter: The Career and Constitutional Philosophy of a Jeffersonian Judge*, has recognized that during or immediately after the War of 1812, decision making on the Court was becoming more collegial. However, considering the monumental decisions in the 1819 term, it was apparent that the chief justice still enjoyed considerable ability to influence the Supreme Court's disposition of important cases. Both *McCulloch v. Maryland* and *Dartmouth College v. Woodward* were announced in that noteworthy term. On the other hand, *Sturges v. Crowninshield*, dealing with state insolvency legislation and the federal Constitution's bankruptcy and contract clauses, appeared to avoid the decision of difficult questions when it was announced in 1819. Subsequently in 1827, Justice Johnson revealed that there was in fact a sharp difference within the justices concerning the complex constitutional issues presented. A compromise, presumably brokered by the chief justice, resulted in a decision based on the contract clause's prohibition of retroactive state legislation impairing contractual obligations.

Coming on for the Supreme Court's consideration in 1824, *Gibbons v. Ogden* has perplexed both public understanding at the time the Court's opinion was announced and understanding also among the legal profession and scholars ever since. This volume suggests that the internal contradictions and complexity of the Court's opinion are because John Marshall was making a valiant attempt to mediate the differences on the Supreme Court and to produce an opinion that, through its dicta rather than its narrow holding, would give guidance to future Courts as they struggled to adjust the commerce clause to growing divergence of opinion concerning the nature and extent of American federalism. *Gibbons* is thus a very important case for the history of the Supreme Court, and for a better understanding of the relationship of Chief Justice Marshall to his colleagues.

The Steamboat Case is also an important piece of constitutional history, and it continues to exercise a formative impact on present-day constitutional discussion and analysis. We know that recently, in a series of decisions beginning with *U.S. v. Lopez* (1995), the Rehnquist Court began to reexamine the hitherto sweeping and broad construction of the commerce clause that began in 1937, and a brief treatment of those, and earlier, consequences of the *Gibbons* decision is included in Chapters 7 and 8. It is not an exaggeration to say that the commerce clause, with the possible exception of the Fourteenth Amendment, is the most important provision in the federal Constitution. That certainly is true in terms of economic regulation both within the federal union and in international affairs.

Quantitatively, the commerce clause has provided a rich source of litigation at the Supreme Court level. When in 1952 Edward S. Corwin provided Supreme Court annotations to an edition of *The Constitution of the United States*, later published by the Government Printing Office, approximately half of the total number of pages were devoted to the clause covering foreign and interstate commerce. A close second in terms of page count was those sections devoted to the Fourteenth Amendment or its application of the federal Bill of Rights to the various states. Obviously that situation has reversed itself since Chief Justice Earl Warren took office in 1953, but commerce clause adjudication has continued to define economic federalism within the federal union.

Beginning in 1824 with *Gibbons v. Ogden* until the ratification of the Thirteenth, Fourteenth, and Fifteenth Amendments (1865–1870), Supreme Court elaborations of commerce clause doctrine have defined the nature and scope of U.S. government power. After 1870 that function was shared with new considerations of individual rights and liberties and their guarantee by the Constitution and its post–Civil War amendments. From 1937 to 1995 the Supreme Court proved willing to allow Congress virtual plenary power in regulation of commercial matters, and it also broadly construed what might be included within the "commerce" category. Not until the decision of *U.S. v. Lopez* was there once more a judicial restriction of federal power under the commerce clause. One hundred seventy-one years after the Court's opinion in the Steamboat Case, the Court once more began the task identified by John Marshall: respecting the internal economic life of the states while at the same time protecting the federal common market from state-based interference.

Professor Kent Newmyer has correctly pointed out that Marshall-era cases have acquired a certain mythological status in American law, even though in many instances they are cited either in support of principles they never decided or as window dressing that appears to enhance more relevant, and more modern, precedents. The narrowness of the Court's holding in *Gibbons* renders nearly all of the lengthy opinion subject to being identified as dicta. A dictum is an observation in a judge's opinion that was not necessary to the court's holding in the case; as we have mentioned, and as contemporary observers complained, the Court's opinion in *Gibbons* is certainly packed with dicta. As a result, most references to the Steamboat Case in modern litigation are bound to rely on the persuasive quality of a mere observation, rather than ruling case law. Yet the materials cited, be they the product of Marshall's thought or contributions from those of his associate justices, are extremely useful in arriving at a wise and equitable solution to the controversies that come before the Supreme Court. What is remarkable about Marshall's verbiage in *Gibbons* is that, like Sir Edward Coke's maxims and adages in his *Reports* and *Institutes of the Law*, it captures in a usable and accessible expression form some of the basic principles of American constitutional law.

As I have suggested, the *Gibbons* case arrived at the Supreme Court at a turning point in the dynamics of decision making within the Court. Although Chief Justice Marshall's dominance of Court leadership had long passed, the judges had benefitted greatly through the innovations introduced by Marshall when he became chief justice in 1801. When in *Marbury v. Madison* (1803) he solidified the place of judicial review in federal constitutional law, the chief justice also introduced the unitary opinion of the Court as the preferred method for publicly justifying the decisions of the Supreme Court. At some point between the *Sturges* compromise of 1819 and John Marshall's first dissent in a constitutional law case (*Ogden v. Saunders*, 1819), the justices must have retained a preference for the Court issuing unitary opinions. However, they also recognized that when they had strong reservations about the explanation of the Court's opinion, they might feel free to issue either a concurring or dissenting opinion. Perhaps that occurred in *Gibbons*, but even if it did not, it is apparent that achieving a single Court opinion in the Steamboat Case represented a serious challenge to the unitary opinion system. As a corollary, John Marshall's opinion in *Gibbons* demonstrated that a skillful draftsman could arrive at a narrow but mutual decisive rationale that would please all of the justices. At the same time, the acceptance and integration of concurring and dissenting views might be expressed in dicta, and thus be preserved for future use by counsel, or perhaps even adoption as ruling case law by a subsequent and different panel of Supreme Court justices.

Leadership on the Supreme Court is exercised in a variety of patterns, and it was John Marshall's mission to adapt to two different situations: first, a Court composed of elderly justices faced with overwhelming political power in both the executive and judicial branches of a federal government on the brink of impeachment for partisan judicial behavior, and second, a growing and increasingly vocal minority of Jeffersonian and Jacksonian justices whose political, economic, and social views sharply contrasted with those of Marshall and his conservative colleagues on the bench. The first situation faded away with the death of Justice Samuel Chase in 1811; the second situation was arguably in place with the confirmation of Justice Smith Thompson in 1823. Thereafter, Chief Justice Marshall played the difficult role of leading by encouraging consensus rather than by exercising influence with men who shared his political views and profited from the anonymity offered by a chief justice who wrote unitary opinions in which they could concur without political reprisal. In this second role, Marshall was demonstrably less successful than he was in the first, but the task was infinitely more delicate and demanding.

It has become a commonplace to assert that Chief Justice Marshall laid the foundations for the greatness of the Supreme Court in American history, and it is also customary to point to the achievements up to and including the 1819 term to justify that conclusion. Yet it cannot be denied that it was Marshall who took the lead in establishing a pattern of collective leadership after 1823, and that the new dynamic was given its first serious test in *Gibbons v. Ogden*, followed by *Brown v.*

Maryland (1827). It was a task for which the chief justice was well qualified, and indeed, before 1823 there was already evidence that he was adept at mediating differences of opinion among his fellow justices. At the same time, it would prove to be of growing importance to the smooth administration of Court business and public confidence in its decision making. Conversely, the first situation in which Marshall found himself from 1801 through 1811 has not repeated itself in the history of the Court. If that is the case, then *Gibbons* has additional importance not only in judicial history, but also in its contribution to our growing understanding of judicial leadership and the role of the chief justice of the Supreme Court since Marshall's incumbency in that office.

It has long been uncritically accepted that Daniel Webster's argument dominated the Court's decision in *Gibbons*. Indeed, Webster himself not immodestly asserted that he alone had triumphed over ineffectual opposing counsel. Yet a reading of the arguments of counsel, and a reconsideration of Chief Justice Marshall's opinion for the Court, would indicate a contrary interpretation. Indeed, the evidence suggests that both Webster and his co-counsel, William Wirt, were overconfident, ill-prepared, and outgunned by the opposition. In any litigation, and especially in appellate practice, careful preparation is essential to achieving success.

In addition, the delay of the final hearing of the *Gibbons* appeal from its original 1821 appearance on the Supreme Court's docket until the final decision in 1824 may well have impacted the Court's reception of the case. Politically, the climate shifted away from concern about congressionally launched internal improvements. Constitutionally, the Court asserted its "federal question" appellate authority in *Cohens v. Virginia*. Associate Justice Brockholst Livingston died and was replaced by Smith Thompson, who had served on the New York court of impeachment and errors when it denied Thomas Gibbons relief, thereby triggering the appeal to the U.S. Supreme Court. And then two unforeseen events occurred. Newly confirmed justice Thompson was delayed in taking his seat on the Court during the terminal illness and death of his daughter, thus removing him from advocating the steamboat monopoly position in the Court's conferences. Then immediately after the conclusion of oral argument, Chief Justice Marshall injured his arm in an accident, slowing the announcement of the Court's opinion by a month and adding Justice Story to assist the chief justice in the preparation of the Court's opinion. That delay gave rise to much speculation and facilitated the issuance of Webster's self-serving claims that have colored both contemporary views and historical interpretations of the Supreme Court's decision in *Gibbons*.

As a contribution to the Landmark Law Cases & American Society series, this volume is intended for classroom use and as a quick introduction to *Gibbons v. Ogden* for the general reader. Like many other monographs in this series, it strives to provide readers with an understanding of the major scholarly interpretations dealing with the commerce clause, and it also attempts to place the Steamboat Case in a new perspective, thereby encouraging continued study of the relationship between economic regulation and constitutional government. It is appropriate that *Gibbons* and its impact on Court history, Marshall studies, and federalism be reconsidered as we move closer to the 2 March 2024 bicentennial year of its announcement.

CHAPTER I

The Background of the Commerce Clause

Gibbons v. Ogden, the so-called Steamboat Case, stands at the junction of economic, technological, and constitutional history. It brings to a close a tentative and uncertain phase in American legal and economic development, but it also launches a new era in federalism and lays a firm foundation for centralized regulation of American commercial activity. Neither Marshall's encyclopedic exposition of commercial regulation nor the federal Constitution's commerce clause itself represented novel issues for the new nation. Indeed, the history of trade and the record of political regulation of commercial activity extends even before classical periods of Greek and Roman civilization. Doubtless even those remote antecedents impacted *Gibbons,* but it is sufficient to limit this introductory consideration to the colonial period of American history, the Revolutionary War, and the critical period of our national development under the Articles of Confederation.

Two constitutions preceded our present federal Constitution, which was ratified in 1788. The first was that of the British empire and its constituent colonies, and the second was the Articles of Confederation. Good constitutional history demands that we examine these earlier governmental systems and that we briefly assess the degree to which the Constitution's commerce clause and the Supreme Court's decision in *Gibbons* were shaped by America's collective memory of government under both earlier constitutions. That influence was both positive and negative. Historical recollection can provide sound foundations on which to build new institutions, but it can also mislead men and nations by generating irrational fears that inhibit constructive and innovative thought and action.

Were it not for England's quest for commercial advantage over European rivals, it is likely that the American colonies that became the United States would never have been established. Long-standing but elusive efforts to find a northwest passage to China, Japan, and the East Indies drove the exploratory and early settlement efforts of the Elizabethans and the new Stuart dynasty. However, as colonial populations became stabilized and staple crops such as tobacco, and later rice, indigo, and cotton, became of economic significance, organization of the expanding empire demanded growing attention from imperial administrators in London. Ironically, the first statutory effort to control empirewide trade was launched not by royal officials, but by the bureaucrats of the Interregnum Parliament, which in 1651 introduced balance-of-trade mercantilism into colonial administration. Fine-tuned by Charles II's colonial administrators and reenacted early in the Restoration era, this scheme required that colonial exports and imports be carried in vessels constructed either in England or its colonies. It also stipulated that any commercial transactions with European nations or their colonies were to occur only after colonial cargoes were transshipped through a port located in England. These so-called navigation acts, frequently amended and with enforcement gradually tightened, applied until the eve of the American Revolution. They greatly increased the profitability of empire building and ensured that trade balances accrued to the English (and later the Scottish) merchants who traded with the New World. In addition, colonial export and import duties provided a reliable and increasing crown income that was not dependent on the willingness of the English (and later British) Parliament to impose additional taxes or to allocate additional revenues to the monarch's "civil list," which was money provided for the support of the ruler, his family, and his retainers.

During the eighteenth century, the North American colonies began to diversify into manufacturing activities, thereby threatening competition with goods imported from England and Scotland. To ensure that trade balances continued to favor Britain, Parliament enacted statutes that specifically prohibited colonial production of iron (1750 and 1757) and that drastically reduced the number of apprentices who could be trained by American master hatters (1732). Well before the American Revolution, and indeed almost from the inception of the empire itself, colonial commercial arrangements were so structured that benefit accrued almost entirely to those British merchants and industries that depended on North American trade for their markets.

Subordination of colonial economic growth to British commercial prosperity accelerated after the 1689 accession of William of Orange to the English throne in 1689. As the de facto leader of continental Protestantism, William III and his royal successors involved England, after 1707 Britain, in protracted and expensive wars with France and its allies (1689 through 1763). Several of those conflicts were triggered by clashes between English, French, and Spanish settlers in the New World. Although colonial troops played a variety of roles in these wars, British military and naval units bore the brunt of defending the empire. Understandably, the Cabinet and Parliament sought new sources of income to support the military forces during the wars and to maintain sizable troop garrisons in the major North American colonial cities. When the Grenville administration in 1765 secured legislation imposing a stamp tax on the colonies, the Stamp Act Congress loudly protested that although external taxation of trade was in accordance with the British constitution, an internal excise tax might be imposed within the colonies only with the consent of the colonial assemblies. In response to these intercolonial objections demonstrated by the formal protest of the Stamp Act Congress, by violent rioting, and by compelled resignations of royal stamp tax collectors, Parliament repealed the stamp tax but simultaneously enacted the Declaratory Act of 1766, asserting its right to tax the colonies in all things whatsoever. As a consequence, trade regulation became the rationale for a series of parliamentary statutes that either imposed importation duties on goods brought into the colonies or, alternatively, subsidized British goods or Indian tea imports into the colonies, threatening to establish increased monopolization of colonial markets.

Plainly, the economic manipulation of Britain's colonial empire emphasized centralized regulation of colonial trade; it provided many benefits to the crown, to Parliament, and to the mercantile community. Against this experience from their colonial history, newly independent Americans feared that even an American-controlled central government might well use taxes, or other restrictions on trade, to control and exploit the states, even as Britain had dominated its colonies. Consequently, the Articles of Confederation, which went into effect in 1781, not only provided a weak revenue base for the central government, but also failed to give the Congress any authority to regulate commercial activity between or among the various states.

Several proposals to amend the Articles and to permit Congress to tax imports were defeated. Although the Confederation Congress was empowered to regulate foreign commerce and trade with the Indian tribes, it lacked any authority over interstate trade, nor could it tax that commerce to relieve the central government's precarious financial situation.

During the Revolutionary War, a modicum of cooperation necessarily existed between the states and the Continental Congress, but victory removed pressing demands that the several "sovereign" states and their national congress work together against the common enemy. At the same time, the onerous wartime task of supplying America's military forces highlighted a critical need for improved systems of transportation. When campaigns stalled in one geographical area for an extended period of time, vital supplies of food and clothing for troops, forage for horses, fuel for fires, and shelter from the elements all became scarce. Overland transport was difficult even in the best of times, and the large rivers that carried supplies more easily were most frequently under British military or naval control. Rivers provided easy transportation in only one direction: downstream. Moving troops and supplies upriver was in all cases difficult, and when dealing with large streams marked by rapid and forceful flow or tidal action, virtually impossible. These wartime challenges were a portent of the difficulties that would arise when Americans attempted to settle, and trade with, the vast western territory secured to them by the peace treaty in 1783.

Even before independence, certain provinces and cities enjoyed commercial advantages originating from their geographical characteristics or well-established trade patterns. Large protected harbors suitable for oceangoing vessels were the most fortunate; they included the seaports of Boston, Providence, New York City, Philadelphia, Baltimore, Norfolk, and Charleston. When a harbor's tidal flow and bottom characteristics precluded silting, maintenance costs were low and safety conditions were optimal. Also important were the size and productivity of the hinterland served by the harbor. The rich farming areas of New York, Pennsylvania, Virginia, and Maryland did much to enhance the flow of traffic through their colonial seaports, while Providence, with a relatively small backcountry, early began to rely on the oceanic slave trade for much of its commercial activity. Colonial New Jersey found access to markets through the major neighboring port cities of New York and Philadelphia. Alexandria in northern Virginia found its commercial growth jeopardized by the proximity of Baltimore, even as its hinterland was within the service area of Philadelphia. These inequities generated resentment between the colonies and subsequently among their successor state governments; they also gave added emphasis to state-based initiatives designed to give commercial advantages to local merchants and producers to the detriment of interstate competition.

Over the past century, historians have debated whether the years from the end of the Revolution to the implementation of the new federal Constitution in 1789 constituted a critical period. Certainly many contemporaries viewed this transitional time as being marked by economic distress. There is undeniable evidence of economic hardship and popular discontent brought on by difficulties in restoring or re-creating international trade patterns. And unquestionably there were numerous examples of competition for commercial advantage among the various states. These included state efforts to monopolize their internal markets as well as legislation to impose duties or tariffs on exports, imports, or both. At the same time, it is also true that the several state governments were able to minimize suffering; in some notable instances, two or more state governments were willing and able to work collectively to mitigate the effects of economic depression. Gradually, the states and the American people began to make progress toward recovery even as the Philadelphia convention was preparing its proposals for a new central government. In retrospect, it seems most plausible to conclude that these difficult postwar years were times of experimentation in a broad spectrum of areas. Seeking a constitutional remedy for economic imbalances, statesmen explored the possibility of reshaping federalism, of innovating new forms of state government, and of testing new means and systems by which they might achieve both economic regulation and interstate cooperation. To many leaders in the early republic, both goals seemed to be of vital concern to all Americans and essential to national survival.

Given the importance of commerce to the well-being of the United States, it is not surprising that even under the Articles of Confederation there had already been substantial cooperation among the states. Indeed, the Articles themselves provided some of the instrumentalities within which joint interstate efforts might be made. Within the British empire, there had been a system for the adjustment of colonial boundary disputes through a mixed commission, followed by Privy Council appellate review if the arbitrated decision was unacceptable. A similar mixed commission arrangement was included within the Articles and used to adjust territorial disputes between New York and Massachusetts, and between Connecticut and Pennsylvania. During the Confederation period, the mixed commission achieved two goals. First, it preserved the then-existing preference for individual state sovereignty, and second, it provided a neutral and peaceful method for adjusting critical interstate territorial issues. Significantly, the mixed commission arrangement was applied internationally in the 1794 treaty negotiated by John Jay between the United States and Great Britain. The Jay treaty adjusted outstanding commercial and territorial claims between the two nations, and the mixed commission was tasked with arranging for an amicable settlement of trade debts owed by Virginia planters and other American agriculturalists to their British merchant creditors.

Although the Articles of Confederation delegated limited powers to the central government, it was necessary to provide Congress with specifically enumerated powers without which it could not function as a nation within the expectations of international law. This included Congress's supervisory authority over the decisions of state prize courts. These were wartime tribunals authorized by international law to condemn and dispose of enemy vessels and cargos captured by American warships and privateers. In the exercise of its military and diplomatic functions, Congress needed the power to review state prize decisions for conformity to international law and treaties. Unfortunately, this need for a unitary central supervision of wartime prize jurisdiction was not duplicated in regard to peacetime commercial affairs involving foreign nations. As a consequence, American foreign trade fell within the discretionary regulatory powers of the state governments, leaving the United States in a weak and embarrassing diplomatic situation.

Historically, Americans during the Confederation period were aware of the value of solidarity in economic matters. Before the Revolutionary War, intercolonial cooperation was achieved in the 1774 Continental Association. This association was an embargo imposed by the First Continental Congress on the importation of British goods. It was extremely effective in bringing colonial grievances to the attention of the mercantile community. Historians estimate that British imports into the North American colonies decreased 97 percent between 1774 and the following year. Although the association was dependent on the voluntary cooperation of the colonies and on the pressure of public opinion for its enforcement, it demonstrated that unified economic action was in some situations an extremely powerful political instrument.

Paramount among these examples of successful intercolonial cooperation was the Revolutionary War itself. Because the Articles of Confederation did not come into effect until 1781, the longest and most active period of military engagement took place without any formal system of central government being in place. Undoubtedly, efforts to supply the needs of American forces through voluntary state support proved to be inadequate; yet the war was conducted, treaties of alliance were negotiated, and victory was achieved over a determined and well-trained professional army.

With the end of the Revolutionary War, the United States acquired new territories west of the Appalachian Mountains and east of the Mississippi River. Opportunities beckoned Americans to seek prosperity in the west; the mountain ranges and seemingly vast distances raised a daunting challenge. Against this background, Virginia and Maryland turned their attention to their shared interests in the navigation of the Potomac River. Although the Articles of Confederation required the states to obtain Congress's approval before entering into interstate compacts, the needs of the two states were such that their joint action and a request for congressional approval were imperative. Addressing the Virginia House of Delegates in March 1785, George Mason suggested that the commissioners negotiating on behalf of both states should ask Congress to authorize a compact that would (1) provide for sharing expenses incurred to protect Chesapeake Bay from invasion, (2) establish a uniform law concerning negotiability (of bills of exchange and promissory notes) among the two states, (3) provide a uniform value for gold and silver circulating between the states, and (4) impose a uniform system of duties on imports and exports between the two states.

At about the same time, the Virginia commissioners took the initiative of writing to the president and executive council of Pennsylvania concerning the upper reaches of the Potomac River. They anticipated that the future navigation of the Potomac might lead to a cross-mountain linkage with the Ohio River. Because the route would pass through Pennsylvania, they asked about the operation of Pennsylvania import duties on goods in transit through the Keystone State. They suggested that unopened goods being transported through Pennsylvania should be exempt from any Pennsylvania import duties.

These joint efforts of Virginia and Maryland would ultimately generate more widespread efforts to bring all states together at Philadelphia to consider such modifications to the Articles of Confederation as might not only facilitate this type of interstate cooperation, but also empower the central government to occupy a more active role in commercial enhancement and regulation. In August 1785 James Madison wrote to James Monroe,

> The true question is whether the commercial interests of the States do not meet in more points than they differ. To me it is clear that they do, and if they do, there are so many reasons for, than against, submitting the commercial interest of each State to the direction and care of the majority.

He concluded that if commerce was to be regulated at all, the authority should rest with Congress, not with the states acting individually. Most clearly, if the post-Revolutionary United States were to retaliate against Britain for the destruction of American trade, results would be possible "only by harmony in the measures of the States."

The lessons of the Continental Association merged with the demonstrated need for interstate economic cooperation; both reinforced a powerful 1782 argument advanced by Alexander Hamilton in support of the much-debated, and continually aborted, 1781 proposal to authorize Congress to impose a duty on all imports into the United States. In his *Continentalist* No. 5 essay, Hamilton pointed out that market forces would moderate any effort to impose excessively high import taxes. If duties were excessive, trade in the commodities would decrease, and revenue would gradually disappear. Thus there were market-based limits on governmental taxation of imports, just as there were market forces that moderated any advantages one state might enjoy over its sister states in terms of harbors or staple goods produced. Any commercial state that attempted to overly exploit the commercial inadequacies of its neighbors would soon find itself to be encouraging competing mercantile growth within its victims. On the other hand, Hamilton was clearly not advocating governmental laissez-faire in economic regulation. Rejecting the free trade concepts popularized by Adam Smith, the New Yorker pointed out that both English and French trade flourished under the "fostering care" of governments. Within the United States, such benevolent oversight should reside in the Congress, for because the states were "parts of a whole with common interests in trade, as in other things there ought to be common direction." The goal of national policy should be the preservation of a favorable balance of foreign trade, and that could best be achieved with unified action under congressional control.

Hamilton and Madison, along with their fellow nationalists, focused on the central administration of foreign trade, and more specifically the use of import duties to raise a revenue for Congress and the general needs of the entire United States. In addition, centralized direction of internal or interstate trade would facilitate a unified approach to commercial activity within the nation and also enhance the standing and credit of the United States throughout the world.

The movement that resulted in the 1787 Philadelphia convention evolved out of a number of interrelated economic and constitutional needs. First and foremost, the central government needed a steady and reliable source of revenue, heavily reliant on import duties but shielded against protective state initiatives that might diminish this source of steady income. Second, more uniform protection of property rights and regularization of commercial transactions were required to build the new nation's reputation for financial responsibility. This was critically important if foreign capital investment and transatlantic trade were to be attracted to a radically new political entity (a group of former British colonies now formed into republican and independent states). Third, the role of the Continental Congress as the U.S. representative in world diplomacy should no longer be undermined by individual state initiatives that ignored broader national considerations. Fourth, centralized administration of both international commerce and internal trade among the states was essential to the creation of a prosperous and stable national economy.

Collective concerns about Potomac River transportation had, as we have seen, occupied Maryland and Virginia since 1785, and this practical problem of forming an effective partnership between state governments exposed some of the weaknesses of the Articles of Confederation. Throughout the various states there were leaders who wished to see the Articles amended to bring the states together into a stronger union. Such a constitutional change might also deflect what many saw as the threat that three distinct regional blocs of states might evolve, either as independent confederacies or as economic satellites to the neighboring empires of Britain, France, and Spain. The problem of federalism was at the bottom of the inadequacies many saw in the Articles. While the looseness of the confederacy threatened to dissolve the American union, its economic impact, coupled with destructive competition between the states, undermined the prosperity of the United States.

After approval by the Continental Congress and its call for a meeting, all of the states except Rhode Island sent delegates to the Philadelphia convention. The established goal was to amend the Articles of Confederation, but Virginia's delegation seized the initiative and presented a draft for a new constitution. Their proposal was to add an executive and a judicial branch to the legislative authority already held by Congress; it provided a second house to the national legislature and increased the legislative powers of those two houses. This "Virginia Plan" triggered sharp debate, and much energy was spent on compromising differences between the states. By the time alternative plans were submitted, the Virginia Plan had been thoroughly debated, and most difficulties concerning the form of government and representation of the states in Congress had been the subject of compromises.

Almost as an afterthought, a Committee on Detail, appointed to prepare a draft of the new Constitution, came to the question of commerce and its regulation. Despite earlier neglect on the floor of the convention, this subject proved to be among the most controversial that would face the delegates. And by the time the committee reported to the convention, the moderate heat that oppressed delegates as they assembled in June had escalated into a humid and debilitating August heat wave. The outdoor temperature in downtown Philadelphia was bad enough, but the delegates' comfort and magnanimity were further stretched by the fact that because they had voted to hold their proceedings in secret, the windows of their meeting room could not be opened to catch whatever breeze that might arise to relieve the doldrums of August.

A substantial part of the hot month of August was devoted to the issues and colored by the innate suspicions that each delegate brought to the convention. The least tangible but most universal objection to federal trade regulations was the consideration that we touched on previously. The regulation of interstate and foreign commerce was frequently referred to as empowering Congress to enact "navigation laws." Sensitive to the colonial antecedents of the term, the delegates' aversion to centralized control was well described by constitutional historian Charles Warren, who commented that

> the term "navigation act" while in general applying to any regulation of commerce, had a particular significance at that date. The principal of such acts, then familiar to Americans, were those obnoxious statutes of Great Britain which confined shipment of goods to English-built and English-owned ships.

Having fought a long and costly war for freedom from British commercial regulation, the delegates at Philadelphia found it unpalatable to accept centralized control, even from a government of their own making.

Regionalism also gave a special urgency to the discussion of centralized regulation of commerce. The northern states, and particularly those in New England, had extensive involvement in shipbuilding and provided the largest group of ship's officers and seamen in the United States. Obviously they would profit directly from the expansion of American shipping and most likely dominate the new nation's commerce. Planters south of the Mason-Dixon line, which divided Maryland from Pennsylvania, were particularly alert to the possibility that giving the commerce power to the central government would facilitate the termination of both the international and interstate slave trade. In their opinion, this would leave the south without access to its main source of labor. These southern delegates also had reservations about congressional regulation of trade, anticipating that this would facilitate monopolization of trade in certain key exports such as tobacco, cotton, rice, and indigo. Perhaps this concern drew its impetus from disclosure of the post-Revolutionary commercial maneuvers of Robert Morris, the so-called financier of the American Revolution. A few years before the convention met, he had secured a monopoly of the French tobacco trade through a lucrative contract with the Farmers General of the French Excise. At the time, tobacco was one of the leading American exports to France.

In addition to the threat of similar monopolies arising under federal auspices, southerners and several northern delegates were concerned that some of the northern states with strong shipping interests might influence Congress to eliminate foreign vessels from competing for trade through their harbors. Such an elimination of foreign shipping would leave southern planters and some northern merchants at the mercy of New England shipping firms. Freight rates would be raised to exorbitant levels. As a defense against this possibility, it was suggested that the Constitution should require supermajorities to approve congressional trade legislation.

The most heated discussion, however, dealt with the fear that once Congress had authority over foreign and domestic commerce, the international slave trade would be abolished. Support for provisions protecting the slave trade from legislative action was centered in the delegation from South Carolina, with additional votes from North Carolina and Georgia. The northern tier of the southern states — that is, Virginia and Maryland — tended to favor limitation of the slave trade. In part, this may have been due to a declining economic place of plantation agriculture in Virginia and Maryland; there was also a strong upper south faction that favored emancipation followed by transportation of freedmen out of the states in which they had been enslaved. Finally, states like Maryland, which had developed an extremely profitable commercial economy, strongly opposed any transfer of regulatory power to the central government.

A final point of discussion was whether Congress might be authorized to impose export taxes. Anticipating that the central government would be controlled by northern commercial interests, the southern states objected strongly to any form of export duties. Other noncommercial states feared that Congress would exercise favoritism and use the export tax authority and other powers to discriminate against them.

This intricate web of self-interest and long-held fears provided the occasion for strong and heated debates. It also produced a complex compromise that ultimately satisfied the majority of convention delegates. Neither the states nor the federal government would be empowered to enact export duties. The powers of regulating foreign and interstate commerce were vested in Congress, subject to the proviso that neither the states nor Congress might enact export taxes, and that no federal law might be enacted concerning the international slave trade before the year 1808. In addition, the convention agreed that Congress might not grant preferences to the ports of one state over the ports of another, and that vessels bound for a state would not be required to clear through a sister state. Except to cover the cost of implementing its inspection laws, no state might impose duties on imports or exports.

Wisely, the Philadelphia convention included within the text of its proposed federal Constitution the provision that the document would go into effect when approved by the positive vote of only nine states. Significantly, Rhode Island, the smallest and most commercial of all the American states, did not join the union until 29 May 1790, thirteen months after President George Washington was inaugurated. The ratification process gave rise to a massive pamphlet and newspaper debate over the proposed constitution, making available far more details concerning political thought than are accessible to historians from the meager surviving records of the Philadelphia convention. This material, emerging from authors both supportive of the Constitution and others who voiced sharp opposition, has formed a powerful gloss on the text of the federal Constitution itself. The principal federalist apologia, the *Federalist Papers*, remains one of the most often cited nonjudicial interpretations of our current Constitution. However, the writings of the antifederalist opposition are important because they provide historians with insight into the origins of states-rights sentiment in the United States, and also because they demonstrate the powerful influence that state loyalty played in the late eighteenth century, which, one might argue, is not to be ignored even as we move into the third millennium.

The war of words that greeted the work of the Philadelphia convention reminds us that state ratification of the current federal Constitution was by no means a foregone conclusion. As political scientist Robert E. Cushman has noted, the supporters of the convention's work, or federalists, were better organized because they, in contrast to the antifederalists, had "built up the business and commercial centers along the Atlantic seacoast." Many were also officer-veterans of the American Revolution, whose loyalty to George Washington was second only to their memory of the suffering that state recalcitrance had wreaked on the Continental army. Their service either in Congress or in the administration of the Confederation government provided them with detailed knowledge of the dynamics of federalism and the inadequacies of the Articles as a fundamental law for national government.

The antifederalists justly accused their opponents of perverting the purposes for which the Philadelphia convention was called — that is, the amendment of the Articles, not the erection of a new form of government. On the other hand, the Philadelphia meeting had been assembled to address the narrow questions of commercial regulation and interstate cooperation, and the antifederalists found themselves in the position of defending a relatively unpopular status quo. They also were tasked with opposing a carefully considered and radically new concept of national government that might prove to be a profitable unification of American economic policy and commercial regulation. Cushman again hits the nail on the head:

> Having escaped by separation from England the authority of an outside power to dictate to them in the management of their affairs, they were now to be placed in many important matters under the power of a strong national government. This national government could control their relations with their neighbors in trade and commerce, and, of even greater importance, could move in and impose taxes upon persons, property, and interests, a power which had never existed before.

They were, in Cecilia Kenyon's title derived from the Bible, "Men of little faith." In *Federalist* No. 6, Alexander Hamilton described them as "visionary or designing men" who sought, or purported to seek, "perpetual peace between the States, though dismembered and alienated from each other," and in *Federalist* No. 40, James Madison pointed out that the antifederalist complaint about lack of authorization was spurious. For what had the Philadelphia convention been called, and what were the universal expectations of the American people, except to consider the regulation of trade by the "general government" and the imposition of taxes on trade to provide a source of general government revenue?

In regard to foreign and interstate trade, the ratification publications and debates reflect and clarify the issues considered by the Philadelphia convention, and the coverage and analysis of those questions are much more exhaustive. The need for central and unified regulation of commerce and import taxation was perhaps more closely tied to the nation's need to exercise economic control domestically because of the interconnection of interstate and foreign trade and its impact on the conduct of foreign relations. Hamilton in *Federalist* No. 22 and Madison in *Federalist* No. 42 made this connection quite forcefully, and John Jay in *Federalist* No. 4 pointed out that the United States stood to enjoy substantial advantages in conducting the transoceanic shipping trade once the proposed Constitution was ratified.

One striking contribution of the attenuated ratification process is its elaboration of the economic benefits of a centrally directed economic trading territory coextensive with the national boundaries of the United States. This is what has come to be known as a common market. From the unlikely platform of agrarian South Carolina, David Ramsay, after asserting that America would become a "nursery for seamen," expounded a vision of national self-sufficiency. He rejoiced that "commanding our own resources and acting in concert, we can become a little world within ourselves, and smile at those who are jealous of our rising greatness." Alexander Hamilton in *Federalist* No. 11 stressed the value of states trading among themselves to supply reciprocal wants — a system highly desirable considering the diversity of production among the states and the geographical size (and hence climatic and natural resource differences) within the United States. Tench Coxe, urging ratification by the Convention of Virginia in May 1788, was even more specific:

The capacity of some parts of America are admirably adapted to supply the wants of others. New-England, destitute of iron and deficient in grain, can be plentifully supplied with both by the middle states. Possessed of fisheries, and strongly inclined to ship building and navigation, they can be furnished with the choicest timber from the Carolinas and Georgia.

And even Rhode Island, the last state to ratify the Constitution, provided a supportive writer, who commented that having Providence within a common market would make it one of the major trading cities of New England: "the whole extended country [*would be*] opened to her industrious and enterprising spirit." But David Ramsay had the most succinct and enticing phrase for his South Carolina contemporaries: "The more rice we make, the more business will be for their shipping: their interest will therefore coincide with ours."

Alexander Hamilton might consider his opponents "visionary men," but were the antifederalists the visionaries of that age? Given the transportation difficulties that stood in the way of interstate travel, given the interstate suspicions and disparate laws in the separate and highly independent states, and given the complexities of governing a federal union, were not the federalists the visionaries? Did they not project not only a new construct for federal union, but also an intriguing proposal for an economic system that would serve a vast semicontinent and weld Americans into a true nation? And they proposed this fully aware that the technological problems of transportation were far from being solved, the mechanics of economic unification were but dimly understood, and the divisive forces of separation over slavery had been powerfully demonstrated at Philadelphia and in the ratifying conventions. Converting such a dream into a reality would require time, patience, and deft statesmanship.

Patents and Monopolies, Profits and Personalities

As the 1787 Philadelphia Constitutional Convention busied itself with last-minute details of their proposed draft, they allowed themselves a break from their labors to view the launch of John Fitch's experimental steamboat *Perseverance* on the Delaware River. Conspicuously absent from among the delegate-observers was Benjamin Franklin, who had, two years before in a presentation to the American Philosophical Society, advocated a steamboat that operated by jet propulsion rather than paddle wheels. Along with several other politicians, the sage of Philadelphia had given his support to inventor James Rumsey, who, in addition to experimenting with steamboats, was the proprietor of a Philadelphia inn and tavern frequented by the most influential men in the Confederation Congress and the state government. Convention delegates who watched the vessel's first trial, as well as Franklin and Rumsey, who did not, had a focused interest in the demonstration. Just a few days before, the convention had briefly considered whether the proposed federal government might institute a system of patents to recognize inventive genius and thereby grant a limited monopoly as a reward to the inventor. The matter had been referred to the Committee on Detail, then involved in preparing the final text of the new Constitution, and upon ratification, it ultimately became part of the eighth clause of Article One, Section 8, of the federal Constitution.

Fitch and Rumsey were the earliest American inventors who tried their hands at developing a steamboat, and each possessed the engineering skills that were required to deal with the numerous technical problems that steamboat production demanded. Both had achieved a modicum of success in gaining financial support for their activities. James Rumsey had received a conditional land grant from the Confederation Congress to encourage his experiments; in this, he happened to be first to ask, and Fitch was refused a similar grant by the same body. Undaunted by this refusal, Fitch raised $300 from private sources in Philadelphia and established a steamboat company there in April 1786. State land grants from Virginia, Maryland, and Pennsylvania were offered as rewards should Rumsey succeed in inventing and operating a steamboat. Yet neither Fitch nor Rumsey possessed the political connections or financial patronage necessary to fund the substantial capital investment needed to complete their experiments and turn their discoveries into fully operational steamboats. That combination was first achieved by Robert Fulton.

Characterized as a gifted engineer and a shameless self-promoter, Fulton was in Europe when New York's former chancellor, Robert R. Livingston, arrived in Paris to help James Monroe negotiate the purchase of the Louisiana Territory from France. Four years previously, Livingston had become interested in steamboats through the experimental work of John Stevens, an engineer and Livingston's brother-in-law, who lived in Hoboken, New Jersey. In 1802 Livingston entered into partnership with Fulton with a view toward the development of an operational steamboat within two years.

Although Fulton failed to meet this deadline, he spent the biennium profitably by constructing one vessel that demonstrated considerable promise, which was used in a demonstration before French officials interested in the possibilities of steamboat navigation. He also studied diagrams of competitor European inventions and developed a careful summary concerning the propulsion and engineering of European steamboats. After failing to secure either patents or substantial financial support for his inventions, he decided in 1805 to return to the United States. Shortly before he sailed, Fulton attempted to purchase a lightweight steam engine from English inventor Matthew Boulton. Again he was unsuccessful, and he returned empty-handed but armed with a substantial mass of technical data that might prove useful in his work with Livingston. Once on American soil in early 1806, he pored over recent U.S. patent filings and spent time cultivating political contacts. During the same year, the federal government agreed to stage a trial run of Fulton's steamboat on the Hudson River, an event that eventually took place in August 1807 when the *North River Steamboat* made an upriver voyage from New York to Albany in thirty-two hours. As a result of this demonstration, Fulton was awarded a United States patent in February 1809. Yet there was something of a cloud over his bright sky of success: earlier, and therefore prior and superior, U.S. patents had been awarded to John Fitch, James Rumsey, and the partnership of John Stevens with Nicholas Roosevelt. In addition, Fitch's earlier contacts with Chancellor Livingston raised troubling speculations that the partnership had possibly infringed the Fitch patent. It was also obvious that Fulton had gained engineering advantages from his exhaustive research in prior European and U.S. patent filings. This raised questions concerning the originality of Fulton's steamboat design, and this was essential to the legal validity of a federal patent as the law was then established.

Ostensibly the award of a United States patent should confer a monopoly on the inventor for a fixed time. However, the value of a patent and the exclusivity of its grant of a limited monopoly are directly proportional to the holder's ability to assemble the capital necessary to develop the invention for practical use, prosecute infringers of the patent rights, and then successfully market the invention to the general public or license its use to potential competitors. John Fitch had not been able to develop a commercially profitable steamboat, and his 1798 monopoly rights from the New York state legislature were transferred to Chancellor Livingston and Robert Fulton. The Livingston–Fulton grant of monopoly privileges conferred a monopoly of steamboat navigation on New York waters through 1827. Yet it did not discourage others from competing with their North River Steamboat Company. Among the first of these adventurers was Aaron Ogden, a former governor of New Jersey, who in August 1800 established a wind-powered ferry between Elizabethtown, New Jersey, and New York City; he converted it to steam in 1812. In 1814, after the settlement of litigation between himself and Livingston–Fulton, Ogden secured from the partnership the right to run a steam ferry from Elizabethtown to New York City. This was the commencement of Ogden's identification with the Livingston–Fulton enterprise. With the February 1815 death of Fulton and Thomas Gibbons's establishment of a competing New York–to–Elizabethtown ferry in 1816, Ogden became the primary defender of patent and monopoly rights that would be brought before the U.S. Supreme Court eight years later in *Gibbons v. Ogden*.

Ironically, it was Ogden's Elizabethtown–to–New York City

{ *Chapter 2* }

infringement that brought Thomas Gibbons into the steamboat business. Aaron Ogden launched his steamboat enterprise in 1813 and soon added John Stites and Jonathan Dayton as partners. Subsequently, Ogden bought out Stites's interest, and Gibbons secretly purchased the shares owned by Jonathan Dayton. As a Georgia land speculator and onetime loyalist during the Revolution, Gibbons found steam navigation a more promising future than what awaited him in Georgia, where his past was more widely known. Transferring his business location and residence to New Jersey in 1811, he benefitted from Ogden's social and political contacts. Through Ogden's influence, the New Jersey legislature enacted retaliatory laws designed to neutralize the Livingston–Fulton monopoly in New Jersey. The New Jersey statutes imposed fines and forfeiture on Livingston–Fulton vessels operating in New Jersey waters. Armed with this protection, Ogden and his new partner, Gibbons, prepared to challenge the New York monopoly grant on three levels: they would try to secure repeal of the monopoly by the New York legislature; they would attack the monopoly in New York and New Jersey courts; and they would challenge the monopoly in federal courts, asserting that it violated the commerce clause of the federal Constitution. Their efforts to secure repeal of the New York monopoly ultimately failed, as did the efforts of Robert Fulton to obtain repeal of New Jersey's retaliatory legislation. And before a judicial attack could be mounted, a personal feud between Ogden and Gibbons over Gibbons's treatment of his married daughter aggravated the financial relationship between the two men. Gibbons left the partnership in 1816 and established his own steamboat company, designed to challenge the constitutionality of the New York monopoly over the New York City–Elizabethtown route. As we have already noted, by this time, the death of Robert Fulton in 1815 and the squabbles of the Livingston family left Ogden, the Livingston–Fulton licensee of the New York–Elizabethtown route since May 1814, the principal defender of the Livingston–Fulton monopoly.

Because the inventive claims made in the various federal patents were vague and overlapping, none of the parties was willing to sue for infringement in the federal courts. Instead, the Livingston–Fulton strategy centered on the political influence of Chancellor Robert R. Livingston with the New York legislature, augmented by the Livingstons' independent wealth to finance both engineering development and state-based litigation and legislative lobbying. Despite Robert Fulton's success building a large steamboat capable of sustained operations on the Hudson, he had drawn heavily on a variety of prior patented designs, including patents in the United States, England, and Europe. And as we have noted, the Livingston–Fulton conglomerate had been liberal in licensing its patent and monopoly rights to a variety of firms operating in limited areas within New York State. Not infrequently, litigation based on the state monopoly resulted in a settlement that licensed other steamboat operators under the protection of Livingston–Fulton's grant from the New York legislature. Revenues from licensing operations served to fill the Livingston–Fulton war chest, facilitating further protective lawsuits as well as lobbying the New York legislature to maintain or extend the original 1807 legislation.

The profitability of Hudson River navigation between Albany and New York City gave birth to the most serious challenge to the Livingston–Fulton interests. Led by James Van Ingen, a group of Albany businessmen commenced operating a New York–Albany steamboat line in April 1811. Livingston–Fulton promptly brought suit in the federal circuit court for New York, only to have their action dismissed for lack of jurisdiction. As Justice Brockholst Livingston, the federal circuit court justice, pointed out, all of the parties named in the case were citizens of New York; hence, there was no diversity of citizenship upon which to establish jurisdiction. Because neither Livingston nor Fulton asserted rights as inventors, and because they did not proceed on the basis of Fulton's 1809 patent, they waived any right to trial in federal courts on the basis of the federal patent law. Undoubtedly the complexity of overlapping patents made it unwise for them to rely on Fulton's patent, but the failure to plead any other basis for federal court jurisdiction doomed the Livingston–Fulton action to failure. Undaunted, they brought an equitable suit in the New York chancery court, requesting, in addition to other relief, an injunction against Van Ingen's further navigation in violation of the New York monopoly grant. In October 1811 Chancellor John Lansing Jr., a former mayor of Albany, denied the injunction, and Livingston–Fulton took an appeal to the court of impeachment and errors.

Composed of justices of the New York supreme court augmented by a few legislative representatives from the New York Senate, the court of impeachment and errors, known more popularly as the court of errors, was then the highest court of appeal in New York State. In *Livingston v. Van Ingen* (1812), the senators deferred to the judges' opinions that reversed the chancery court and remanded the case with instructions that an injunction be issued. As Justice Joseph Yates, Justice Smith Thompson, and Chief Justice James Kent indicated, the chancellor was incorrect in asserting that an injunction could not issue until the claimants' property rights were established at common law. Quite the contrary, the statutory direction prescribing injunctive relief for violating the monopoly was more than adequate authority for issuing an injunction. It is worth noting that the judges sitting in the court of errors ignored Chancellor Lansing's extended contention that the legislature could not grant a monopoly over the use of air, water, fire, and steam, because by natural law and Justinian's *Digest*, these were common properties of all citizens. Quite clearly, the monopoly was not over the use of navigable waters or the implementation of steam, fire, and water. The New York legislators had simply restricted access to state waters by steamboats other than those of the grantees. Undoubtedly, Chancellor Lansing had been led into this irrelevant discussion in the hope of raising public opinion in favor of the Albany syndicate, and also with an eye toward impugning the Livingston–Fulton monopoly, which had already become extremely unpopular with the general public.

Similar considerations may have led the court of impeachment and errors to go beyond a narrow procedural basis for reversing the chancellor. There were serious issues concerning state and federal constitutional interpretation, as well as the impact of the Livingston–Fulton monopoly on the public good, that demanded some consideration. Those supreme court justices who gave opinions in the court of errors elected to examine at length the extended arguments of counsel, which set forth strong reasons whether the Livingston–Fulton monopoly did or did not violate federal constitutional law. In effect, *Livingston v. Van Ingen* became a significant forerunner of *Gibbons v. Ogden* and established a formidable rationale upholding the exercise of state legislative power for the protection of technological innovations and improvements independent of the federal Constitution's patent and commerce clauses. Given the national stature of Chief Justice James

Kent, it is not surprising that his discussion was both the most comprehensive opinion and the most influential.

Both Yates and Thompson heavily stressed the constitutionality of New York's grant of exclusive privileges to the Livingston–Fulton entity. They emphasized the restriction of the grant to territorial waters of New York State, an exercise of the state's traditional governing power that existed before the American states ratified the federal Constitution. In addition, they emphasized the limited nature of patent rights authorized by the Constitution; only inventors and authors might obtain patents under the Constitution's provisions, and Livingston–Fulton asserted only that they possessed the right to navigate, based on their succession to the rights originally granted to John Fitch and legislatively transferred to them.

Neither Yates nor Thompson anticipated any repugnancy between state grants of monopolies and the Constitution's patent provisions or commerce clause. Chief Justice Kent was unwilling to make such a categorical distinction between state and federal authority. However, he did point out that no congressional regulation of commerce had been enacted. In such a circumstance, he was unwilling to speculate whether the Livingston–Fulton monopoly might at some future date come into conflict with a federal statute pertaining to commerce. Pointing out that "it may be difficult to draw an exact line between those regulations which relate to external and those which relate to internal commerce, for every regulation of one will, directly or indirectly affect the other," Kent continued that it would be a "monstrous heresy" to interfere with an existing state grant when there was neither an existing federal regulation nor a constitutional inhibition against such state action.

Kent, addressing federalist aspects of both the commerce clause and the federal patent provision, agreed with Justices Yates and Thompson that in the event a state law or grant came into conflict with the United States government's exercise of a concurrent power, the federal action would prevail. That was the very essence of the supremacy clause in Article Six of the federal Constitution. But of course the threshold question was whether Congress's authority over commerce was concurrent. To that problem, Kent's answer was both cautious and comprehensive. He observed, "The legislative power, in a single, independent government, extends to every proper object of

{ *Chapter 2* }

power, and is limited only by its constitutional provisions, or by the fundamental principles of all government, and the unalienable rights of mankind." And because the Livingston–Fulton monopoly pertained only to steamboat travel within New York State, the issue at hand was not what powers were granted to the federal government by the federal Constitution, but rather what authority remained with, or was reserved to, the state of New York.

Chief Justice Kent buttressed this conclusion with a "safe rule of construction" that he phrased thusly:

[I]f any given power was originally vested in this state, if it has not been exclusively ceded to congress, or if the exercise of it has not been prohibited to the states, we may then go on in the exercise of the power until it comes practically in collision with the actual exercise of some congressional power. When that happens to be the case, the state authority will so far be controlled, but it will still be good in all those respects in which it does not absolutely contravene the provisions of the paramount law.

Citing Alexander Hamilton in *Federalist* No. 32 for his conclusion, Kent took care to approve of what today would be characterized as an originalist view of the *Federalist* and the debates of the state ratifying conventions. These were for him the best evidence of the sense of the authors of the Constitution. As such, these principles "solemnly sanctioned at that day, and flowing from such sources, . . . [were] to be regarded by us, and by posterity, as coming in the language of truth, and with the force of authority."

A comprehensive view of the whole Constitution persuaded Kent that the framers intended that the commerce clause be concurrent. Not only was it not designated to be exclusive, but it was also arguably concurrent by virtue of the fact that the states were prohibited from imposing duties or taxes on exported goods. The narrowness of this prohibition against state action, coupled with its express inclusion in the constitutional text, suggested to the chief justice that many other commerce-related actions remained available to the states. Indeed, for him the situation in regard to the patent clause suggested the strong likelihood that a concurrency construction facilitated the basis for an exercise of state power that would augment the limited federal power authorized by the patent and commerce clauses. While United States patent laws protected actual authors and inventors, state financial grants, prizes, and monopolies encouraged the importation of foreign technology, augmenting the federal system. The Livingston–Fulton New York legislative grant was an outstanding example of this supplementary function of state legislative power, and therefore would not be in conflict with the interstate commerce powers should Congress elect to exercise those powers.

Lawyers may well characterize as dicta virtually all of the opinions submitted by the judges in the court of impeachment and errors. The judgment of the court, entered after those opinions were given, highlights the only matter at issue in *Livingston v. Van Ingen*: the Chancellor acted improperly in refusing injunctive relief authorized by the legislative grant to Livingston and Fulton. And yet it is important to recognize that although this was an unnecessary elaboration of the court's reasoning, it was ominously predictive of any future New York disposition of a challenge to the Livingston–Fulton monopoly. Furthermore, that decision would remain operative in New York from spring 1812, when it was delivered, until Chief Justice John Marshall's decision in *Gibbons* more than a decade later.

The *Van Ingen* opinions in the court of impeachment and errors provided a strong foundation upon which attorneys subsequently could build their arguments for a narrow construction of the commerce clause in the federal Constitution. One extremely persuasive rationale was the contention that a state had virtually plenary authority to regulate commercial activity within its own boundaries. It is interesting that even as *Van Ingen* was decided, states other than New York had enacted retaliatory legislation, restricting the New York monopoly's right to operate steamboats within their territorial waters. Already it had become obvious to the general public, if not in the submissions to the *Van Ingen* court, that transactions and activities limited to a single state could have a substantial economic impact on one or more sister states, or even on foreign commerce. In fact, New Jersey, Connecticut, and Pennsylvania retaliatory legislation imposing penal sanctions against New York steamboat operations in their respective territorial waters was clear evidence that New York's monopoly had launched the same sort of interstate legal struggle that had undermined the economy during the Confederation period.

Although the *Van Ingen* judges recognized the subordinating power inherent in the federal Constitution's supremacy clause, they were willing to stretch the logic of concurrency and to argue that exclusive powers of Congress had to be based on an express grant to Congress or on an equally clear prohibition of state exercise of the power. Chief Justice Kent asserted that "necessary implication" might also play a role in ascertaining whether a power was exclusive or concurrent in its application. Both Kent and his colleagues on the court of errors chose to ignore the possibility that the federal Constitution's commerce clause might, standing alone, nullify state regulation of interstate commerce. At the same time, they refused to hold that Congress had legislated under the commerce clause by enacting the 1793 federal Coastal Licensing Act, which established guidelines for the issuance of licenses to American vessels that would engage in coastal shipping, and would by compliance enjoy exemption from certain taxes and inspection procedures. Sharply declining to speculate on what effect the constitutional grant might have in the absence of congressional enactments, Kent observed:

> [W]hen there is no existing federal legislation which interferes with the [New York state] grant, nor any pretense of a constitutional interdict, it would be most extraordinary for us to adjudge it void on the mere contingency of some future exercise of congressional power. Such a doctrine is a monstrous heresy. It would go in great degree, to annihilate the legislative power of the states.

Neither Kent nor Marshall after him was willing to accept the broad modern recognition of a dormant commerce power existing independently from an actual congressional enactment.

After *Van Ingen*, the Livingston–Fulton interests might well have rested their case, but a variety of factors intervened to further complicate their situation. Chancellor Robert R. Livingston died in 1813, and inventor Robert Fulton followed him in 1815, leaving the numerous shareholders, including a substantial number of Livingston relatives and in-laws, to squabble over future North River Steamboat Company activities. Thomas Gibbons, goaded on by public disapproval of the North River Steamboat Company's monopoly as well as by his personal feud with Aaron Ogden, continued to expand his operations in defiance of New York injunctions. Profitability of eastern steamboat ventures, and growing success west of the Appalachian Mountain chain, inevitably drew more entrepreneurs into the field.

The *Van Ingen* victory in the New York court of impeachment and errors produced two major reactions. For the time being, it proclaimed that state-based monopoly grants operating within the territorial limits of the granting state were valid under the federal Constitution. That led inevitably to the next consequence: those states with oceanic harbors, states with navigable rivers entirely within their borders, and states controlling the mouths of navigable rivers obtained lucrative competitive advantages over states that lacked those geographical assets. Steamboat travel on the Hudson River north of the New Jersey–New York boundary became subject to the sovereign control of New York State. Understandably, New Jersey, with a competing territorial claim to the more southerly waters of the Hudson River and portions of New York Bay, enacted retaliatory legislation; so did Connecticut regarding steamboat navigation of Long Island Sound.

Even more notable was the monopoly situation facing the transmontane west. Although antimonopoly sentiment blunted Livingston–Fulton efforts to gain grants from the western states and territories, the Territory of Orleans, which controlled the delta of the Mississippi River, was persuaded in 1811 to grant sole steamboating rights to Livingston–Fulton. In effect, the entire central portion of the United States, from the present state of Montana to the southern border of today's Arkansas and eastward to Ohio and the northern borders of the present-day states of Alabama and Mississippi, was subordinated to the Territory of Orleans and the commercial power of New Orleans. It was here that the greatest opportunity existed for the exploitation of the steamboat, and Robert Fulton's visionary scheme for a vast economic empire now came within reach.

The potential economic bonanza of steamboat travel was enhanced by an upsurge of public interest in the new form of travel, a phenomenon that would repeat itself after 1850 by adulatory enthusiasm for the steam railroad, and after 1903 by widespread and bombastic attraction to aerial flight in balloons, airships, and airplanes. The steamboat thus became not only an innovation in transportation systems, but also the first of many American enthusiasms for rapid, comfortable, and reliable modes of conveyance across the vast continental landscape. As a consequence, legislative and judicial actions that touched on steamboats became a matter of widespread concern among the citizenry, and public opinion either for or against the Livingston–Fulton monopolies became an important factor in shaping the actions of public officials after 1811. What was at stake was not only profits, but also election to public office, as universal white manhood suffrage increasingly became the growing standard in pre-Jacksonian America. Just as most western states and territories fought for freedom from monopolistic control, based on public resentment against economic privilege, so did the established eastern seaboard states react to protect the economic and cultural interests of their citizenry, either in monopolistic control of or free access to the new steamboat travel.

By the fall of 1807, a few months after the successful New York City–to–Albany trials, the North River Steamboat Company realized a rapid increase in passenger traffic, due in part to Robert Fulton's active and aggressive marketing of the service and publishing passenger endorsements of this mode of travel. Almost immediately, lawsuits or threats to sue became an established part of the business; in addition, the New York legislature was harassed by petitions for the repeal of the Livingston–Fulton monopoly, but the influence of Chancellor Livingston and his heirs proved impervious to these applications. After the 1811 *Van Ingen* decision, the monopoly profits began to soar. In 1814 the North River Steamboat Company earned $85,000, most of which was reinvested in constructing more and improved steamships. The interest was not entirely commercial, for excursion sailings on steamboats became available to the average citizen, and evening dinner parties aboard the vessels were the frequent resort of the social elite. Recreational steamboat travel, although briefly curtailed by World War II, remained a fixed part of New York–New Jersey cultural life until well past 1950.

Immediate and conveniently available profits on the Hudson did not tempt Robert Fulton to ignore the enormous potential for travel on western waters despite Chancellor Livingston's political and technological doubts about the enterprise. In June 1809 Livingston–Fulton dispatched Nicholas Roosevelt to Pittsburgh with the assignment of setting up operating locations on the Ohio River and the upper

Mississippi. In addition, Roosevelt invested in coal mines and made a flatboat trip downriver to chart the currents. However, Chancellor Livingston's concerns about antimonopoly and anti-eastern sentiment proved to be partially correct. It was not until March 1811 that the Orleans Territory legislature, urged on by territorial governor William C. C. Claiborne, issued a monopoly grant to Livingston–Fulton. Encouraged by that grant, Roosevelt in January 1812 sailed his steamboat from Pittsburgh to New Orleans, braving the rapids at Louisville and a series of earthquakes that racked the Mississippi Valley. The heroic effort launched Livingston–Fulton in western waters, but it would not continue unopposed, for Henry N. Shreve shortly thereafter launched his large steamboat, the *Enterprise*, in time to carry much-needed supplies to Andrew Jackson's army before the battle of New Orleans in January 1815. Shreve's vessel proved to be a better mousetrap. It had a very shallow draft, facilitating travel in shoaly tributaries of the Mississippi. To minimize below-water construction, the machinery and boilers of Shreve's steamboats were located above deck. Shreve experimented and ultimately perfected a high-pressure steam boiler, in contrast to the low-pressure boilers of the Livingston–Fulton monopoly. And finally, Shreve introduced a superstructure of decks, arriving at what currently has become our general picture of a Mississippi River steamboat. This added both elegance and carrying capacity to Shreve's boats.

If technological innovation was on Shreve's side, so too was the political and judicial atmosphere in the west. When Edward Livingston sued him on behalf of the monopoly Livingston–Fulton in 1815, the action was dismissed on the ground that the 1811 Orleans Territory monopoly was in violation of the territorial constitution that guaranteed freedom of navigation of the Mississippi River. Two years later, U.S. district court judge Dominick Augustus Hall held that the territorial grant was invalid because it attempted to confer exclusive use of a federally protected highway. Hall's decision not only ended the monopoly in western waters, but also proved to be vastly popular throughout the west. By 1819 the Livingston–Fulton venture into western waters was almost moribund, with over twenty-five competing steamboats in operation against the monopoly. To add insult to injury, Henry Shreve was appointed federal superintendent of western river improvements in 1817, and he continued in that office until 1841.

Landmark cases that leave their imprint on U.S. constitutional history are quite rare. Even in the early nineteenth century, it was expensive to carry appeals to the United States Supreme Court, and most private litigants were compelled to either settle their cases or, alternatively, abandon the opportunity to appeal. Only matters that involved great promise of profit made extended litigation an acceptable business proposition. Perhaps the only exception to that economically determined result was a case in which a "matter of principle" was involved, and most matters of principle were closely intertwined with personal animosity. The situation that gave birth to the Steamboat Case was unique in that it combined all three: the potential for vast profit, an antimonopoly principle strongly supported by public opinion, and animosity, if not outright hatred, between Thomas Gibbons and his onetime partner, former governor Aaron Ogden.

American enthusiasm for an improved system of transportation dated from the end of the American Revolution. Independence brought liberation from English restrictions on commercial and industrial enterprise. It also nearly doubled the land area of the United States through Britain's 1783 cession of western territory stretching from the Appalachian Mountains to the Mississippi, and that vast landmass was doubled again by the 1803 Louisiana Purchase. This territorial acquisition laid open a vast and virtually unexplored empire. Its potential for economic development was both challenging and inspiring. And it created a desperate need for adequate and cheaper means of transportation. Historian Merrill Jensen pinpoints the impact of transportation enthusiasm on national behavior: "Americans got together as they had never done before in creating societies for social and economic improvement, digging canals, building bridges, and improving roads." Yet it also was a major challenge in the east, where road transportation was prohibitively expensive and unreliable for marketing agricultural products to the major population centers. Transportation historian George Taylor estimated that two-thirds of South Carolina's market crops were raised within five miles of a river, and the remaining third were harvested not more than ten miles from a river. River transport, in turn, was only feasible for downstream transport; return trips could not draw on sailing vessels to any substantial degree because of the uncertainty of wind patterns.

As Louis Hunter, the historian of western steamboating, emphasized, "The urgent need of the time was for a source of power by which vessels could be propelled quickly and cheaply both up stream and down on our great inland waterways."

Even greater obstacles lay in the path of those seeking to transport goods in the west. The short-lived Livingston–Fulton monopoly of steamboating in the Orleans Territory was mainly operative between New Orleans and Natchez, where oceangoing vessels were also able to navigate. It was left to Henry Shreve to begin the redesign of vessels for the shallow waters of the Mississippi and its tributaries to the north, and with the judicial invalidation of the Orleans monopoly grant in 1817, the entire length of the river was again available for commerce in goods and passengers. So great was the demand for free navigation that it seems likely that public opinion would have soon secured the repeal of the Livingston–Fulton monopoly had the courts not intervened. When the news of the Orleans monopoly reached the midwestern states and territories, the reaction was strong. Inhabitants of towns on the Ohio River were highly incensed, and mass meetings of protest in Ohio and Kentucky petitioned Congress to cancel the territorial grant.

Professor Hunter points out that a difficulty in the path of western steamboat monopolies was the fact that because many western rivers were the boundaries between states and territories, no one legislature could issue an exclusive monopoly for steamboat operation. In addition, the expense of litigation and legislative lobbying sapped the strength of original grantees in their attempts to protect their legal monopoly. Even with Louisiana territorial and state law protecting the Orleans monopoly, these economic factors virtually eliminated any advantage the Livingston–Fulton licensees enjoyed in western waters. Hunter asserts that seven years before the U.S. Supreme Court decision in *Gibbons*, the western rivers were freely available to all who wished to operate steamboats.

Antimonopoly sentiment was also operative in New York State. A year after the 1824 decision in *Gibbons v. Ogden*, the legislature repealed all steamboat monopoly grants within the internal waters of the state. There was a rapid increase in steamboat traffic, primarily in the transport of passengers rather than cargo. Shorter distances between farm and market, coupled with a denser population in the east, resulted in continued reliance on land transportation of goods, but in the west, rivers remained the principal avenue of commercial transport and a critical component of economic prosperity.

Western river navigation by steamboats was the backbone of economic development throughout the vast Mississippi River drainage basin. Not surprisingly, it was navigation of western rivers that stimulated the evolution of steamboat design throughout the United States. The need for shallow draft vessels by 1838 led to a ship that needed only thirty inches of water, and by 1841 the minimum draft was reduced to twenty-two inches. As Taylor comments, "little wonder that western river men boasted that for successful navigation their steamboats needed only a heavy dew." It was the west that developed the now-familiar stern wheel, which was more efficient in pushing barges and riverboats, and also developed increased speed by exposing more water to the thrust of the paddles. One year after Chief Justice Marshall's decision in *Gibbons*, steamboats on the Mississippi River were making an average of a hundred miles per day, thanks to the design innovations encouraged by the elimination of the Orleans monopoly in 1817 and the enthusiasm of western steam navigation entrepreneurs.

Even in the east, the invalidation of the Livingston–Fulton monopoly after 1826 resulted in a substantial expansion of competition in the industry. Thomas Cox notes that in November 1825, there were only 43 steamboats competing for passengers on the Hudson River; but by 1838, 150 steamboats on the Hudson carried 2 million passengers. In the west, by 1820 there were only 69 vessels operating on the Mississippi. By 1855 there were 727 steamboats traveling the river system between Montana and New Orleans. Opening steamboat travel to free competition vastly increased the availability of transportation throughout the United States and contributed greatly to economic growth. Although the 1824 *Gibbons* decision was a major factor in producing this benefit in the east, it is clear that in the west, where cheap and available transportation was more urgently needed, the combined impact of public opinion and judicial action in the lower federal courts was much more influential than the Supreme Court's opinion.

Ironically, the same considerations that led to the rapid growth of steamboat transport also led to its demise by 1850. Land transport by steam railroad was not restricted by the meanderings of riverbeds, and its reliability was less affected by flood or drought. Railroads proved to be faster than steamboats, and they were able to operate in winter, when ice closed the northern rivers to navigation. Only in the coastal trade, and in connection with inland canal traffic, such as the Erie Canal after its 1825 completion, did steamboat travel continue to be competitive with the railroad. Economically, *Gibbons v. Ogden* had only a quarter century of impact on American life. However, before 1830 the promise of wealth through steamboat operation was more than adequate to generate dogged litigation either to maintain or to destroy monopolistic rights in this new and promising innovation in transportation.

Occasionally history is shaped by the personality of individuals. It is possible that even with the high financial stakes available to the winner in *Gibbons v. Ogden* the case might have been settled before it was argued in the U.S. Supreme Court. Countless other disputes were mediated, and compromises negotiated, that eliminated challenges to the Livingston–Fulton monopoly. The tide of what would become Jacksonian democracy was beginning to run against the encrusted wealth and privileges of the old social elite, and doubtless some would-be entrepreneurs were willing to wait until free competition overwhelmed the steamboat monopolies. But Thomas Gibbons was a driven man, and Aaron Ogden, although much less flamboyant, was a stubborn man also. Historians have not agreed concerning their relationships or their quarrel, but there is a consensus that Gibbons's harsh behavior toward his married daughter was the focal point of the Gibbons–Ogden clash. Apparently Ogden had intervened in support of the daughter and Gibbons's wife, triggering Gibbons's resentment. By 1816, words had given way to action on Gibbons's part, and the Georgian unsuccessfully attempted to attack Ogden with a horsewhip. Shortly afterward, Gibbons tacked a challenge to a duel on Ogden's front door, and Ogden replied with an action at law for trespassing on his land. Despite many efforts, by both friends and counsel, to ameliorate the quarrel and begin steps toward settling the *Gibbons* litigation, the antagonism persisted until Ogden's death in 1839.

This was a case destined to enrich the reputations and the pocketbooks of leading American lawyers. Fueled with the malice and conflicting personalities of two individuals of widely different backgrounds, it was the climax of a long and exhausting contest between monopoly rights, inherited privilege, and political influence, on one hand, and free competition, energetic pursuit of new wealth, and demands for equality and economic opportunity in a rapidly developing young republican society, on the other hand. Yet in normal times and with more reasonable principal litigants, it might never have arrived at the door to the Supreme Court's chamber in the basement of the Capitol in Washington.

CHAPTER 3

Commerce in the Lower Federal Courts before 1824

Given the importance of commercial activity to American national prosperity before 1824, it may be surprising that no cases involving the Constitution's commerce clause reached the U.S. Supreme Court before *Gibbons*. We may surmise that both economic and legal factors contributed to this situation. Lack of a diversified domestic economy limited incentives for interstate trade but encouraged international commercial contact, primarily with Britain, as in the colonial period. American oceanic shipping and New England shipbuilding flourished, and the United States continued to supply agricultural produce to European and Caribbean markets. The Napoleonic wars increased the United States' role in transatlantic trade and provisioning, but at the same time, French and British efforts to destroy American trade with their rivals produced tense diplomatic confrontation. Ultimately this drove the Jefferson administration into imposing restrictions on oceanic and coastal trade. These included prohibitions on the importation of British or French goods, which were expanded to restrictions on both exports and imports in nonintercourse acts, and finally the embargo acts, which provided a detailed system of regulation designed to ensure that American vessels did not participate in any foreign trade whatsoever.

The embargo acts were enacted from December 1807 through April 1808; each successive legislative change was designed to more effectively distinguish between strictly coastal navigation and attempts to engage in prohibited trade with foreign nations or their colonies throughout the Atlantic basin. Although the intent of the legislation was clearly based on Congress's authority to legislate in support of the president's power to conduct foreign relations, the statutes also constituted a regulation — indeed, a prohibition — of foreign commerce. Even though the full Supreme Court did not hear embargo cases until well after the 1809 repeal of the statutes, there were numerous cases in the U.S. circuit courts, which were presided over by circuit-riding justices of the Supreme Court. Circuit riding was a major part of the duties of Supreme Court justices before 1892, and in the case of the Marshall Court, it ensured that the chief justice and his associates were painfully aware of the executive branch's efforts to control or entirely eliminate foreign commerce. Their dockets were strong reminders of the diligence required to prevent the United States' entry into war with either France or Great Britain. For the purposes of this study, the litigation in the federal circuit courts is important because it and the embargo statutes represent the first concerted congressional effort to control both foreign and domestic commerce. Circuit court decisions began to explore the complexity of commercial regulation in the light of federal and state sovereignty, and they represent the commencement of the Court's long involvement with defining the nature and scope of the commerce clause, as well as the dynamic relationship between federal commercial control and state police powers. In addition, enforcement of the embargo acts required the establishment of an expanded administrative apparatus, and this in turn required the circuit courts to review the constitutionality of the statutes and their application on one hand, and on the other hand to examine the relationships of executive branch officers to each other. Ultimately the embargo statutes were held to be a constitutional exercise of federal authority, and for the most part, executive branch action was approved.

Among the circuit court cases, the most interesting in terms of commerce clause jurisprudence is that involving the *William*, a Massachusetts vessel licensed to engage in coastal trade. The ship and crew were charged with transferring goods to a non-U.S. ship bound for a foreign port. Among other positions taken by the defense attorneys, it was argued that the embargo legislation was unconstitutional. Normally a circuit court opinion would be written by the Supreme Court justice sitting on circuit, but in this instance, the elderly and ailing Justice William Cushing assigned the opinion to the district judge, John Davis, who wrote a forceful defense of federal power to regulate commerce and an eloquent assertion of federal supremacy in support of the embargo.

Judge Davis began his opinion with the observation that it had been one of the "great procuring causes of the Federal Constitution" that the then-existing economic distress should be relieved by creating a federal power over interstate commerce. In addition, for congressional legislation to be declared invalid, he insisted that there had to be a "clear repugnancy" or conflict with an express constitutional provision; absent such a showing, the federal statute must be presumed to be valid. He rejected counsel's contention that the commerce power did not carry with it such a general and unlimited authority as was required to enact an embargo of foreign commerce. The commerce power was not restricted to commercial objects alone, but might also be "considered as an instrument for other purposes of general policy and interest." Citing *Federalist* No. 23, Davis asserted that like the powers of taxing and war, the commerce clause permitted Congress, in dealing with great national matters, to "make all regulations which have relation to" the enumerated powers. That included enacting the embargo statutes.

Not content with this broad interpretation of the Constitution's commerce clause, Judge Davis wrote that through ratification of the Constitution,

> [a] national sovereignty is created. Not an unlimited sovereignty, but a sovereignty, as to objects surrendered and specified, limited only by the qualifications and restrictions, expressed in the constitution. Commerce is one of those objects. The care, protection, management and controul, of this great national concern is, in my opinion, vested by the constitution, in the congress of the United States, and their power is sovereign relative to commercial intercourse.

That was particularly the situation in time of war or impending peril. At such times, "[f]oreign intercourse becomes . . . a subject of peculiar interest, and its regulation forms an obvious and essential branch of the federal government."

Interestingly, Judge Davis also was asked to hold that navigation was not included within Congress's power to regulate foreign and interstate commerce. After observing that navigation is not necessarily "contained" within commerce, he asserted that Congress can nevertheless regulate commerce as a proper object of attention under the commerce power. Adjudicating embargo cases thus brought the circuit courts into issues that would subsequently be of Supreme Court concern in *Gibbons*. Another example of a similar embargo act influencing subsequent events was the 1813 condemnation of the cod-fishing boat the *Active*, for lying in harbor with goods that would have violated the embargo act restrictions. Unfortunately for the prosecution, the prohibition in the embargo acts was against leaving harbor with prohibited goods on board. The *Active* was still within the harbor when it was apprehended, and thus could not be condemned under the embargo statutes. However, the federal Coasting Licensing Act of 1793 prohibited fishing vessels from possessing commercial goods even within a harbor, and thus the ship was legally seized and indicted under the provisions of this federal statute rather than the embargo legislation.

This generous construction of the commerce clause proved not to be popular in all situations, as the South Carolina circuit court case *Elkison v. Deliesseline* (1823) demonstrates. In December 1820, the South Carolina legislature enacted a law requiring that all black seamen who arrived in South Carolina ports were to be imprisoned in the local jail until their vessel departed. The recent Denmark Vesey uprising had aroused public fears that a renewed slave insurrection might be instigated by free black sailors in the port cities. Because of diplomatic protests to the federal government, enforcement of the law had been suspended by the state, but a local group of citizens took on itself the responsibility of ensuring that the statute was enforced. Henry Elkison, a British subject born in Jamaica, was imprisoned in accordance with the South Carolina law and petitioned U.S. Supreme Court Justice William Johnson to secure his release under the terms of the British–U.S. treaty of 1815.

Justice Johnson's opinion abruptly announced that the constitutionality of the state statute "will not bear argument." Indeed, arguments submitted to justify the state's legislation and subsequent private action proved the invalidity of both under federal constitutional law. For the so-called Negro Seamen's Act to be valid, it would be necessary that the state have constitutional authority that was "paramount to the treaty-making power of the United States, expressly declared to be part of the supreme Legislative power of the land." Such a unilateral renunciation of treaty provisions might constitute a cause of war between the contracting nations. Indeed, counsel's arguments in favor of state authority included a clear acknowledgment that "if a dissolution of the Union must be the alternative [to enforcing federal supremacy in the matter], he was ready to meet it." Johnson pointed out that Massachusetts had many black sailors serving in its merchant ships, and the South Carolina law would apply similar imprisonment requirements on them. In a strong affirmation of federal supremacy, he asserted that "the right of the general government to regulate commerce with the sister states and with foreign nations is a paramount and exclusive right." His nationalism carried him even further in the direction of asserting a dormant authority that even if Congress did not regulate commerce, "the words of the [constitutional] grant sweep away the whole subject, and leave nothing for the states to act upon."

In a fearless assertion of defiance against local public opinion, Johnson ordered that the seaman be released from jail. As he might have expected, the order was disregarded, and he was reduced to continue his assertion of federal authority in essays published in the Charleston newspapers. Eventually, local animosity to Justice Johnson rose to the level that he migrated from his home state and resided in New York State until his death in 1834.

John Marshall had been less impetuous — and, as he later wrote to Justice Joseph Story, less willing — to butt against a stone wall. The case of *Wilson v. U.S.*, decided in his Virginia federal circuit court in 1820, involved three black seamen who entered the port of Norfolk on a Venezuelan privateer ship. The captain was prosecuted under a 1799 federal statute that prohibited the importation of slaves and free blacks into states that had excluded them from the class of acceptable immigrants; Virginia had enacted such an exclusion statute. The main issue was whether the three seamen were "imported." Marshall pointed out that the crew of a vessel is not imported, and furthermore, the state statute imposed sanctions for leaving such seamen behind when the ship left port. When the prosecution of the captain took place, the seamen had not been left behind, and therefore the state law was not violated. In passing, Marshall noted that the federal government possessed extensive authority over commercial activity:

> [T]he power of congress to regulate commerce, comprehends, necessarily, a power over navigation, and warrants every act of national

sovereignty, which any other nation might exercise over vessels, foreign or domestic, which enter our ports.

It was Marshall's good fortune to find a technical basis on which to reverse the captain's conviction in the U.S. district court. As a consequence, the constitutionality of the Virginia statute was not brought into issue. This good fortune was the subject of an interesting interchange between Marshall and Justice Story. Writing to Story on 23 September 1823, some time after Johnson's opinion in *Elkison*, Marshall commented, "Our brother Johnson, I perceive, has hung himself on a democratic snag in a hedge composed entirely of thorny state rights in South Carolina, and will find some difficulty, I fear, in getting off into smooth open ground." The chief justice admitted that he might have considered the constitutionality point in the *Wilson* case, but because it was not absolutely necessary to do so, he avoided construing the Virginia act in light of the federal Constitution. Quite clearly he recognized the heated political atmosphere and the fear in southern states that elaboration of Congress's commerce power might well be used to undermine the institution of slavery, or at the least, restrict the interstate slave trade. Coming as *Elkison* did just nine months before the arguments in *Gibbons*, the case could not have failed to impress all of the justices with the fears of the southern slavocracy, and also alerted them to the wisdom of being circumspect in balancing the interests of increased commercial activity within the nation against the instinctive states rights' protectionism of the south.

Corfield v. Coryell, a case of trespass for the seizure of a vessel brought in the federal circuit court for Pennsylvania, directed professional and public attention to still another aspect of commerce clause interpretation. A New Jersey statute restricted access to territorial oyster beds; it required that those harvesting oysters be residents of New Jersey, and that the vessel involved in the activity be owned by a New Jersey resident. Contrary to the New Jersey law, a group of Pennsylvania oystermen were harvesting oysters in New Jersey waters of Delaware Bay. They and their vessel were seized by New Jersey authorities and they were convicted, fined, and deprived of their boat. They elected to sue the New Jersey officials for trespass to their vessel, and their attorneys brought their action on diversity grounds in the U.S. circuit court for Pennsylvania, asserting that the New Jersey law was repugnant to the commerce clause of the federal Constitution. The trial was held in April 1823, and given the pendency of the *Gibbons* appeal in the U.S. Supreme Court, Justice Washington continued the matter until the Supreme Court had decided the Steamboat Case at its February 1824 term.

The issues raised by *Corfield* were thus very much in Washington's mind as he participated in the Supreme Court's conference discussions of *Gibbons*. *Corfield* raised serious questions concerning the traditional authority of state governments to conserve natural resources for the benefit of their own citizens. It presented Washington with the possibility of conflict between those local governmental powers and the commerce clause. In addition, it involved the scope of the privileges and immunities provisions contained in Article Four of the federal Constitution, which in turn had been derived from a similar provision in the old Articles of Confederation. Like many of the other issues touching on interstate commerce, *Corfield* raised complicated issues of federalism as well as sensitive matters of political balance in the allocation of governmental power. Justice Washington had already begun to contemplate the complexity of rendering a decision in *Corfield* nearly a year before *Gibbons* was argued before the Supreme Court. Although Washington was traditionally a justice who tended to acquiesce silently in Supreme Court opinions, he doubtless was an active participant in the Court's discussions concerning state residual powers and the commerce clause.

This admittedly sparse harvest of lower federal court cases may suggest the answer to two questions: First, why was Supreme Court attention to the commerce clause so long delayed? And second, why was the *Gibbons* decision so ambiguous? The *Wilson* and *Elkison* cases strongly suggest that as early as 1820, the chief justice and his colleagues were well aware that clarification of the commerce clause might raise strong political repercussions based on fears that the federal commerce power might be exercised to restrict the interstate slave trade. With the depletion of southeastern soil through intensive agriculture, planters began to move westward to newer and more fertile farmlands. As demand for slave labor grew in the new states and territories, there was an increasingly lucrative trade in the interstate transportation and sale of slaves from their native states. Consequently, interstate commerce in African Americans held in slavery was deemed essential to the economic well-being of both the older Atlantic seaboard states and the newly admitted states of the former southwest territory. Admittedly the balance of the federal union had been carefully preserved in the U.S. Senate by the simple expedient of matching free state entry with slave state admissions. However, heavy European migration into the northern states and the midwest threatened southern interests with growing free soil legislative majorities in the U.S. House of Representatives. Sectional conflict over the morality of chattel slavery and heightened fears of slave insurrections united to create widespread apprehension over the extension of federal power to either regulate or prohibit commerce. Indeed, oral argument in *Elkison* had degenerated into a sharp interchange between counsel and the bench over the possible dissolution of the union if federal supremacy meant unlimited entry of free black seamen into South Carolina. To the extent it was possible, the Supreme Court wisely avoided dealing with these issues. Ever the wary politician, Marshall in *Wilson* finessed an opportunity to further enunciate federal supremacy, just a year after he had expounded the doctrine in *McCulloch v. Maryland.* Perhaps the same considerations dictated the Court's equivocal opinion in *Gibbons.*

These lower court cases graphically illustrate the interdependence of the foreign commerce grant's language and that of the interstate commerce clause. The very placement of the two powers within the same phrase of the Constitution leaves little doubt that this intimate relationship was both recognized by the Philadelphia convention and constitutionally intended in the course of the drafting process. Although foreign commerce had been assigned to centralized congressional regulation by the Articles of Confederation, Congress's oversight of commerce among the states was introduced by the new federal Constitution. The threat of international reprisals and perhaps even war led Justice Johnson in *Elkison,* and later in *Gibbons,* to insist on exclusivity in the Court's interpretation of Congress's power over all commercial relations. Yet it was the merger of the two clauses that elevated the status of the interstate regulatory authority into a matter of national importance. The growing commercial role of the United States demanded that Congress possess a sharply defined and pervasive power over both foreign and interstate commerce. On the other hand, the nature of the federal system, and indeed perhaps even the existence of the union itself, demanded that the Supreme Court and its justices on circuit be not only circumspect but also equivocal in their interpretations of the two commerce powers. That they continued to do so in the course of deciding *Gibbons* should not surprise us.

Finally, as we shall consider at length in Chapter 6, there was considerable debate over the nature of the union before the Supreme Court's 1819 decision in *McCulloch v. Maryland.* States' rights political theories flourished unchallenged in October 1818, when Aaron Ogden brought an action against Thomas Gibbons in the New York chancery court, and even after the *McCulloch* opinion was issued, the newspaper and pamphlet debates over the Court's ruling left major issues of federalism a matter of conjecture. The strong opinion of the New York court of impeachment and errors in *Livingston v. Van Ingen* reminded the legal profession and politicians that state powers were established on the right of sovereign governments to control their own land and their territorial waters. Simply put, the broad questions of federalism needed to be examined and determined before it would be timely for the commerce clause to be explicated by the Supreme Court.

Of course, it was not then within the province of the Supreme Court to determine which cases should reach its docket, or indeed the extent of the record subject to review. Modern readers will be familiar with a much newer method of handling appeals to the U.S. Supreme Court through the Court's discretionary issuance of writs of certiorari. Virtually all appeals are subjected to a screening process by the justices of the Court; this is designed to identify those appellate applications that are entitled to receive the full attention of the Court. Only if a minority of four justices decide that the case is of sufficient importance, and that there is a pressing need for decision, will the Court issue a writ of certiorari directing that the matter be placed on the Court's docket for argument. In the Marshall Court, as today, original jurisdiction cases of litigation between two or more states, or of certain cases involving diplomats or foreign nations, must be accepted for argument before the Court.

However, when Marshall was chief justice, the Supreme Court could not restrict the cases that were brought before it on appeal. One of the vagaries of early federal procedure was that as a general matter, the procedural rules of the states controlled practice before the federal courts operating within that state. Thus when cases were brought before the Supreme Court on appeal, either from federal or from state tribunals, the record to be considered by the Court varied from state to state, depending on the scope of review applied in the highest court of the state. Many such appeals, like *Gibbons*, were based on the condition that in the state courts, a party had raised on his own behalf a provision of the Constitution, a federal statute, or a treaty right, and that the highest court in the state that had jurisdiction over the case had denied the defense on the basis of these federal questions. However, in such cases in Marshall's time, as today, there was no need for the litigants to be citizens of different states.

More expeditious, and also more susceptible to the Supreme Court's docket control, were cases either brought in the lower federal courts or transferred from state courts at the request of a party. It was required that cases brought in or transferred to federal courts be above the monetary minimum established for U.S. court jurisdiction, and that the parties be of differing states or foreign citizens. Once within the federal court system, virtually all commercial cases would be tried in a circuit court, presided over by a justice of the U.S. Supreme Court. As Professor G. Edward White has noted, justices riding circuit were alert to identify cases that raised important points of law, and they were careful to share these findings with their colleagues. After 1805 there was a statutory procedure whereby points of law raised in the circuit courts might be referred to the Supreme Court if the Supreme Court justice and his associated district court federal judge disagreed on these issues. A number of these "certificate of division" referrals to the Supreme Court resulted in the expeditious decision of matters that finally determined the outcome of circuit court litigation. Significantly, the procedure made possible an appeal to the Supreme Court even if the litigants themselves would not otherwise have undertaken either the time or the expense of appealing the circuit court's decision.

However, there was a downside to litigating in the U.S. circuit courts, which also involved the circuit-riding duties of Supreme Court justices. Assuming that a party lost his or her case in the circuit court, any appeal to the Supreme Court would bring the case before the trial justice's colleagues, and perhaps even the circuit justice himself. There was then no binding rule of judicial ethics requiring the circuit court justice to remove himself from participating in the appeal or abstaining from voting on the outcome. In a few instances the justice not only sat with the bench and voted, but he was actually assigned the task of writing the opinion that affirmed his decision below. More frequently, the trial justice did not participate in the hearing or in deciding the appeal, but contented himself with reading his opinion below into the Supreme Court record. And much to the relief of many appellants, it was usually the case that the circuit justice would neither participate in hearing the case nor take any part in its discussion or in preparing the Court's opinion. These uncertainties made appeals from federal circuit courts more problematic than they otherwise would have been, and we may surmise that this inconsistency in handling appeals from lower federal courts may have dissuaded many litigants from carrying their cases on appeal to the Supreme Court.

Prosecuting an appeal by either route was expensive, primarily because of the stature of counsel who most frequently appeared before the High Court. Not infrequently, they were members of the U.S. Senate or House of Representatives, and uniformly, all successful Supreme Court counsel could demand high fees for their advocacy. Uncertainties concerning procedure, judicial ethics, and constitutional issues made the outcome of appeals tentative at best. And finally, it took time and determination to persist through the years of effort required to obtain a hearing in the crowded and dimly lit chamber of the Supreme Court located in the basement of the Capitol building. It took sixty-four months, or five years and four months, for Aaron Ogden's original case to reach the U.S. Supreme Court. To that saga we now turn our attention.

Initial Litigation in *Gibbons v. Ogden*

By July 1816 Thomas Gibbons was well into the process of successfully attacking the Livingston–Fulton steamboat monopoly. His
steamship had successfully navigated in New York waters, contrary to
the express terms of the monopoly legislation, and as we have seen, he
had done so to the applause of a substantial portion of the public who
opposed monopolies in general and/or the partnership of Livingston
and Fulton in particular. Yet Gibbons was acutely aware of the fact
that issues of law were not necessarily subject to the influence of public opinion. Wisely, he needed to know where he stood before he took
steps that would compel the Livingston–Fulton syndicate or its
licensee, Aaron Ogden, to sue him in either the New York state courts
or the federal circuit courts for New York. More specifically, the New
York court of impeachment and errors' opinions in *Livingston v. Van
Ingen* needed to be carefully evaluated for two reasons. The *Van Ingen*
opinions had quite clearly laid down a strong argument for the territorial sovereignty of the state over its waters. On the basis of that
foundation, it had been powerfully demonstrated that New York was
entirely within its rights to encourage steam navigation by granting a
monopoly to those who first succeeded in operating a steamboat connection between New York City and Albany. In addition, the leading
opinion in *Van Ingen* had been written by James Kent, then chief justice of the state supreme court, but who subsequently in 1814 had
became chancellor of New York State. In his new office, Kent would
be the judge empowered to issue injunctions against violators of the
monopoly grant's terms. The new chancellor had also begun to earn a
national reputation as a prominent scholar and judge, which added to
the weight and persuasiveness of the *Van Ingen* precedents.

Lawyers consulted by Gibbons were understandably cautious in
predicting his chances for success should he be sued either for

infringement of the 1809 U.S. patent to Livingston–Fulton or for violation of their state monopoly. In July 1816 William Alexander Duer, a midcareer member of the New York bar and son of Revolutionary leader and speculator William Duer, was asked to evaluate Gibbons's proposed course of action. Duer advised Gibbons that in light of the federal Coasting Licensing Act of 1793, the New York monopoly grant to Livingston–Fulton could not limit Gibbons's rights to engage in steamboat navigation of New York Bay. In further support of Gibbons's legal position, he contended that federal power over commerce was "necessarily exclusive," as was U.S. authority under the patent clause. He also calmed the Georgian's well-founded concern about the constitutional positions adopted by Chancellor Kent in the *Van Ingen* case. As Duer interpreted the *Van Ingen* decision, it merely held that New York and the federal government had concurrent authority to reward Robert Fulton for his engineering achievements in steamboat construction and extended operations. Astutely, Duer read *Van Ingen* to deal only tangentially with the potential clash between patent rights and state monopolies. As he read the *Van Ingen* opinions, they held that federal patents and state monopoly grants were based on differing constitutional powers, permitting the exercise of either without violation of constitutional limitations. Most importantly, in Duer's opinion *Livingston v. Van Ingen* left open the question of federal and state power under the commerce clause.

Although Duer's analysis of the situation was most encouraging, Thomas Gibbons still had doubts a year later, at which time he secured an opinion from former vice president Aaron Burr, who after a period of European exile had resumed practice in New York City. Burr's primary concern was whether Gibbons as defendant could have the case transferred to the federal courts in the event the Livingston–Fulton syndicate or its licensee, Ogden, elected to commence litigation in New York state courts. On this point, Burr was confident that the diversity of state citizenship between the litigants would result in an "instant removal" to the federal circuit court. And in federal courts, according to Burr, it was doubtful whether any U.S. court would refuse to declare the New York monopoly laws to be "unconstitutional & Some of them to be highly absurd & tyrannical." Litigation in federal courts would circumvent Chancellor Kent's known partiality toward the New York steamboat monopoly. It also provided

a quicker route to appellate review and more sympathetic consideration before the Marshall Court. Unfortunately Burr's counsel proved
to be less accurate than his marksmanship in the duel that killed
Alexander Hamilton; transfer did not materialize as readily as pre-
dicted. This was one of those situations in which federal practice considerations had not become a matter of precedent. Burr was astute in
recognizing the problem, but understandably, he was unable to predict future decisions of the federal courts.

Nevertheless, encouraged by both legal opinions, Gibbons continued to harass and challenge Ogden's exclusive control of New York
City–Elizabethtown steamboat travel. Hard-pressed and humiliated
in a hostile public press, on 20 October 1818 Aaron Ogden filed a bill
in equity in James Kent's chancery court requesting an injunction
against Gibbons. Within the petition for other relief was a request for
forfeiture of Gibbons's steamboat, the *Bellona*, the extraordinary sanction stipulated by New York statute for violation of the monopoly
grant. Predictably, Chancellor Kent issued a preliminary injunction
the following day. It was this injunction that would bring the litigation to the U.S. Supreme Court in the February 1821 term after an
appeal within the New York state court system.

Chancellor Kent's injunction stopped Gibbons for a very short
time. By December 1818 he had entered into a contract with a Livingston–Fulton licensed syndicate authorized to conduct steam navigation between Staten Island and New York City. Under this
arrangement with Livingston–Fulton, the syndicate headed by U.S.
vice president Daniel Tompkins was authorized to stop in New York
City, and Gibbons asserted a similar right to do so on the basis of his
contract with Tompkins and his associates. Although Gibbons was
interested in clarifying the constitutional meaning of the commerce
clause, it is readily apparent that he did not mean to sacrifice business
opportunities or to suspend operations while litigating the fine points
of constitutional law.

On the other hand, December 1818 may have been the best of times
for Gibbons because of his obtaining the Tompkins contract, but it was
also the worst of times because Gibbons's attorneys inadvertently lost
their chance to transfer the case to the U.S. circuit court for New York.
This left them with no alternative to litigating the case before Chancellor Kent and the New York court of impeachment and errors. Their

error was excusable, especially in light of Aaron Burr's opinion, but its significance would not become apparent for several months. It was on 15 December 1819 that William N. Dyckman, a Manhattan attorney serving as Gibbons's solicitor, made a motion in the chancery court asking for the production of certain documents mentioned in Aaron Ogden's complaint. Solicitors in the chancery court were responsible for filing papers and serving as the attorney of record for their clients; trials were conducted and court appearances were made by counselors in equity. Along with his motion papers, Dyckman submitted what he doubtless considered to be a pro forma notice of his appearance in the case on behalf of Thomas Gibbons. Eight months after Dyckman's appearance in the case, he and Peter Jay Munro, Gibbons's trial counsel and a nephew of former U.S. chief justice John Jay, would learn of their error. In August 1819 — that is, before Dyckman filed his notice of appearance — the New York chancery court ruled that requests for a federal court transfer had to be made before a notice of appearance was filed in the New York state proceeding. This new rule of practice, overlooked by Gibbons's lawyers, made transfer to the federal courts impossible. Because state procedures were binding in the federal courts meeting in that state, there was no possibility of applying to the United States courts for relief. The Steamboat Case would therefore have to be litigated in the highest New York state court having jurisdiction before it could be appealed to the U.S. Supreme Court.

Dyckman escaped Gibbons's wrath; ironically, he had already been fired for not moving the case forward more quickly. His successor as Gibbons's solicitor, Gilbert L. Thompson, after obtaining access to additional documentation, proceeded to prepare an answer to the petition, taking care to assert in defense both Gibbons's rights under the Tompkins syndicate's license and his status as a holder of a federal coasting license under the 1793 statute. Diligent to the extreme — at least by New York chancery court standards — Thompson then moved to dissolve the preliminary injunction. In his 6 October 1819 ruling denying the motion, Chancellor Kent went well beyond the scope of the motion to observe that the 1793 federal statute did not confer any ownership rights or privileges to navigate on holders of such a license. In the chancellor's view, such ownership matters were properly decided in accordance with state law. The federal statute simply conferred American status on the vessel licensed under the act.

Clearly Kent's dictum negated Gibbons's legal positions in his answer; on the other hand, the chancellor's statement had been made prematurely because no proofs had been adduced in the case, and the matter had not been set down for hearing before the chancery court. Until these formal steps were taken and a final decree was entered, there was no final determination, and an appeal was improper. However, Gibbons's eagerness to press for a quick resolution of the case drove his attorneys to appeal the chancellor's decision on a preliminary injunction to the court of impeachment and errors, which in January 1820 affirmed Kent's order.

Perhaps in deference to the chancellor, the New York court of impeachment and errors set forth Kent's decree verbatim within its own judgment, then affirmed the decree in a relatively brief January 1820 opinion by Justice Jonas Platt. Kent had taken a close look at the federal Coasting Licensing Act of 1793 and concluded that he could find in its terms "no ground to infer any such supremacy or intention from the act regulating the coasting trade." Congress had made no pretense toward regulating interstate or foreign commerce within the statute. Therefore, New York need not defer to the provisions of the federal Coasting Licensing Act before it granted the Livingston–Fulton monopoly.

In its unanimous decision, the court of errors affirmed the chancellor's decree and reaffirmed on the basis of its prior decision in *Livingston v. Van Ingen*. Justice Platt, who had sat on the *Van Ingen* appeal by virtue of his position as a New York state senator and member of the court of impeachment and errors, commented that the court's reasons for so deciding *Van Ingen* were "now before the public, and I have not the vanity to believe, that I could add anything to their force or perspicuity." Indeed, his modesty may have been justified, for he ignored the notable distinction Gibbons's counsel had made between *Van Ingen*, a case between two New York residents, and *Gibbons*, which was litigation between citizens of different states, and which raised complicated questions concerning the interpretation of a federal statute and the constitutional impact of the Constitution's commerce clause on the validity of the Livingston–Fulton monopoly grant. Unfortunately, Chancellor Kent's decree below also lacked an examination of the novel interstate character of the *Gibbons* litigation. Having decided that the federal Coasting Licensing Act conferred no property rights on Thomas Gibbons, Kent doubtless felt justified in dismissing from further consideration the potential constitutional conflict between that federal statute and the New York state monopoly. Furthermore, *Van Ingen* raised the issue of the validity of the Livingston–Fulton monopoly in light of the Constitution's commerce and patent clauses, but the case resolved that issue in the context of asserting that the U.S. government's authority under the commerce clause was concurrent with the powers of state legislatures under residuary or police powers. Thus the focus of *Van Ingen* was on the interplay of U.S. patenting authority and state monopoly laws. Both Kent and Platt made the erroneous assumption that *Livingston v. Van Ingen* was a binding precedent; that mistake in both Kent's chancery decree in *Ogden v. Gibbons* and Platt's terse affirmation relying on *Van Ingen* left important questions unconsidered as the case was appealed to John Marshall's Court. On a subsequent appeal to the U.S. Supreme Court docketed at the February 1821 term, the Marshall Court, in a per curiam opinion, refused to entertain Gibbons's appeal because the decision by New York courts was not a final disposition of the case. Thereafter, the New York courts wasted little printer's ink on the case. By successive orders, entered without any further opinions, Chancellor Kent made the injunction permanent, and his final decision was upheld by a similarly brief order of the court of impeachment and errors. In effect, this meant that the chancellor's 1819 opinion, and the court of impeachment and errors' January 1820 affirming opinion, became the law of the case when it was taken on appeal to the U.S. Supreme Court in 1824.

Rendering the injunction permanent, followed by the order's affirmation by the court of impeachment and errors, removed the jurisdictional flaw noted in the Supreme Court's refusal to hear Thomas Gibbons's appeal in 1821. Despite Gibbons's impatience with the slow progress of the case, it became impossible to resolve the issues before the Supreme Court in its February 1822 term. Although the case was docketed for argument in 1822, Senator William Pinkney of Maryland, who represented Gibbons along with Daniel Webster, was disabled by his final illness when the Court's 1822 term began, and he died on 25 February 1822. In addition, Thomas Addis Emmet, cocounsel for Aaron Ogden, was not present when the case was called. Attorney General William Wirt, formerly Chief Justice Marshall's neighbor in Richmond, was subsequently retained by Gibbons to replace Pinkney, but the opportunity to litigate the appeal was lost until the opening of the February 1824 term.

However, the three-year delay had somewhat altered the situation of the Supreme Court and the state of federal constitutional law. In 1823 Associate Justice Brockholst Livingston died, leaving a middle-state Supreme Court seat vacant. Although Livingston was a cousin to Chancellor Robert R. Livingston, he also had become closely allied with Chief Justice Marshall's inner group among the justices. His vote on the *Gibbons v. Ogden* appeal was not predictably in favor of Gibbons, but at least it seemed likely to be so. On the other hand, the December 1823 appointment of Smith Thompson to the Court placed on the bench a jurist characterized by biographer Gerald T. Dunne as a "long time exponent of the doctrine of concurrent powers, and one of the most politically active Justices ever to sit on the Supreme Court." Thompson had studied law in Chancellor Kent's law office and had been an active supporter of his mentor as a fellow justice on the New York supreme court from 1802 until Kent's appointment as chancellor in 1814. Thompson then succeeded Kent as the intellectual leader of the New York supreme court until his 1819 federal appointment as secretary of the navy. He remained a member of the Monroe Cabinet until his nomination and confirmation as an associate justice of the U.S. Supreme Court in December 1823. The new justice had already adopted a strong concurrent powers position in his 1811 *Livingston v. Van Ingen* opinion delivered in the New York court of impeachment and errors, and might well have filed a dissenting opinion in the Supreme Court resolution of *Gibbons* in March 1824. However, the serious illness of his infant daughter and her subsequent death delayed his taking his seat on the Court until 10 February 1824, the day after arguments were concluded in *Gibbons*. He therefore did not take part in either the discussion or decision of *Gibbons v. Ogden*.

Another event that followed the 1821 order striking *Gibbons* from the Supreme Court's appellate docket was the critically important opinion in *Cohens v. Virginia*, also decided in the Court's 1821 term. The procedural circumstances in *Cohens* made it possible to assert principles that expanded the Supreme Court's jurisdiction of the U.S. Supreme Court without encountering resistance to the enforcement of its decrees. Also known as the Lottery Case, *Cohens* brought before the Court the question whether a congressional statute enacted to create a lottery within the District of Columbia precluded the Commonwealth of Virginia from prosecuting individuals who sold D.C. lottery tickets within the state of Virginia. The defendants had pleaded before the Norfolk hustings court that the federal statute, being a valid exercise of congressional authority over the District, was the supreme law of the land. As such, it preempted Virginia state law prohibiting gambling and games of chance, including lotteries. Reasoning that it was not Congress's intention to make the federal statute a law of national rather than local application, the Supreme Court rejected this defense and denied the appeal.

On the other hand, the Court also considered Virginia's assertions that because the commonwealth was a party to the action, the U.S. Supreme Court's jurisdiction was valid only if it was based on the Constitution's grant of original and not appellate jurisdiction. Procedurally, the Court was compelled to resolve these questions concerning its jurisdiction before it could subsequently deny the Cohens' appeal on the merits. The initial inquiry drew into consideration the role that the Supreme Court would play in resolving "federal questions" on appeal from the highest state court having jurisdiction in a case. A federal question was a matter that involved interpretations of the U.S. Constitution, federal statutes enacted pursuant to the Constitution, and treaties entered into by the authority of the United States both before and after the ratification of the Constitution. Justice Joseph Story's opinion for the Court in *Martin v. Hunter's Lessee* (1816) had powerfully argued that as a sovereign nation, the United States needed a uniform interpretation of international law and its treaty obligations — and only the U.S. Supreme Court's opinions provided adequate insurance of such uniformity. *Cohens* presented Chief Justice Marshall with an opportunity to assert the need for a similar unitary interpretation of domestic constitutional matters deemed to be of national significance.

John Marshall's opinion for the Court in *Cohens*, which was probably written around the time it was considering its dismissal of the 1821 appeal in *Gibbons*, provides insight into the Court's reaction to commerce clause litigation. In spelling out the critically important functions of the federal government, Marshall stressed situations that in his opinion required national unity: "That the United States form, for many, and for most important purposes, a single nation, has not been denied. In war, we are one people, in making peace, we are one people. *In all commercial regulations, we are one and the same people"* (emphasis added). For Marshall and presumably also for his colleagues, war-making power and treaty-making authority were equal to the power to make commercial regulations. That emphasis on the importance of the commerce clause in the construct of the federal union was reinforced by Marshall's insistence that the primacy of the Court's duty to interpret federal questions was essential to the effectiveness of the national government. He observed,

> No government ought to be so defective in its organization, as not to contain within itself the means of securing the execution of its own laws against other dangers than those which occur every day. Courts of justice are the means most usually employed, and it is reasonable to expect that a government should repose on its own Courts, rather than on others.

Furthermore, he advanced a strong individual rights argument, asserting that natural justice demanded that the rights of parties, even persons accused of violating state penal statutes as were the Cohen brothers, were properly referable to the "federal question" jurisdiction of the U.S. Supreme Court for resolution.

> We are told, and we are truly told, that the great change which is to give efficacy to the present [constitutional] system, is its ability to act on individuals directly, instead of acting through the instrumentality of state governments. But, ought not this ability, in reason and sound policy, to be applied directly to the protection of individuals employed in the execution of the laws as well as to their coercion. Your laws reach the individual without the aid of another power, why may they not protect him from punishment for performing his duty in executing them?

For these reasons, federal questions might be appealed to the U.S. Supreme Court even if a state were a party to the action. Such a forceful defense of the Court's appellate authority evidenced the justices' determination to resolve issues of federalism, recognizing that per-formance of this judicial duty was essential to the effective operation of the federal system. *Cohens* presented the Court with a valuable opportunity to once again stress the supremacy of the Constitution, of federal statutes enacted pursuant to the Constitution, and of treaties entered into by the United States. In case any doubt remained, throughout the opinion, Marshall included close paraphrases and direct quotations from *McCulloch v. Maryland* (1819).

Cohens also confronted the Court with a states' rights argument not dissimilar to the threats leveled at Justice William Johnson in *Elkison*. Counsel asserted that if federal law superseded state criminal law, popular hostility would destroy the union. To this, Chief Justice Marshall asserted the national origins of federal authority, and he appended a rejection of regional separatism:

> The people make the constitution and the people can unmake it. It is the creature of their will, and lives only by their will. But this supreme and irresistible power to make or unmake, resides only in the whole body of the people, not in any subdivision of them. . . . The acknowledged inability of the government then, to sustain itself against the public will, and by force or otherwise, to control the whole nation, is no sound argument in support of its constitutional inability to protect itself against a section of the nation acting in opposition to the general will.

Of course, in *Cohens* the Court decided the merits of the case in favor of Virginia, reasoning that Congress, in enacting a law permitting the District of Columbia lottery, was making municipal rules for the district and not legislating for the nation. As such, the lottery statute was not a "law of the United States" intended to be enforced throughout the United States by virtue of the supremacy clause. Having asserted its jurisdiction, the Court denied relief on the bases of its construction of the Constitution's supremacy clause and its interpretation of congressional intent when legislating for the District of Columbia. Virginia managed to prevail in *Cohens*, and the brothers paid their fine as required by Virginia law. But three years later the Court would be confronted with New York's similar threats that vigorous regulation of interstate commerce would destroy the union. Having dealt with political blackmail earlier, it was better prepared for the 1824 appeal in *Gibbons.*

Events beyond American courtrooms also made patent the need for the Supreme Court to consider the role that the federal government should play in American economic development and diversification. The issue of internal improvements and their funding first came to national attention in President James Monroe's veto of the Cumberland Road appropriation bill on 4 May 1822. Construction on that transmontane route to the west came to a halt as the result of the 1819 financial panic, but the return of prosperity induced Congress to enact a statute authorizing federal expenditures to complete the highway, which was also known as National Road. Monroe's veto message asserted that federal involvement in road construction was not authorized by the Constitution, and that the legislation was unconstitutional. He recommended that if such assistance was necessary, it was imperative that it be preceded by an appropriate amendment to the Constitution. Chief Justice Marshall, in a private letter, indicated that he agreed with this constitutional position, but at the same time, Nathaniel Macon expressed what was a more general fear — that just as Congress strove to extend federal power in the area of roads and internal improvements, it was to be expected that the Supreme Court would attempt to do so in the area of commercial activity.

Popular concern over growing federal intrusion into what had traditionally been local or state responsibilities raised serious questions about the federal system and how the United States, either collectively or individually, might need to adapt constitutional law and principles of federalism to meet emerging economic challenges. Arguably roads would play a decisive role in solving American transportation needs; federal involvement and direction offered many advantages. At the same time, the customary alignment of federal and state powers was both familiar and something of a safeguard against growing sectional differences over the institution of slavery. At the very least, increasing political tension and debate over internal improvements may have tempered the Marshall Court's approach to the *Gibbons* appeal after the case's first appearance on the Supreme Court docket in 1821.

Separate from constitutional law and political developments, Chief Justice Marshall's literary projects may also have impacted his consideration of the 1824 *Gibbons* appeal. The five-volume biography of President George Washington, published from 1804 to 1807, had devoted the first volume to a study of American colonial history before 1776. As Marshall noted in July 1824, the detour into a broader topic was required by the lack of published colonial histories in the first years of the nineteenth century, and Washington's career could not be appreciated without this background. Other historical work published after the 1807 appearance of the first edition of Marshall's study of Washington reduced the need for an extended colonial introduction, if it ever existed. In addition, Marshall's publishers insisted that the five volumes be reduced in scope and coverage with the publication of the second edition. Thus it was that for some time before the argument of *Gibbons v. Ogden* in the Supreme Court, the chief justice had been at work shortening the biography and revising the first volume into *A History of the Colonies Planted by the English on the Continent of North America* . . . , which was completed and filed for copyright protection on 7 July 1824. Among the topics covered in detail was the American colonial insistence that while the British Parliament had the right to regulate colonial trade, it had no right to legislate for the colonies' internal affairs, nor could it regulate trade for the purpose of raising revenue within the colonies.

Although Marshall refrained from applying the results of his historical labors to the task of writing the Court's opinion in *Gibbons*, it seems safe to speculate that the commercial regulatory role of Parliament and the value of centralized trade regulation in a federal union were not far from his thoughts as he considered *Gibbons* and prepared the opinion in that case. The years intervening from the case's first appearance on the Court's docket in 1821 provided time and opportunity for the chief justice to reconsider his own writings on the subject of imperial trade regulation in the British empire. Quite aside from contemporary issues of commerce, internal improvements, and federalism in Marshall's United States, American colonial experience demonstrated the importance of unified direction of commercial matters. If nothing else, Marshall's literary work redirected his attention to historic events that were closely related to the issues and policy considerations presented to the Court in 1824.

As appealed to the Supreme Court in its February 1824 term, *Gibbons* had been significantly simplified by the agreement of the parties to a statement of facts. Given the complex spiderweb of commercial arrangements underlying the positions of both groups of litigants, this was a welcome relief to the justices. In addition, the parties had agreed to a settlement that eliminated the forfeiture of the *Bellona* and the *Stoudinger*, Thomas Gibbons's steamboats seized under the provisions of the New York monopoly grant. Apparently there was some doubt whether such an extraordinary legislative destruction of property rights was valid or constitutional under New York fundamental law. Finally, the judicial opinions in the courts below were those already before the Supreme Court in 1821. They were well-known to the justices who would hear oral argument and participate in arriving at a judgment in the case.

Chancellor Kent's 1819 opinion presented the strongest defense of New York State's constitutional position. He had provided a striking assertion of state power to regulate the use of federally licensed vessels in the interest of public health and safety. Even when the use of a chattel was protected by a federal patent, the state's residual power over that utilization could be limited by the federal Constitution only when (1) the state's authority was impeded or defeated by the need to achieve some lawful and paramount federal objective, or (2) the state law was "absolutely repugnant to some constitutional law of the Union."

Citing English precedents, the chancellor asserted that the New York legislature's grant to Livingston–Fulton, being exclusive, carried with it the right to restrain others from "all contiguous and injurious competition." Chancellor Kent's effort to support a generous interpretation of the Livingston–Fulton grant is notable for introducing an economic analysis of the broad scope of monopoly rights; it may well have triggered Chief Justice Marshall's use of an economic argument to reject a narrow geographical limitation on the commerce clause in favor of the principle that state action should not be permitted to negate the economic advantage of free commercial activity among the states.

Kent's October 1819 chancery court opinion was affirmed at the January 1820 term of the New York court of errors. Samuel Jones Jr., a former member of the New York state assembly who would become recorder of the City of New York in 1823, argued the appeal on Gibbons's behalf, repeating natural law navigational rights earlier rejected in *Van Ingen* and claiming supremacy for the 1793 federal licensing statute. In his response, Josiah Ogden Hoffman, a former attorney general of New York State, stressed the precedents established in *Van Ingen* as well as emphasized the persuasive points made in the chancellor's opinion below. Interestingly, Hoffman elaborated on Kent's point that regardless of patent rights or rights to navigate under the 1793 Coasting Licensing Act, it was the state of New York's traditional authority over police matters that justified regulations for public safety. He chose an example of a circumstance that, as we have seen in the *Wilson* and *Elkison* cases, was ever more present in the nation's consciousness:

> [New York] has reserved to itself the precious and very important power of encouraging art and science, by granting exclusive rights to use improvements introduced from foreign states. Congress may give to authors and proprietors of books, an exclusive right of publication and sale. But would a state, in which slaves exist, allow an author, though he had taken out a copy right, to vend a book inciting slaves to insurrection and murder? The patent right must be subject to such laws as a state may pass for its own security.

Once again the "peculiar institution" and the threat of slave insurrections were urged as reasons to restrict congressional power over commerce and to accommodate state regulatory authority over property and persons within their territorial limits.

In his relatively brief affirming opinion for the court of impeachment and errors, Supreme Court associate justice Jonas Platt relied heavily on *Livingston v. Van Ingen*, which he viewed as binding precedent in *Gibbons v. Ogden*. Following Chancellor Kent's lead, he too rejected the argument that the 1793 federal statute created a paramount right in *Gibbons* to navigate in New York waters in defiance of the Livingston–Fulton state monopoly. The act itself demonstrated no congressional intention to establish such a right or license. When and if such an act of Congress was passed, it would then be timely to address the legal arguments advanced on behalf of *Gibbons*. On a personal note, Justice Platt indicated that he, as a former New York state senator and legislative member of the 1812 court of impeachment and errors, had voted in support of the decision in *Livingston v. Van Ingen;* he could not in good conscience acquiesce in that decision being overruled or ignored.

The record of *Gibbons v. Ogden* in New York's courts is notable for the number of issues left unanswered. The patent issue, even though it had been given detailed coverage in *Livingston v. Van Ingen*, was no longer the focal point. Although the Livingston–Fulton syndicate had belatedly secured a U.S. patent in 1809, neither Chancellor Livingston nor Robert Fulton claimed to be inventors. The New York legislature had awarded the monopoly because they had demonstrated the ability to maintain regular steamboat traffic on the Hudson River. *Gibbons* moved well beyond the narrow patent issue, drawing lines of battle between federal authority under the commerce clause and opposition to an exclusive state-based monopoly of steam navigation. By 1821, the bright promise of a vast interstate trade network and the foreign and interstate commerce regulation on which it depended were being balkanized by state mercantilist incentives. Retaliatory actions by sister states highlighted the possibility that state sovereignty would undermine both foreign and interstate commerce, and destroy cooperation and comity between sister states of the union. Like a threatening and gloomy cloud anticipating the arrival of a thunderstorm, interstate trade in slaves and growing fear of insurrection in the plantation states added urgency to the effort to reconstruct the political and economic aspects of the American union.

Reading the court of errors' 1820 decision in *Ogden v. Gibbons*, the Marshall Court in 1824 must have been puzzled by the degree to which New York justice Jonas Platt accepted *Livingston v. Van Ingen* as binding precedent. *Van Ingen* dealt primarily with the interplay of Congress's power over patents and New York's competence to issue a monopoly to Livingston and Fulton, based on their improvement on steamboat construction through the importation of foreign designs and mechanical arrangements. In his 1812 *Van Ingen* opinion, Chief Justice Kent referred in passing to congressional power to regulate commerce, but then asserted that no such congressional action had been taken. Deciding *Ogden v. Gibbons* in the New York chancery court, Kent in 1819 dismissed the 1793 federal Coasting Licensing Act as a mere revenue statute in regard to which Congress had expressed no intention to attribute supremacy under Article Six of the federal Constitution. Essentially, Justice Jonas Platt's affirming opinion adopted Kent's view for the court of impeachment and errors. At the very least, the New York approach to the 1793 federal act had shifted in its emphasis between 1812 and 1820, notably in the concern for the supremacy clause of the Constitution. In that regard, the 1812 *Van Ingen* opinion was of little significance; indeed, the U.S. Supreme Court's renewed attention to supremacy matters in the 1821 *Cohens v. Virginia* context rendered both *Van Ingen* and *Ogden v. Gibbons* not particularly persuasive in 1824.

As it prepared to hear argument in Thomas Gibbons's second appeal, the Court was driven to look more closely at New York's cavalier dismissal of the importance of the 1793 federal statute. The thirty-seven sections of the act passed on 18 February 1793 repealed thirty sections of a similar statute enacted less than two months earlier, on 12 December 1792. Marked by a precise stipulation of administrative practices and dominated by measures designed to discriminate between coastal and international trade, both versions of this regulatory statute evidence Congress's intention to control navigation in aid of an increasing need for neutrality between the warring nations of Europe. That interconnection between commercial activity and vital national concerns of war and peace had already been noted in John Marshall's opinion for the Court in *Cohens*. Indeed, the chief justice had identified making war and peace as two major functions of the United States government, along with the regulation of commercial activity. What may have been a plausible interpretation of the 1793 statute by the court of impeachment and errors in 1820 had become quite problematic by 1824. Furthermore, the judicial articulation of federal and state power had evolved significantly in the Court's *Cohens* opinion, affirming both federal supremacy and the judiciary's role in its maintenance.

Economy of judicial effort in some circumstances can be a virtue. However, New York's judges badly misjudged the persuasiveness of their antiquated 1820 analysis. Letting that disposition of *Gibbons v. Ogden* remain as the state's last explanation of its constitutional views set the stage for a de novo and exhaustive consideration of Thomas Gibbons's basis for appeal. It represented a defiant but flawed challenge to the primacy of commercial regulation by the federal government.

Oral Argument: A Clash of Titans

Given the financial stakes and constitutional importance of the Steamboat Case, it is not surprising that it was argued before the U.S. Supreme Court by four of the most eminent lawyers of the day. Daniel Webster, newly elected as a congressman from Massachusetts after he relocated his practice from New Hampshire, had earlier represented Thomas Gibbons in the abortive 1821 attempt to obtain Supreme Court review. William Wirt, appellant Gibbons's other attorney, had been U.S. attorney general since 1817 and had joined Gibbons's litigation team in February 1822. Although Wirt did not seek elective political office at either the state or federal level, he had earned an enviable reputation by frequent appearances as appellate counsel before the U.S. Supreme Court. These appeals were argued either for the United States or on behalf of private clients because at the time, there was no professional or ethical objection to a U.S. attorney general accepting briefs from private clients.

Aaron Ogden's attorneys for the appeal were no less distinguished, but their professional reputations were grounded on New York state practice rather than on litigation in the U.S. Supreme Court. Thomas Addis Emmet came from a prominent Irish nationalist family; after training in medicine at the University of Edinburgh, he altered his career path and was admitted to the Irish bar in 1790. He was widely known as defense counsel for political prisoners and for his service as legal counsel to the Society of the United Irishmen. When that society was declared illegal in 1797, Emmet, then its secretary and a member of the executive committee, resided in France, and he attempted to gain French aid for the Irish cause. After the collapse of a rebellion led by his brother, Robert Emmet, he emigrated to the United States, where he was admitted to the New York bar and served as the attorney general of the state from 1812 to 1813. Thomas Jackson Oakley's practice centered at Poughkeepsie after his 1804 admission to the New York bar. A member of Congress from 1813 to 1815, he thereafter was elected, and frequently reelected, to the New York state assembly. Oakley, like Emmet, had a brief term of service as the state's attorney general from 1819 to 1821. Extended periods of service in public office were rare in New York during this time period because rapid change in the state's politicized council on appointments generated turmoil and instability in state officialdom.

The arguments before the Marshall Court were considered by contemporaries as one of the high points of advocacy in the Marshall era. In 1849 Supreme Court justice James Wayne remarked, "the case of *Gibbons v. Ogden,* in the extent and variety of learning, and in the acuteness with which it was argued by counsel, is not surpassed by any other case in the reports of the Court."

Because Thomas Gibbons appealed to the U.S. Supreme Court from an adverse judgment of the New York court for impeachment and errors, his counsel were entitled to open argument when the appeal was called for presentation on 4 February 1824. Earlier Webster and Wirt had differed on the strategy that they should follow in arguing against the monopoly. "Black Dan" Webster insisted that the case should be argued on the basis of the commerce clause, while Wirt preferred to place the emphasis on the patent issue and the general unconstitutionality of the New York legislation. Unable to agree, each accepted the task of using his own strategy, and they decided that Webster would go first in their presentation. Wirt's deference was as much an acknowledgment of his co-counsel's charismatic appeal as it was a concession to the fact that Webster, through his role as a publicist for Marshall Court jurisprudence, enjoyed a special relationship to the Court as a whole and to Justice Story in particular.

Daniel Webster had been prepared to argue the case in 1821, and he reportedly spent the previous night composing his presentation. Although most of Webster's nocturnal endeavors were probably in the nature of revising an earlier text, the summary of his remarks evidences an astute understanding of the legal points at issue in 1824. His argument began with a forceful, but far from watertight, assertion that the federal government's commerce power was exclusive. A second tier of his presentation was based in part on the exclusivity position, asserting that in the "higher branches" of commerce regulation, federal power must be exclusive. State action or legislation might be constitutional if it did not rise to the "higher branch" status. The third level of the brief dealt with concurrent power principles, which undoubtedly would be the central focus of the opposition's position. At the outset, Webster asserted that the principles of concurrency were insidious, but he was willing to concede that state authority might be exercised concerning harbor pilotage, health regulation, and the operation of quarantine facilities. These were areas insufficiently touched on by the federal commerce power, and thus would not be unconstitutional. There were also situations in which the federal commerce power might be exercised to supplement or augment state economic activity. One example was federal funding of major road construction; perhaps the completion of Jackson's military road in 1819 had drawn Webster's attention to the contributions that lengthy or strategically located highways made to national security. At the same time, most road construction properly fell within the ambit of local and state initiatives. The federal admiralty authority might augment state and local law enforcement in waters adjacent to but beyond the territorial waters of a state. However, Webster warned that concurrency of power not only weakened the exclusive nature of the federal commerce power, but conversely, might be a vehicle for eroding traditional state initiatives.

This opening argument demonstrates the accuracy of Justice Joseph Story's evaluation of his friend's approach to appellate advocacy, which was marked by "a clearness and downright simplicity of statement" and a "power of disentangling a complicated proposition, and resolving into elements so plain as to reach the most common minds." Webster's carefully layered approach permitted him to suggest a variety of alternatives to the Supreme Court as it considered Gibbons's appeal. The justices could draw from any combination of the views expressed and still decide against the Livingston–Fulton monopoly. Webster's strategy was to present a cautious and measured group of proposals that gained their persuasive power from a pragmatic assessment of the interplay of national and local requirements and capabilities. As such, the breadth of choices submitted was wide enough to appeal to all of the justices, but narrow enough to direct support to the pro-national position of Gibbons. The argument, which bordered on an outright rejection of concurrent powers in commercial regulation, may well have been revised after 1821 to anticipate the arrival of newly confirmed associate justice Smith Thompson. A protégé of Chancellor James Kent, Thompson, while serving as a judicial member of the New York court of impeachment and errors, had written a strong concurrent powers opinion in *Livingston v. Van Ingen*. Thus Webster had good reason to expect a dissenting opinion from Thompson when *Gibbons v. Ogden* was decided. However, when the case came on for argument on the first day of the 1824 term, Thompson was absent because of his daughter's terminal illness and death. The chief justice denied the appellee's motion asking to delay argument until Thompson arrived from New York. Thus Webster's discussion of concurrency was not as critical as it otherwise might have been, but that phase of the argument undoubtedly suggested that an exclusive interpretation of the commerce clause might overlook some of the complexities of commercial regulation.

Within this broad framework of Webster's argument, several emphases deserve special mention. Earlier in his argument, he deprecated the current state of the American union as a result of the tense circumstances and hostility among the states that was generated by the existence of the Livingston–Fulton monopoly. There was virtual retaliation by New Jersey and Connecticut against the New York monopoly grant, and in response to the harsh penalties that were imposed by New York on anyone navigating by steamboat in what were deemed New York territorial waters. Because this was a situation that had existed during the Confederation period of American history, it was something that the ratification of the Constitution should have eliminated. Apparently, it did not. Webster queried whether it was the responsibility of the Supreme Court to find a way through this impasse and once again restore tranquillity among the states of the union. Shortly thereafter, he called attention to the critical role that commercial regulation had played in the convening of the federal convention in Philadelphia in 1787. He succinctly summarized the growing national concern that commercial activity was disruptive of relations between the states, and that the fear that lack of central oversight of commercial activity undermined American economic prosperity and national unity. The 1786 Annapolis meeting was called for the sole purpose of proposing a "uniform regulation of trade," and it was for that "entire" purpose that the federal convention convened in 1787. To quote Webster,

> Few things were better known, than the immediate causes which led to the adoption of the present constitution; and he thought nothing clearer, than the prevailing motive was to *regulate commerce;* to rescue it from the embarrassing and destructive consequences, resulting from the legislation of so many different States, and to place it under the protection of a uniform law. The great objects were commerce and revenue, and they were objects indissolubly connected. By the confederation, diverse restrictions had been imposed on the States, but these had not been found sufficient. . . . The States could still, each for itself, regulate commerce, and the consequences was a perpetual jarring and hostility to commercial regulation.

This implied that unless the Supreme Court upheld Gibbons's position, it would endorse a return to the Confederation period's commercial chaos and dismantle both the union and the economic system achieved by ratification. Indeed, the union had already been badly undermined by New York's monopoly and the retaliation of two neighboring states. To drive these points home, Webster asserted,

> We do not find in the history of the formation and adoption of the constitution, that any man speaks of a general *concurrent power,* in the regulation of foreign and domestic trade, as still residing in the States. The very object intended, more than any other, was to take away such power. If it had not been provided, the constitution would not have been worth accepting.

Ratification transferred to the general government all of those "high and important powers" necessary to maintain a uniform and general system that would operate as a unit. Of necessity, he asserted, such powers must be exclusive and exclusively committed to a single hand.

Turning to the New York monopoly grants to the Livingston–Fulton syndicate, Webster denounced the state's action as the "exercise of a sovereign political power," which, left unchallenged, could be

{ *Chapter 5* }

expanded into numerous other areas of legislation. Even within the restricted field of maritime navigation, might not an accepted, even tolerated, grant for propulsion by steam encourage a multitude of other restrictive monopoly grants for the navigation of sloops or any other class of vessel? Such restrictions might limit navigation and other commercial activity to favored state residents, to the exclusion of traders from other states and foreign nations. Should the Supreme Court concede such an authority to New York to discriminate against its own citizens as well as nonresidents? What would prevent other states from adopting the same methods? In company with other states taking the initiative of issuing monopolistic and discriminatory grants, New York would fracture all federal attempts to regulate interstate or foreign commerce.

If the New York grant were not held void ab initio, it was invalidated by its collision with the 1793 federal Coasting Licensing Act, which conferred rights to navigate coastal waters on those U.S. citizens who, like Thomas Gibbons, had been granted the privilege of freely navigating the coastal waters of the nation. No state legislation could deprive a citizen of those rights granted by the license of the U.S. government. The right to engage in the coastal trade, like the right to hold land in New York or to sue in its courts, belonged to Gibbons as a citizen of the United States. Although Webster was not more specific in adumbrating his understanding of federal citizenship and related rights, his argument in this regard appears to rely heavily on the privileges and immunities clause in Article Four of the Constitution, which first appeared in virtually identical verbiage in the old Articles of Confederation. Of course, equal access to commercial institutions and facilities, for both states and their individual citizens, was part and parcel of the framework on which a viable national economy would be established and flourish. That was one of the underlying principles of the privileges and immunities clauses that had been augmented powerfully by the Constitution's provision for an interstate commerce power vested in Congress. Implicit in Article Four's privileges and immunities provisions was a clear intention that in commercial activities, discriminatory or retaliatory state legislation against the citizens of a sister American state was in violation of the federal Constitution.

The federal Coasting Licensing Act assumed a critical place in

Webster's argument; it was not, as New York's courts had held, merely an act providing administrative processes by which the nationality and character of a vessel could be determined for the purpose of assessing taxes and duties. Nor was it simply a convenient way to evidence the ownership of the vessel, and the advantages that would accrue from American status. According to Webster, the very phraseology stipulated in the statutory form of the coasting license left no doubt that property rights to navigate were conferred on the licensees. Referring to the Livingston–Fulton grant, Webster noted that it purported to give the syndicate authority to license individuals wishing to navigate by steam in New York waters. The state was attempting to do by its monopolistic grant what Congress already had done by enacting the federal Coasting Licensing Act. Therefore, the New York monopoly grant was invalid and unconstitutional because it was contrary both to the commerce clause of the Constitution and to the 1793 federal Coasting Licensing Act, a federal statute enacted pursuant to the Constitution.

Thomas Jackson Oakley undertook the unenviable task of defending Aaron Ogden and the Livingston–Fulton syndicate against Webster's many-pronged and forceful attack. It also fell to him and Thomas Addis Emmet, his co-counsel, to buttress the case for a concurrent powers construction of the Constitution's commerce clause. The printed records of argument indicate that Webster and William Wirt used slightly less than 30 percent of the time devoted to presenting the case before the Supreme Court. There is much to be said in favor of brevity in oral argument, but the two New York attorneys were faced with a Court reputed to favor the extension of federal authority. And their defense of the Livingston–Fulton monopoly was further hampered by the relatively weak 1820 opinion authored by Justice Jonas Platt in the court of impeachment and errors.

Oakley, opening for the respondent, presented a detailed and well-nuanced analysis of the concept of concurrent state and federal powers. A few days before the 1824 Supreme Court term opened, Oakley was described by opposing counsel William Wirt as being "one of the leading logicians of the age, as much a Phocion as Emmet is a Themistocles and Webster is as ambitious as Caesar. He will not be outdone by any man, if it is within his power to avoid it. It will be a combat worth witnessing." Wirt's assessment of Oakley suggests that Ogden's lawyers were expected to counter Webster's oratorical power with a forthright and analytical presentation, stressing the wisdom of adopting a concurrent powers view concerning interstate and foreign commerce. After that, they would polish Oakley's craftsmanship with the oratorical eloquence of the flamboyant Irishman. As Wirt confided in a letter to his brother, Thomas Addis Emmet was known to "put his whole soul" into the preparation and argument of his cases. This strategy had the dual advantage of coinciding with the then-current localizing preferences of the nation; it was also a well-conceived opening wedge in their logical burden of converting those justices who might initially favor an exclusive approach to the commerce clause. By focusing the Court's attention on the practical difficulties of an exclusive interpretation of federal powers, they could give pause to the Court's tendency to be swept along by the power of Webster's presence and argument.

Chilling the heat of rhetoric with the cold logic of reality also provided a better platform from which to recast colonial and early national history and to emphasize the vast array of residual power that still remained with the states, despite the ratification of the Constitution nearly four decades before. Throughout Oakley's argument, there is a leitmotif stressing the sovereignty of the several states before 1789, and the particular situation of New York State, whose first constitution vested the supreme legislative power of the state in its legislature, without enunciating any restrictions on the exercise of that power. By way of contrast, the constitution of the United States created a limited government of expressly delegated powers; the great principle of federalism was that because the United States was a government whose powers were delegated, and not a restriction on state powers already possessed, "every portion of power not granted, must remain with the State Legislature."

Having tersely laid a historical foundation for concurrent powers analysis, Oakley moved into a consideration of the patent clause of the federal Constitution and its relationship to the reserved police powers of the state. Because the issue of federal patent powers had been treated at length in *Livingston v. Van Ingen*, it was considered binding precedent in *Ogden v. Gibbons* as that case moved through New York's court system. Yet Oakley chose to spend a substantial portion of his argument on the patent issue. We must assume that he, and perhaps also Emmet, saw, in the secondary consideration of state–national conflict over patents, a more neutral way to consider the issue of concurrent powers. That was particularly the case in light of the 1793 federal Coasting Licensing Act, which seemed to hold as little relation to implementing the commerce clause as those existing federal statutes that dealt with rewarding authors and inventors, or controlling use of the new discoveries, or suppressing libel or slander by authors. Discussing the concurrent powers theory divorced from the substantial economic significance of the commerce clause increased the possibility of a more objective hearing before the justices. Indeed, the 1793 statute covering the coasting trade was much stronger evidence of congressional intention to act under the commerce power than was existing federal legislation dealing with patents, their issuance, or their significance within the federal system.

Oakley began by dividing federal powers into those that are expressly granted in the Constitution and those that are implied. Of course, if a power mentioned in the Constitution was to be enforced in a way specified in the Constitution, another means of implementation would not be appropriate. Powers are also to be classified as being either exclusive or concurrent, and exclusive powers are of two types: first, national powers that did not exist before the adoption of the Constitution, and that were created by the constitution's ratification, and second, those powers that by the Constitution have an effect beyond the territorial boundaries of a single state. Exclusive powers were required to be expressly enumerated in the Constitution; all implied powers were therefore concurrent.

Concurrent powers arose in a variety of situations. According to Oakley, concurrency could be determined by considering the follow questions: (1) Did the power exist in the states previous to the Constitution, and did it pertain to their sovereignty? (2) Was the power granted in exclusive terms by the Constitution? (3) Was the power granted to the union and prohibited to the states? (4) Was it exclusive in nature, either because it was operative beyond state boundaries or because it arose in the origin and creation of the union? Or (5) was the federal power so dominant that no state action could be taken without triggering actual conflict with the federal Constitution? In regard to repugnancy, he cited *Federalist* No. 32, that only immediate and inevitable constitutional conflict with the Constitution would suffice to justify invalidation of any state action. The thrust of Oakley's argument is clear: very few delegations of power in the Constitution are exclusive, and concurrency exists in all cases except when conflict with federal constitutional powers is inevitable.

Once it is determined that a power is concurrent, it must be ascertained whether utilization of that power by Congress precludes state legislation. This must be tested by considering the nature of the power. Federal legislation establishing weights and measures or regulating the value of foreign coinage precludes any state legislation on the subject matter, but most other areas of governmental concern are subject to both congressional and state legislation until there is actual and practical collision, in which case Article Six of the Constitution demands that federal statutes be preferred and thus state enactments are rendered invalid. Both the state and federal governments exercise authority to impose and collect taxes, both the United States and the state of New York may impose criminal sanctions for counterfeiting notes issued by the Bank of the United States, and both are responsible for the organization and training of militia, except that the states habitually added additional requirements to supplement those imposed by federal law.

To this point, Thomas Oakley's submissions to the Court ran counter to Webster's assertion that concurrent powers were insidious. Indeed, the New Yorker's analysis emerges as a rational catalog of the hierarchy of constitutional power under the Constitution, replete with examples of how the states and the federal authorities had hitherto allocated their powers in a logical and orderly manner. The foundation was well laid for a closer look at the degree to which concurrency principles should be applied to the question of state monopolies and the Constitution's patent clause.

In rapid succession, Oakley asserted that the patenting authority was not exclusively granted to Congress, nor was it exclusive in its nature; it was simply an affirmative and general power. Neither did the Constitution deny the patenting power to the states. Therefore, the states might exercise this concurrent power until an actual and practical conflict arose between state action and the primacy of the federal government under Article Six. State authority was extensive, as Oakley demonstrated by describing the narrow limits expressed within the Constitution's authorization to Congress. Federal patents might issue only for inventors who made a discovery, thereby excluding individuals who introduced useful machines or inventions from abroad. On the other hand, state patents conferring privileges and rights limited in scope by the boundaries of the state, and without conflict with federal patents, reward importers of new technology into the state.

The issuance of a federal patent recognized certain rights in the grantee, but as Oakley quickly pointed out, the degree to which a patentee used the patented object was subject to control by state legislation. Relying on the justices' awareness of exploding boilers on steamboats, he asserted,

> Patented manufactures may be injurious to the public health, though highly useful as manufactures; or they may be nuisances to private individuals and neighbourhoods, though extremely useful to the public. . . . The right to use all property must be subject to modification by municipal law. . . . It belongs exclusively to the State Legislatures, to determine how a man may use his own, without injuring his neighbour.

The same considerations applied to authors and their copyrighted works. Obviously the issuance of a federal copyright would not operate to permit the author to publish libelous, blasphemous, or obscene matter that otherwise would violate state law.

Oakley asserted that the patenting laws enacted by Congress were "framed on the supposition that the power to prohibit remains in the States." He conceded that although the states might prohibit the use of federally patented objects, they were precluded from granting the use of a federally patented object to other than the patentee. On the other hand, the state's authority over inventions located within its territory was extensive, based on its sovereign control over its public domain. Conversely, in allowing use within its territory, a state might impose conditions, and in situations it deemed appropriate, New York had every right to restrict an invention's use to a given operator, thereby ensuring the safety of steamboat travel on its waters. The discussion of public domain provided Oakley with a smooth transition into his discussion of the commerce clause and the historic authority of a state to control its territorial waters as trustee for the people of the state. It will be recalled that *Corfield v. Coryell* was, as Oakley spoke, awaiting decision in Justice Bushrod Washington's circuit court for Pennsylvania; because it involved oyster beds held by the state of New Jersey in trust for state residents of the state, Oakley's comments were of particular interest to Washington, and perhaps to several other justices.

Moving to the question of commercial regulation, Oakley considered the extensive authority exercised by the states from the Declaration of Independence to their ratification of the Constitution. He pointed out that in 1776 as in 1788, the states had the right to permit, deny, or limit trade from and to sister states of the union and foreign nations. This power rested solidly on the *ius commune* and thus was part of customary international law, subject to alteration by treaties and other arrangements between sovereign nations. With the ratification of the Constitution, two things occurred: (1) states were required to obtain the consent of Congress if they wished to impose import or export duties, and (2) state authority to regulate commerce was subjected to the superior power of Congress to regulate trade among the states, with Indian tribes, and with foreign nations. As to the second point, Oakley was quick to assert that Congress had yet to act under this constitutional authorization.

Furthermore, Congress's power to regulate commerce was limited by the requirement that it could not act on commerce entirely internal to the state, nor might it intrude on the state's authority to govern affairs within the state even if they might thereby impact interstate commerce. Emphasizing the extensive residuum of power within state legislatures, Oakley explained,

> Internal commerce must be that which is wholly carried on within the limits of a State: as where the commencement, progress, and termination of the voyage, are wholly confined to the territory of the State. This branch of power includes a vast range of State legislation, such as turnpike roads, toll roads, exclusive rights to run stage wagons, auction licenses, licenses to retailers, and to hawkers and ped[d]lers, ferries over navigable rivers and lakes, and all exclusive rights to carry goods and passengers, by land and water. All

such laws must necessarily affect, to a great extent, the foreign trade, and that between the States, as well as the trade among citizens of the same State. But, although these laws do not thus affect trade and commerce with other States, Congress cannot interfere, as its power does not reach the regulation of internal trade, which resides exclusively in the States.

More specifically, absent any congressional legislation to the contrary, a state might, under the *ius commune*, withhold entry into its territory, or restrict that right to a single individual or firm of its own choice. The Livingston–Fulton monopoly did not prohibit navigation but only restrained navigation by steam within New York; it represented a valid attempt to "exclude from the right of navigation on its waters in a particular mode, because they deem that mode injurious to the public interest, unless used by particular persons."

Indeed, the federal government, in the organic acts admitting Louisiana and Mississippi into the union, demonstrated Congress's understanding that states within the United States retain the authority to control and regulate navigation of their territorial waters. Both acts required as a condition of admission that the petitioning territory agree that navigable rivers and waters leading to the Gulf of Mexico would be common and forever free, without any tax, duty, impost, or toll imposed by the petitioning territory or admitted state. That freedom of access was to be accorded to its own inhabitants and to the citizens of all other states of the American union. Why should such express waivers be required unless Congress anticipated that otherwise the newly admitted states could prohibit or tax commercial activity passing through their waters?

Before concluding, Oakley made a final point distinguishing between trade and the carriage of passengers for hire. Congress was empowered to regulate commerce, which included the purchase or sale of goods, and the transportation of goods for those financial purposes. It did not include the transportation of persons, which was a distinct business. Therefore, Gibbons's reliance on the 1793 federal Coasting Licensing Act was improper because his vessel was not engaged in the coasting trade, but rather navigated for the sole purpose of transporting people and not goods.

Oakley's tightly organized argument raised the matter of concurrent powers in terms that did not challenge the primacy of the federal government in the regulation of commerce, but it did point out the large overlap that existed between possible federal commercial regulation and the vast amount of state legislative competence that existed under what have come to be recognized as police powers. He had also suggested that a bare constitutional grant of power without supplementary congressional enactment under that power would leave a residuum, or a default authority in the state governments. In Oakley's view of concurrent powers, there was no room for dormancy in the Constitution's commerce clause. In practical terms, Congress would have to use it or lose it for the time being.

Although Oakley had taken pains to conform to states' rights history and analysis, he was careful not to rely heavily on these theories. Rather, he emphasized the practical need to consider the interconnection of federal and state powers in the regulation of interstate and foreign commerce. His presentation had done much to leave the Supreme Court with a well-considered basis for a decision that would support Aaron Ogden's case and the Livingston–Fulton monopoly but still be consistent with the Constitution's supremacy clause. It also left to future generations a rich discussion of concurrency that would, in time, find its way into the opinions of later Supreme Courts. A historian of the Supreme Court, Charles Warren, quotes a New York newspaper's judgment of Oakley's argument:

[He] set about attacking the ramparts of the law which had been erected, with his usual coolness and deliberation. He broke ground at a great distance from the immediate question, and commenced a system of mining . . . one of the most ingenious and able arguments ever made in this Court.

If Thomas Oakley worked with the diligence of a subterranean termite, his senior counsel erupted with flamboyant rhetoric along with a superabundance of precise and overwhelming detail.

Although we cannot evaluate Thomas Addis Emmet's eloquence, the version of his comments printed in the Supreme Court reports provides one good example of his oratory. The concluding segment of his address praises the foresightedness of New York State in encouraging, then rewarding, the efforts of Livingston and Fulton. In his moving tribute, he extolled their achievements, which adapted preexisting steamboat technology to the state's need for a reliable and utilitarian ship designed for regular navigation of the Hudson River from New York City to Albany. This gift to the nation was made possible by the unselfish and generous support of the state of New York, which,

> by a patient and forbearing patronage of ten years, to Livingston and Fulton, by the tempting inducement of its proffered reward, and by the subsequent liberality of its contract, . . . called into existence the noblest and most useful improvement of the present day. . . . She has brought into noon-day splendor, an invaluable improvement to the intercourse and subsequent happiness of man, which, without her aid, would, perhaps, have scarcely dawned upon our grandchildren. . . . The Ohio and Mississippi, she has converted into rapid channels for communicating wealth, comforts and enjoyments, from their mouths to their headwaters. . . . New York may raise her head, she may proudly raise her head, and cast her eyes over the whole civilized world; she there may see its countless waters bearing on their surface countless offsprings of her munificence and wisdom.

How could the Marshall Court ignore such a magnanimous legislative gesture that had been so richly rewarded with the progress of mankind? To do so would, according to Emmet, deny to Fulton's widow and child the support they richly deserved, and it would disappoint investors who had "confided their wealth and means to the stability and observance of these laws."

Even in the drab skeleton of Emmet's argument that survives in the printed Supreme Court reports, his plea emerges as an eloquent passage, marked by the emotionalism and romanticism of the day. Its appeal is magnified when the reader is aware — as the Supreme Court undoubtedly was — that Robert Fulton had saved Emmet's life almost a decade before. While the two men were walking across the frozen Hudson River from Hoboken to New York City, the ice gave way under Emmet. It was Fulton who leapt into the frigid water to sustain the lawyer until help could arrive. Emmet survived the incident unscathed, but Fulton was taken ill with the pneumonia that eventually took his life. Arguing in the Supreme Court, the Irish patriot was acutely aware that unless his advocacy was successful, Fulton's child and widow would be left virtually destitute.

Yet it would be unwise and inaccurate to dismiss Emmet's argument as simply a rhetorical gloss on Oakley's presentation. Quite the contrary—Emmet's argument supplied the Supreme Court with an overwhelming abundance of precisely documented and footnoted examples from which one could confidently flesh out the principal points emphasized by Oakley. Emmet provided a catalog of five states in addition to New York that had enacted steamboat monopoly statutes. An extended footnote discussed New York and Georgia statutes providing for ferries, toll roads, and stagecoach monopolies within their territories, many of which had interstate significance. To illustrate the capacity of states to restrict both interstate and foreign trade from entering their territories, he provided a footnote on the slave trade, followed by a reference to an 1803 congressional statute that recognized the right of the states to enact such legislation. In still another footnote, Emmet drew on legislation and case law from at least eight states that illustrated the broad and sweeping authority over both exports and imports exercised as part of a state's inspection laws.

Clearly, this detail would be unsuitable for oral argument, lest its full impact be lost on the attention of the listening justices. However, to the extent that the court would have access to the transcript of arguments printed in the Supreme Court reports, these would emerge as critically important details that would lend substance and weight to Oakley's and Emmet's major contentions that commerce was already regulated on a concurrent basis. They seriously undermined the opposition's argument that the commerce clause conferred on the federal Congress exclusive regulatory power over interstate and foreign commerce. Emmet's exhaustive research also demolished Webster's fallback position: that in major areas of commercial regulation, Congress possessed exclusive power. Documented past practice suggested that although federal power was entitled to paramount roles in dealing with commercial activity, the states were by no means minor participants in economic regulation touching on, or substantially supporting, both interstate and foreign trade. Nor did this involve only routine day-to-day interaction between state and federal commercial law, but it was also clear that in many situations, Congress had tacitly accepted this situation and in several circumstances had expressly recognized the extent and importance of state collaboration with federal initiatives.

Emmet was also a canny fisherman, baiting his hook with insects, worms, and alluring dry flies that would have special appeal to his judicial quarry. This task was rendered more difficult when circumstances prevented Justice Smith Thompson from attending the argument of the case, and therefore being disqualified from discussing it in conference or the Court's decision. Without an advocate on the bench for state authority and concurrent exercise of commerce regulatory power, the Irish angler's skills were tested to the extreme. The personal appeals to the interests and inclinations of the justices are even more striking when we realize that when Emmet wrote his brief, he could not have anticipated Thompson's absence. These circumstances only became obvious the day before argument was scheduled to begin, and even then, he and Oakley had attempted unsuccessfully to delay the hearing until Thompson could be present. Discussing the impact of the supremacy clause on the case, Emmet took care to cite Justice Thompson's earlier opinion in *Livingston v. Van Ingen*, where the future Supreme Court justice, as a judicial member of New York's court of impeachment and errors, had insisted,

> All fears and apprehension of collision in the exercise of these [state] powers, which have been urged in argument are unfounded. *The constitution has guarded against such an error, by providing that the laws of the United States shall be the supreme law of the land, any thing in the constitution of any State to the contrary notwithstanding. In case of collision therefore, the State laws must yield to the supreme power of the United States.* [Italics in original]

While planning to flatter Justice Thompson with a citation to his words, Emmet was also able to argue that only direct conflict — collision between federal and state laws — would justify resort to the federal Constitution's supremacy clause. This narrow construction of federal supremacy was characteristic of the concurrent powers position. Indeed, in *Van Ingen*, Chief Justice James Kent applied the same standard — collision — in his opinion.

More importantly, Emmet cited Justice Joseph Story and Chief

Justice Marshall as resorting to the same limiting construction in their respective opinions in *Houston v. Moore* and *Sturges v. Crowninshield*. Pointedly, he quoted Story as writing,

> In cases of concurrent authority, where the laws of the States and of the Union are in direct and manifest collision on the same subject, those of the Union, being the supreme law of the land, are of paramount authority, and the State laws, so far only as such incompatibility exists, must necessarily yield.

In other words, although supremacy was the Constitution's mandate, invalidation of state legislation was appropriate only to the degree that it was necessary to resolve the incompatibility.

Of course, unlike the *Gibbons* situation, in *Houston*, state–federal concurrency in administering the militia was based on express constitutional language, and in *Sturges*, the Court was faced with deciding whether, in the absence of a federal bankruptcy law, they should declare a state insolvency law unconstitutional for being a violation of the Constitution's bankruptcy and contract clauses. However, in both *Houston* and *Sturges*, concurrent power was conceded by the parties; in *Gibbons*, it was very much in debate. Given these distinctions, Emmet's assertion alerted the Court that at the very least, two justices sitting in judgment on the *Gibbons* appeal previously had been open to a collision-only standard for applying the supremacy clause in constitutional situations.

The Irish barrister resorted to legislative history and a precise reading of the Constitution to counter Daniel Webster's emphasis on the commercial incentives that played a major role in convening the 1787 Philadelphia constitutional convention. As ratified, the Constitution provides only that Congress "shall have power" to regulate commerce. Resorting to the journals of the convention, Emmet demonstrated that the drafting committee had intentionally omitted "the" from that delegation of power, and it was after considerable redrafting that the phraseology presented to the full convention did not read "shall have the power" to regulate interstate and foreign commerce. The deletion, according to Emmet, implied that the drafting committee and the full convention, while intending to confer some authority on the federal Congress to regulate trade, had intentionally omitted "the" from the phrase, thereby refraining from transferring *all* power to the national legislature. That inference, he argued, was supported by *Federalist* Nos. 32 and 82, as well as by the debates in the Virginia ratifying convention, to which John Marshall had been a delegate.

Furthermore, the Supreme Court in *Sturges* had rejected arguments of counsel that contended that unless expressly limited in the Constitution, all powers granted to Congress were exclusive. Finally, U.S. district judge St. George Tucker, in his widely acclaimed annotations to Sir William Blackstone's *Commentaries*, asserted that "the powers delegated to the federal government are, in all cases, to receive the most strict construction that the instrument might bear, where the rights of a State, or of the people, either collectively or individually, may be drawn into question." There was thus both strong historical evidence and recent judicial precedent favoring concurrent construction of Congress's authority over trade.

Continuing the process of elaborating on Oakley's submissions, Emmet took a detailed look at the 1793 federal Coasting Licensing Act, asserting that Webster's argument on behalf of Gibbons had misunderstood the statute. Beginning with the 1789 statute that first controlled coastal navigation, he asserted that the law conferred no right to enter ports, but simply exempted certain vessels from certain duties if they complied with the procedures of registering and being enrolled under the act. Rights to enter a port, to trade, or to navigate existed independently from the 1793 federal statute. They were conferred by the international *ius commune* and the common law. The act and its predecessors limited that right to trade, and it did so by prohibiting the carriage of foreign goods from state to state without the payment of poundage and certain entry fees. Thus in Emmet's opinion, the federal Coasting Licensing Act simply provided an exemption from those taxes for formally registered or enrolled vessels. It had no impact on property rights, nor did it authorize Gibbons, as a licensee, to enter a New York port contrary to provisions of New York law.

Furthermore, he argued that New York's legislation did not impose a blanket limit on entry into New York harbor. Much narrower in its operation, it merely required that vessels powered by steam discontinue the use of steam power and use their sails while in New York territorial waters. Because all steamboats then in operation carried sails, there was no burden on the conduct of interstate or foreign commerce.

Perhaps sensing that this interruption might be construed to be a state-based limitation on interstate and foreign commerce, Emmet made a concession that this might be the case, but he added that under the provisions of *Federalist* No. 32, "it is not a mere possibility of inconvenience in the exercise of powers, but an immediate constitutional repugnancy, that can by implication, alienate and extinguish a pre-existing right of sovereignty." Actually, transferring from steam power to sails while entering the narrow confines of a harbor may not have been as simple a task as Emmet implied. It would require shutting down the steam-powered mechanism and reducing the pressure in boilers to avoid an explosion, all while unfurling and trimming sails. And how did one ascertain entry into New York state waters without some complicated calculations or careful sightings to the shore, if visible?

Turning to the question of patent rights, Emmet was quick to pose the question of standing. Thomas Gibbons neither had, nor did he allege he possessed, a federal patent. While Robert Fulton, and thus the syndicate, were perhaps entitled to claim rights under Fulton's 1809 patent, neither Fulton nor Livingston was an inventor, as required for the issuance of a patent, and the then-current state of U.S. patent law did not recognize improvement patents. There were thus serious questions of standing and mootness that stood in the path of litigating or deciding the patent issue.

Despite his doubts about the relevance of federal patent law to the case before the Court, Emmet pressed forward with an analysis that both stressed the interconnectedness of federal and state law in the area of protecting inventors and writers and questioned whether the Constitution's patent clause precluded any possible action by a state that would encourage useful inventions. After examining several suppositions that might support such a construction, he concluded that "the extraordinary boldness of this position must surprise and astonish." Quite to the contrary, the Constitution gave Congress a limited power to issue an exclusive right to use an invention for a limited period of time. However, an inventor, even before securing a patent, possessed certain property rights in his invention that were created by state law. Recognition of such property rights predated the adoption of the Constitution and remained the legal foundation on which the patent would issue. Pointedly, he noted that the Constitution does not use the word *patent,* and he continued that the federal statute establishing the patent system improperly uses the term, which had a different meaning in England and throughout the legal systems of the world:

> A patent, in England . . . , and in every country but this, implies the creation and gift of a right, by force of the sovereign power, conferring upon an individual a monopoly, in which he had no pre-existing right. This can be done by the States, and only by the States. The power delegated to Congress, does not authorize it to *create* any right, or to *give* any *right;* it only enables that body to *secure* a pre-existing common law right, and for that purpose it may *create* and *give a remedy.* [Italics in original]

This was not to say that the Constitution's authorization of a remedy was insignificant — quite the contrary:

> The object of a patent, granted in pursuance of the delegated power, is to perfect an imperfect right, by exactly ascertaining, if I may say so, its means, and boundaries, and identity, and by affording an adequate remedy for its violation. . . . The object of this power, and of the law made under it, is to give to the pre-existent but imperfect right, the security and attributes of *actual* property. When the law of Congress has done that, it is *funtus officio;* and it leaves that right, . . . to be enjoyed . . . conformably to the laws of the place where it is to be enjoyed. [Italics in original]

Moving on to the use of the term *exclusive* in the Constitution's patent clause, Emmet engaged in word definition and semantics that closely mirrored Chief Justice Marshall's legendary facility in using these verbal skills to shape legal meaning. The word *exclusive* carried two possible meanings. It might simply refer to the fact that one individual possesses a particular right or privilege. But more commonly, the word is used with the connotation that a given person possesses a right or privilege that is denied to all others: "All error would have been avoided, if the adjective had been utterly omitted, or the word *individual* substituted." In effect, Emmet stressed that a patentee's rights were conferred by state property laws. All that the federal statute did was to create a federal cause of action as a remedy for a competitor's violation of those rights.

The distinction between a right and a remedy was one that had troubled the Court in its consideration of state insolvency laws (*Sturges v. Crowninshield*), and it correctly highlighted the frequency and the complexity of the cooperation between state and federal authorities in regulating commerce and other economic matters. It argued for a concurrent approach to the regulation of interstate and foreign commerce, or at the very least, it pleaded for caution in eliminating state power by hastily adopting a rigid exclusive construction of the commerce clause. The caution was one with which the Court might readily agree, for it was state action concerning insolvent debtors that provided relief in 1819 when Congress failed to act promptly in the face of financial panic.

In conjunction with New York's grant of a monopoly to Livingston–Fulton, Emmet made his final appeal — to the contract clause of the Constitution, and the right of the state to use a contract to confer privileges in the use of its domain upon those it chose:

> The waters of the State are the domain and property of the State, subject only to the commercial regulations of Congress. Why should not the contract of a State in regard to its domain and property, be as sacred as those of an individual?

Again he touched on an issue fresh in the minds of the justices. Although a state's being bound by contract was established in *Fletcher v. Peck* (1810), and more recently involved in the controversial case of *Green v. Biddle* (1823), there was no small amount of judicial debate over the contract clause and its impact on the administration of state governments. He inferred that more than a gratuitous monopolistic grant was involved in *Gibbons*. New York State had promised to grant substantial privileges to Livingston and Fulton should they succeed in navigating the Hudson through steam power. Acting on those inducements, the partners had expended time, funds, and energy in achieving that objective. Had New York State then refused to issue the monopoly, would not the U.S. Supreme Court find this to be a breach of the obligations of contract and order the state to issue the monopoly grant? The Court's commitment to regularity in the per-formance of contracts was evidenced by its controversial decisions in *Fletcher* and in *Green v. Biddle*. Both were hard cases where basic principles of justice and considerations of equity demanded contrary decisions. *Fletcher* rewarded individuals who acquired rights through their grantors, who had bribed the Georgia legislature. *Green v. Biddle* took land from pioneer settlers and awarded the realty, along with the settlers' improvements, to nonresident land speculators. Did not Thomas Gibbons now ask the Court to invalidate a New York state legislative grant that Livingston and Fulton had earned through their efforts and dedication?

Thomas Addis Emmet's argument stands as a classic example of outstanding appellate advocacy. Extensively researched and well reasoned, it could not fail to be persuasive. Yet success depends as much on reading the judges as it does on understanding and explaining the cases. In its careful attention to judicial personalities, Emmet's argument is particularly notable; he knew the bench before which he spoke. He had studied their preferences. He knew their judicial positions, and he had worked through the legal and constitutional issues that had been focal points of their attention in the immediate past. In his brief and advocacy, in his professionalism, and in his passionate representation of his client, he left to the American bar a legendary piece of appellate argument that deserves far more extensive attention than it has been given to date.

Attorney General William Wirt, representing Thomas Gibbons as a private client, bore the responsibility of replying to the substantial and lengthy presentations of Oakley and Emmet. Contemporaries have noted Wirt's eloquence and his use of literary allusions as well as his passionate flights of nonlegal language in the course of argument. Unfortunately, these characteristics do not survive in the reported version of his argument. The chief justice's Richmond neighbor also enjoyed the advantage of being the final advocate to address the Court.

As Daniel Webster and he had agreed, the main thrust of Wirt's presentation dealt with the patent clause and its relationship to the Livingston–Fulton monopoly grant by New York State. He began by suggesting that the tests of exclusivity and concurrency proposed by his opponents were inadequate measures for constitutional analysis in

Gibbons. The situation under consideration was not one in which there was a clear clash between state and federal power. Rather, it arose from a regulatory situation in which the subject to be regulated was both "multifarious and complex":

> One branch alone, of such a subject, might be given exclusively to Congress, (and the power is exclusive only so far as it is granted), yet on other branches of the subject, the States might act without interfering with the power exclusively granted to Congress. Commerce is such a subject.

The same situation would apply in regard to the grant of patents, as but one part of the overall responsibility of both national and state governments to encourage useful inventions. But the patenting power was created for the benefit of the entire nation, so that inventive activity might redound to the benefit of all states and their citizens. The very nature of the power required that it extend uniform rights throughout the federal union, and therefore it necessarily must be exclusive to Congress.

New York's monopoly grant moved steamboat navigation beyond the limits of the federal patenting power. Even if the Constitution's grant of patenting power were concurrent, such a state action would be invalid because it would be inconsistent — indeed collide — with the federal power. The act of Congress limited the grant of exclusive rights of use to a term of fourteen years. New York's grant was for thirty years, subject to extension thereafter at the will of the legislature. The state statute therefore expanded an inventor's exclusive right to use his invention beyond the federal limitation, and was directly contrary to Congress's patenting power. The short term of a federal patent was designed to provide for its general availability to the public at the termination of the inventor's exclusive right to sell, use, or license. In granting the Livingston–Fulton monopoly for thirty years, the state legislature attempted to deny the public the right of access to the invention and its use for a period longer than that provided by federal law.

Procedurally, Wirt contended that even though Gibbons did not have a patent, the issue of the validity of the New York monopoly statute was justiciable and germane to consideration of the case. The question was not whether a party claimed under a U.S. patent, but rather whether the New York monopoly act was invalid by virtue of its inconsistency with the U.S. Constitution. Any citizen of the United States was entitled to treat the New York statute as a nullity and to raise the issue of constitutionality whenever an attempt was made to enforce it.

He rejected Oakley and Emmet's arguments that contended that New York had the right to restrict the use of steamboats under its police powers. Navigation by steam was not noxious, immoral, or impious. No legislative claim was made to enact the monopoly statute under those pretenses; indeed, it would be logically inconsistent to ban the unlicensed use of steamboats on policy grounds, and then to permit its grantee to conduct the very activities it had earlier prohibited under its police powers. This argument was a weak attempt to blunt Emmet's insistence that because steam navigation was dangerous, the state had the right to select those persons it believed would use the invention safely and for the benefit of the public.

Turning to a brief consideration of the federal commerce clause, Wirt rehearsed Webster's arguments for the exclusivity of the commerce power in Congress. The subject matter was such that uniformity was demanded. State legislation under quarantine laws and the imposition of limits on commerce through inspection laws were not regulations of commerce, but rather enacted under residual powers left with the states. Echoing Webster, he insisted that even if these state regulations might be absorbed into the "immense mass of commercial powers," certainly the intent and language of the Constitution were designed to make certain aspects of commercial regulation, including navigation, subject to the exclusive control of Congress. As a final point, he suggested that whether navigation was an exclusive or concurrent power was immaterial to the case because when federal and state powers were concurrent, once Congress acts in a given area, if subsequent legislation by a state interferes with that federal statute, the state statute is void.

True to his division of duties with Webster, Wirt had focused on the invalidity of the Livingston–Fulton monopoly due to the patent clause of the Constitution and legislation implementing that federal power. Necessarily, his summary of arguments on the commerce clause and his restatement of Webster's assertions were designed to leave the Court with a clear recollection of the arguments made by his associate nearly a week before. Yet in dealing with the commerce clause and in summarizing Webster's contentions, he probably erred in favoring brevity and neglecting the advantage of having the last word before the oral presentation of the case was concluded. However, he could not resist correcting Emmet's reference to Aeneas at the conclusion of the Irishman's argument. It was more than a matter of classical one-upmanship; it gave Wirt a chance to press upon the Court the danger to the federal union that would result if state competition and commercial litigation were permitted to continue under a Supreme Court decree favoring the New York monopoly statute. As Professor G. Edward White describes the interchange, Emmet had quoted Aeneas's statement of triumph and exultation about the greatness of his country's achievements, but Wirt pointed out that the Latin passage had been quoted out of context. Contrary to Emmet's understanding, it had been uttered as a lamentation over the losses that Aeneas had endured and the misfortunes of his beloved country. Wirt then referred to the distressing spectacle of American states passing legislation and entering judicial decrees against each other's citizens in light of the Court's resolution of the Gibbons and Ogden conflict:

> It is a momentous decision which this Court is called on to make. Here are three states almost on the eve of war. It is the high province of this Court to interpose its benign and mediatorial influence. The framers of our admirable constitution would have deserved the wreath of immortality which they have acquired, had they done nothing else than to establish this guardian tribunal, to harmonize the jarring elements in our system. But sir, if you do not interpose your friendly hand, and extirpate the seeds of anarchy which New-York has sown, you *will* have civil war.

New York would then have reason to cry, rather than exult, over how its unilateral attempt at monopolization of steamboat traffic damaged or destroyed the Constitution and irreparably broke the federal union.

Marshall's fellow Virginian undoubtedly exaggerated the degree of tension that existed because of the widespread legislative reaction to the Livingston–Fulton monopoly. We have already seen that the syndicate's interests in western waters had been successfully challenged, both legally and economically. In interstate navigation of the Hudson River south of the New York–New Jersey boundary, there was widespread defiance of the monopoly's exclusive privileges, and even within New York State itself, legislative support for the syndicate was ebbing rapidly. On the other hand, the implications of federal commerce authority regulating the interstate slave trade were already becoming obvious, and the Supreme Court's decisions in *McCulloch, Dartmouth College*, and *Green v. Biddle* were further evidence of a tendency to rapidly augment federal power at the expense of state authority. The Court itself was beginning to feel the pressure of public opinion arrayed against its recent pronouncements. It was not a stranger to the growing sense of crisis in federal–state relations, nor was it unaware of chronic congressional efforts to isolate state law from Supreme Court appellate review in federal question cases. Wirt thus succeeded in introducing broader public policy considerations into his argument for invalidating the monopoly; in doing so, he also inadvertently reminded the Court that serious consequences might follow from an ill-considered exclusive commerce clause construction in *Gibbons v. Ogden*.

Historian Charles Warren commented that some spectators preferred Wirt's argument to that of Webster. Newspapers reported that the Virginian was to be praised for a presentation that was "powerful, tender, picturesque, and pathetic. The manner was lofty and touching." George M. Bibb, then former chief justice of the Kentucky supreme court, wrote that Wirt's "legal argument was very strong; his peroration was beautiful and grand." Scholars who have looked carefully at Wirt's printed argument in the Supreme Court reports have concluded that his comments must have been sharply edited in the printed version. In delivery time, they were only slightly less than the much more detailed brief of Thomas Addis Emmet. Of course, what is printed in the U.S. *Reports* is what the reporter sent to the printer and not necessarily what William Wirt said or what was included within his brief. Because, as we shall see, the Supreme Court summarily dismissed the need to discuss the patenting aspects of the case, Wirt's presentation was not essential to understanding the Supreme Court opinion, and it may very well have been summarized or sharply edited at the discretion of Henry Wheaton, the official reporter.

Oral argument in U.S. Supreme Court cases was critically important in the Marshall era. However, by 1824 it is likely that lists of major points to be made by counsel had become the rule. We cannot be certain that these points of argument were submitted for the justices' review before argument, but it is most likely that they would have been delivered to the justices either at the time of argument or immediately thereafter. Court rules required that printed records of cases to be argued were to be submitted to the justices well in advance of argument, but these materials would not provide the detailed arguments of counsel before the Court. Thus the major evidence of oral argument available to the justices would be their notes taken in the course of presentations, augmented by whatever outlines of points to be argued that had been submitted.

In the unusual circumstances involved in *Gibbons v. Ogden*, nearly a month would pass between the close of argument and the announcement of Marshall's opinion for the Court, along with Justice William Johnson's dissent. There was more than ample time for the justices to consult, and perhaps compare, their notes, providing an exceptional opportunity to reconstruct the oral submissions of counsel. What were the issues that arose from oral argument and written briefs, and how did they influence the Court's decision?

Much time had been spent on the matter of exclusive congressional authority over commerce, or the sharing of power concurrently between Congress and the states. Webster and Wirt leaned heavily toward an exclusive approach, but they had been careful to offer an alternative based on concurrent power, with interpretive difficulties resolved by the Constitution's supremacy clause. Oakley and Emmet, anticipating the Court's bias favoring federal power, prepared a much more extensive attack on exclusivity than might otherwise have been the case. Emmet's brief in particular provided a powerful demonstration that the commerce clause did not eliminate state residuary authority concerning trade. Indeed, provision of the very channels and instruments necessary for the conduct of commercial business rested heavily on a foundation of individual state law. Although differences between federal and state commercial provisions might be resolved by the supremacy clause, counsel for Ogden painstakingly argued that a direct clash or clear conflict between state and congressional regulation was the narrow ground upon which supremacy considerations should be determinative. On these issues, Emmet and Oakley were able to blunt Webster's sweeping assertion of exclusive federal power over commerce. They also succeeded in convincing the justices that the regulation of commerce was so complex that it could not be accomplished solely through congressional legislation. Indeed, the issue of complexity arises from submissions on each side of the controversy, and cautioned the Court that exclusivity was a weak foundation upon which to erect its decision.

Throughout the oral argument, there were several references to federalism, but Emmet's presentation tellingly identified the need to divide commerce regulations into two operational categories. There were large areas in which uniformity of regulation was required, and there Congress necessarily had to be the regulatory authority. However, in many other aspects of commercial control, situations unique to individual states made local legislation imperative. As American settlement moved west and new states were admitted, state determinations in these areas would become more varied than they were in the old union of the original states. Not only would it be impossible for Congress to deal with this diversity, but it would also result in oppressive and unworkable uniform regulation in the years ahead. Again, the complexity of implementing the commerce clause and the need to reshape federalism to accommodate that need became major themes in the *Gibbons* decision.

Countering Emmet's plea for localism in some areas of commercial regulation, the Supreme Court's experience before 1815 suggested that uniformity was difficult to achieve by judicial methods alone. Trade between the two counties of the District of Columbia had been greatly burdened by the fact that at common law, promissory notes were negotiable in only one of the counties; a long series of Supreme Court decisions ameliorated the problem, but had not eliminated it. The memory of that effort would leave the justices with a clear perception that commercial regulation could only be effective if Congress legislated in those critical areas where national rules were required. That being the case, the Court's function would be limited to resolving constitutional issues raised by disparity between federal statutes and state legislation.

It is revealing that Daniel Webster, never known to underestimate his own forensic ability, asserted that Chief Justice Marshall intensely followed his argument, drinking it in as a baby devours its mother's milk. That may have been his perception, but if Webster was mother, the other three counsel must be considered wet nurses. Professor G. Edward White points out that the sequence of topics in the chief justice's opinion closely follows that adopted by Webster's co-counsel, William Wirt. And a close reading of the presentations by Oakley and Emmet suggests that Ogden's attorneys scored a significant victory in raising and defending the complexity of commercial regulation, along with the need that it be treated as if the power were concurrent. Although Marshall never directly resolved the exclusive power versus concurrent power conflict, the very ambiguity of his opinion suggests that concurrency construction became ruling case law even though *Gibbons* was decided in favor of federal legislative power. Oakley and Emmet may have lost the battle, but they had laid a firm foundation in an ambiguity that would enable others to win the antebellum commerce clause war.

Contemporaries and subsequent students of the case have unwisely accepted Webster's self-evaluation. Indeed, the first reactions to the Court's decision were that Webster and Wirt had won. They accepted the decision that the Court had invalidated the Livingston–Fulton monopoly, but they also understood that the commerce power was exclusively federal. Even before the end of Marshall's chief justiceship, the latter interpretation of the Court's holding was demonstrably incorrect. Can it be said that Webster and Wirt "won"? The evidence would suggest that Webster, despite his unquestioned skill as an appellate advocate, badly underestimated the substantial task before him, and he discounted the talents and diligence of opposing counsel. Wirt, on the other hand, found himself so fixated on the clash between the patent statutes and the New York monopoly that he sacrificed an opportunity to exhaustively attack the concurrency argument in his concluding remarks.

Appellate argument can be invigorated by eloquence, but it rests on the sound foundation of thorough legal research. That was as true in Marshall's day as it is today. Legal research, writing, and advocacy take time and concentrated attention. The record demonstrates that Webster spent the night before argument polishing his presentation, and he very likely drew heavily on the brief he had prepared three years earlier. Given the importance of *Gibbons* to American federalism and economic prosperity, was it adequate to polish an argument by means of a single nocturnal vigil? William Wirt, in a letter to his brother three days before argument began, reported that he would have the honor of concluding the case for Thomas Gibbons. He then admitted, "I . . . have yet to study the cause; but I know the facts and have only to weave the argument." Have only to weave the argument, indeed! How many third-year law students have followed the same course, only to be brought low by a professor's probing questions?

Are we not justified in wondering about the extent of appellant counsel's preparation? In the case of Webster, a lesser degree of preparation may have been deemed adequate because of the extensive preparations he had already made for the 1821 appeal to the Supreme Court. At the same time, as we have suggested, the situation of the Court and the nation had shifted considerably in the interim, providing good cause to make careful revisions and some adjustments in appellate strategy. Wirt, as new to the case, might well have expected to devote more time and attention to his argument. If he failed to do so, it might have been attributable to a lack of adequate time for preparation. In a recent extensive consideration of Wirt's practice, Galen Thorp has pointed out that Wirt's private practice in Baltimore and his appearances before the Supreme Court, coupled with his time commitments as attorney general of the United States, threatened his health and restricted the time he could devote to any given case. Furthermore, most of the contemporary praise concerning Wirt's contribution to the *Gibbons* argument emphasizes his eloquence and his literary flourishes, but not the legal scholarship supporting his argument.

Within the opposition, Emmet brought exhaustive research and sound reasoning to the bar of the Court, notwithstanding his misinterpretation of Aeneas's statement. He had read the Marshall Court bench very well. He followed the chief justice's way with word definition; he knew the opinions filed in prior cases by each of the associate justices. In his brief treatment of patent law, he brought his knowledge of English practice to bear on the task of distinguishing between rights and remedies. Oakley and Emmet's task was to undermine the exclusivity position taken by counsel for Thomas Gibbons; this was a difficult and almost impossible task. The Court's opinion suggests that they succeeded admirably. In addition, they dissuaded the Court from accepting Webster's sweeping assertion of federal power under the commerce clause. In doing so, they showed the path that the Court might take, invalidating the unpopular monopoly but at the same time upholding Congress's paramount right to establish an effective commercial system both within the United States and in international trade. Finally, in terms of the political sensitivity to a pro–federal Court decision, they gave Marshall the fulcrum point of complexity upon which to rest the lever of concurrency between national and state authority. As Professor White perceptively comments, it was the Oakley and Emmet presentations that would shape commerce clause jurisprudence from the era of Chief Justice Taney to that of Chief Justice Hughes — quite an accomplishment for a pair of attorneys who "lost" their case!

CHAPTER 6

The Supreme Court Opinions

The Marshall Court's resolution of the issues raised by *Gibbons v. Ogden* is remarkable in many ways, beginning with the fact that it is one of the few constitutional law decisions of that era that was delayed for nearly a month after oral arguments were concluded. It also generated a concurring opinion by Justice William Johnson that provided a stronger endorsement for national power and an exclusive construction of the commerce clause than did the opinion for the Court written by Chief Justice Marshall. Although Marshall's opinion was encyclopedic in its scope and coverage, it is so Delphic in its content and conclusions that most contemporaries and subsequent scholars were, and are, perplexed concerning the Court's position on many of the major issues raised in oral argument. Professor David Lightner, struggling with the task of assessing the implications of *Gibbons* for the interstate slave trade, characterizes Marshall's opinion as "a masterpiece of bold assertion, coupled with discrete sidestepping." Remarkably, the opinions do not make any clear distinction between foreign commerce and domestic interstate commerce, and Marshall's opinion virtually ignores the foreign affairs implications of state interference with international trade. Despite these disturbing characteristics, the Court opinion in *Gibbons* continues to be cited in most, if not all, federal and state precedents dealing with the federal Constitution's commerce clause. Its perennial flowering as we approach the bicentennial of its announcement makes it truly a landmark decision. Despite constant use and notoriety, the major difficulty still remains to identify exactly what it decided, and why.

Closing argument by William Wirt was completed on behalf of appellant Thomas Gibbons on Monday, 9 February, and the Court reserved opinion before adjourning on that day. Normally, the chief justice announced the Court's opinion within three or four days after completion of arguments. However, in *Gibbons*, the opinion of the Court, representing the views of a five-to-one majority, was not announced until 2 March 1824, three weeks later than most contemporary Court watchers expected. This caused great anxiety on the part of the litigants, and William Gibbons was making arrangements to have copies of Webster's argument sent to his father when it was announced that Chief Justice Marshall had injured his shoulder in an accident on 23 February. Somewhat earlier, Thomas Gibbons wrote to his son suggesting that Daniel Webster undoubtedly had a copy of the Court's opinion in hand, but that he would not release it because the matter of Webster's fees had not been settled. The comment suggests that not only was Gibbons confident of success, but he believed that Webster's close association with the Court, and particularly with Justice Joseph Story, might provide information about the success of Gibbons's appeal.

Following contemporary rumors, some scholars have suggested that during Marshall's incapacity, the task of opinion writing had temporarily been assigned to Justice Story, and some internal evidence lends support to that supposition. The opinion does reflect some similarities to the chief justice's opinion-writing practices. For example, following the chief justice's opinion-writing style, some care was taken with supplying definitions of terms, and those definitions then laid the foundation for subsequent legal conclusions. The logical sequence in the arguments seems to reflect Marshall's usual practice, even though many conclusions appear to be contradictory of others. On the other hand, the Court opinion seems to have an uncharacteristic attention to research detail, and an extensive citation to legal scholarship that is more suggestive of Story's authorship than that of Marshall. Whether there was collaboration in analyzing the case or simply assistance in the physical task of writing out the text is something about which we are forced to speculate. Certainly it is relevant that Justice Story, writing at the time the opinion was under consideration, indicated that Marshall was busy writing the opinion. The chief justice's authorship is also supported by the fact that its delivery was postponed until the first day that Marshall returned to his duties and was physically able to deliver the opinion in person.

What is certain is the fact that as of 23 February, the opinion of the Court was still being drafted, and it was not announced until nine days after the accident. The unusually long delay in the announcement of the Court's opinion, and particularly the fact that the chief justice was not injured until two weeks after argument concluded, would suggest that this was a matter on which the justices disagreed, making the preparation of a majority opinion especially difficult. We know from his concurring opinion that Justice William Johnson held firm for an exclusive construction of Congress's power to regulate commerce, while the chief justice and his five other colleagues joined in the Court opinion, which vacillated between an exclusive and a concurrent construction. Furthermore, Justice Johnson argued that even in the absence of legislation concerning commerce, the Constitution standing alone would invalidate the Livingston–Fulton monopoly. On this point, the Court opinion declined to comment. Discussion of these issues alone would have occupied much of the Court's time in conference, and oral argument had revolved around a large number of other issues in constitutional law and public policy that bore directly on the Court's consideration of the appeal. Just a year earlier, the Court had issued a second and revised opinion in *Green v. Biddle* in an attempt to deflect the public outcry that condemned Justice Story's original opinion as being abrupt and seemingly undiplomatic in denying what some considered to be Kentucky's right of legislative self-determination concerning its local real property law. These factors gave the Court additional incentives in *Gibbons* to exercise caution in deciding complex issues of constitutional construction, fine points of federal–state relations, and delicate matters of public policy. Building consensus in *Gibbons* may well have given the chief justice more pain than did the physical injury to his shoulder.

Although there was widespread speculation concerning what the Court's opinion might be, both teams of counsel were inclined to claim a partial victory in their own cause. It was widely rumored that the Court opinion had been written and that copies had been distributed to preferred individuals, particularly to Daniel Webster. Somewhat later, in 1830, President Andrew Jackson denounced Joseph Story as a "miserably frivolous bookworm; but the wretched tool of Mr. Webster." The comment was prejudiced, unfair, and untrue, but it did reflect the general public's identification of Webster as the recipient of favoritism from some justices of the Supreme Court. Webster's predictions of success for his client ultimately proved to be correct, but for the Boston advocate's nationalist and exclusive power construction, it proved to be a Pyrrhic victory. However, as we have seen, the magnitude of Oakley and Emmet's efforts had a profound impact on the Court majority. Webster and Wirt may well have been lulled into overconfidence, and they probably misjudged the abilities and diligence of their opponents. In any event, they were ill-prepared to achieve exclusivity in commercial regulation for the federal government.

Even more significant than counsels' arguments may have been the changing nature of the Supreme Court itself, as well as the shifting sands of constitutional consensus, both within the Court and in the broader political community of a territorially expanding United States. Before argument took place in *Gibbons v. Ogden*, the Supreme Court had passed through two internal changes while under Marshall's leadership. Historians have generally agreed that from Marshall's joining the Court in 1801 through about the 1812 term, the chief justice had assumed a dominant role based in large part on a seniority rule that permitted him to deliver, and probably to author, virtually all opinions of the Court. With the arrival of Joseph Story on the Court's bench, the chief justice's intellectual and institutional preeminence began to fade, a tendency that was accelerated by the emergence of dissents and concurrences in admiralty and marine insurance cases before and during the War of 1812. In part this period was dominated by Justice Story's efforts to enhance the maritime jurisdiction of federal courts and Justice William Johnson's opposition to that pressure. By 1819, the year in which the Court decided the landmark cases of *McCulloch v. Maryland* and *Dartmouth College v. Woodward*, the ostensible unanimity of the Court's decision on important constitutional issues obscured the sharp differences of opinion that we now know divided the justices in *Sturges v. Crowninshield* (1819). Only in 1827, when the bankruptcy and insolvency issue would once more occupy and divide the Court, would the true magnitude of these disagreements become obvious to the general public. What is important to our understanding of *Gibbons* is that the pre-1812 uniformity of opinion had been shattered by 1819, thrusting John Marshall into a new role as conciliator and mediator. To the extent that his efforts to create consensus were successful, he would continue to author and deliver the Court's opinions. However, until he died in office in July 1835, he would exercise those functions only by gaining the agreement of his colleagues on the bench.

The Marshall Court's dilemma in deciding *Gibbons* is clarified when the Court's opinion in *Sturges*, and its implications for federalism, is examined more closely. *McCulloch v. Maryland* firmly established the federal government's supremacy when it acted within its enumerated powers; the case also sharpened the "necessary and proper clause" into a strong instrument for implementation of the Constitution's enumerated powers. The *Dartmouth College* opinion broadened the construction of the federal Constitution's contract clause by applying its protection to corporate charters. This created an effective check on arbitrary state economic actions that threatened the security of investment capital in the new nation. Unquestionably, these cases represented the high tide of federal power in the Marshall era. Yet high waters bring a certain amount of flotsam and jetsam with them. The troublesome and controversial opinion in *Sturges v. Crowninshield* was putrid litter on the ostensibly clean beach of judicial solidarity and constitutional nationalism. Very likely it proved to be a weighty factor in the extraordinarily extended conferences of the justices as they pondered how to shape the Court's *Gibbons* opinion.

Sturges involved the New York State insolvency statute enacted in April 1811, which, in addition to releasing a qualifying debtor from prison, discharged the debt if certain procedures were followed. Arguably this legislation might be seen to conflict with Congress's power to enact a uniform bankruptcy act. However, because the debtor's promissory notes were signed before the enactment of New York's new insolvency provision, the 1811 act also impaired the obligations of an existing contract, and hence violated the federal Constitution's contract clause. At all of these times, no federal bankruptcy provision was in effect, and state and federal authority was unclear. In the absence of congressional action, might the states provide discharge of indebtedness to insolvent debtors? The U.S. circuit court for Massachusetts certified the constitutional questions in *Sturges* to the Supreme Court for decision.

Chief Justice Marshall's opinion for the Court speculated that "the mere grant of a power to Congress did not imply a prohibition on the states to exercise the same power." Furthermore, the interrelationships between insolvency provisions and bankruptcy laws made it "difficult to say how far they may be blended together." Although the mixture of state and federal legislation might result in "inconveniences" to both,

> [i]t does not appear to be a violent construction of the constitution, and is certainly a convenient one, to consider the power of the states as existing over such cases as the laws of the Union may not reach. But be this as it may, the power granted to Congress may be exercised or declined, as the wisdom of that body shall decide. If, in the opinion of Congress, uniform laws concerning bankruptcy ought not be established, it does not follow that partial laws may not exist, or that state legislation on the subject must cease.

Specifically avoiding entry into more detailed discussion of the nature of exclusive and concurrent powers, or the degree to which an unexercised congressional power might impose limits on state action, Marshall continued,

> [I]t is sufficient to say, that until the power to pass uniform laws on the subject of bankruptcies be exercised by Congress, the states are not forbidden to pass a bankrupt law, provided it contains no principle which violates [the contract clause of the federal Constitution].

Having conceded, albeit in dictum, the residual authority of states to enact bankruptcy provisions, Marshall then held that the operation of New York's statute impaired the obligations of an existing contract, and thus was unconstitutional. Essentially, *Sturges* held that applying a bankruptcy provision retrospectively to contracts entered into before the effective date of the legislation violated the contract clause and was unconstitutional.

From Justice William Johnson's 1827 disclosure in *Ogden v. Saunders*, we now know that the unanimous opinion in *Sturges* cloaked a serious division within the Supreme Court. It is safe to speculate that to secure agreement on the disposition of the case, Marshall took the option of making retroactivity of the New York legislation the *ratio decidendi*, thereby postponing the Court's open discussion of the nature of exclusive and concurrent powers under the Constitution. However, in assembling the Court behind him on this narrow ground, he included language that seriously undermined federal primacy in the area of bankruptcy. He also delayed consideration of the dormancy issue: that the federal Constitution standing alone could confer powers on Congress, and merely by that authorization, could prevent the states from acting in that area. Unfortunately, *Sturges* presented a much stronger textual basis for an exclusive construction of the bankruptcy clause than was present in *Gibbons* concerning the commerce clause. The Constitution expressly provided that Congress should provide a "uniform" law of bankruptcy, and a federal law according uniform relief to merchants and traders doing business in all of the states would greatly encourage both international and interstate trade. On the other hand, the Constitution's commerce clause did not stipulate that Congress enact uniform laws for the regulation of foreign or interstate trade.

Unanimity in *Sturges* had been too dearly bought. Marshall's opinion for the Court would stand for only eight years, until the sharply divided opinion in *Ogden v. Saunders,* from which the chief justice felt compelled to dissent. It also had a profound impact on *Gibbons v. Ogden,* placing a heavy burden on Marshall to undo in the Steamboat Case the markedly concurrent construction of the Constitution he had grudgingly accepted in *Sturges.* Ogden's attorneys had cited *Sturges* no fewer than six times as precedent for the proposition that the commerce clause should be given a concurrent interpretation. They also argued that despite the views propounded in the *Federalist,* *Sturges* had accepted the antifederalist position that when the regulatory powers granted to Congress originally were exercised by the colonies or independent states, they should continue within a state's residuary legislative authority in the absence of an express constitutional provision removing those powers from the states. Whether a federal power was classified as being either exclusive or concurrent, it should be strictly construed against the authority of the federal government.

In an attempt to sweep away this debris on America's constitutional beach, a chastened John Marshall narrowed the *Gibbons* case to holding that the federal Coasting Licensing Act precluded the states from legislating monopolies that conflicted with activities licensed under the federal statute. It was in dictum that he would establish a sand castle on which future, and erratic, commerce clause development would take place, and the swelling tide of states' rights would not be a congenial environment. For these reasons, and perhaps for others unknown to us, much of the text of *Gibbons v. Ogden* must be considered dicta — principles and reasoning not deemed essential to resolving the narrow legal issues of the case. However, even as dicta, these statements provided the bar and the public with guidelines concerning the thinking of the Court in rendering the opinion, as well as a basis on which to predict future Court action in the area. Given the uncertain state of constitutional theory following *Sturges v. Crowninshield*, the dicta in *Gibbons* provide a welcome clarification of constitutional theory as it relates to the interstate and foreign commerce power. To this extent, in *Gibbons* Marshall may have succeeded in restoring some of the federal constitutional power intended by the Founding Fathers for the regulation of the American national economy.

Chief Justice Marshall's opinion for the Court was sufficiently attenuated that it elicited his apology at the end of the Court opinion, citing its length and the "tediousness inseparable from the endeavor" of demonstrating principles that "might have been thought axioms." Both characteristics — length and tediousness — make it advisable at the outset to identify five major subdivisions of the opinion, their sequence within the text, and their relationship to each other.

The opinion begins with a strong statement of the nature of the American union under the provisions of the Constitution, synopsizing the extended discussion of federalism and supremacy earlier established in *McCulloch v. Maryland*. It continues with an analysis of the commerce clause that stresses the preeminence of congressional regulation in the field. The third and very extensive section is devoted to refuting the appellee's arguments for a concurrent interpretation of state and federal authority in the regulation of commerce. A fourth section discusses the impact of the supremacy clause on state regulations that touch on the regulation of interstate commerce. The concluding and fifth section, containing both an apology and a brief summary of the earlier discussion, ends with a powerful statement supporting Gibbons's case and asserting once more the primacy of federal legislation in interstate commerce.

The sequencing of topics within the opinion parallels the format that attorneys before the Court were accustomed to follow in presentation of appellate arguments. Because the appellant bore the burden of proof that the decision below was incorrect, his or her lawyer had the advantage of opening argument and concluding with a rebuttal to the points presented by the appellee. Marshall's opinion for the Court seems to adopt this format, with strong statements upholding congressional authority in sections one, two, and five, bracketing the chief justice's painstaking work of analyzing and then rejecting in the third section Ogden's advocacy of a concurrent power in the states to share in regulating commerce. In the fourth section, having found that the federal Coasting Licensing Act empowered Thomas Gibbons to participate in coastal navigation, Marshall determined that the supremacy clause in Article Six of the Constitution invalidated the Livingston–Fulton monopoly as a state measure that unconstitutionally interfered with Gibbons's rights to navigate under the federal license.

Because the first two sections lean heavily toward supporting an exclusive interpretation of the commerce power, they also suggest that, assuming that the opinion as delivered reflects the chronology of its preparation, we may gain insight into the basis on which Webster was so certain that he had won his exclusivity argument. Had John Marshall's accident occurred after these two sections were written, and a preliminary draft containing only those sections was leaked to the press or to the bar, Black Dan's confidence would be justified. Yet the more moderate treatment of the federalism questions in the third section of the final draft was destined to dampen the hopes of ultranationalists who at first eagerly applauded Thomas Gibbons's victory.

At the outset in the first section of the opinion, Marshall set forth a powerful statement of American federalism:

> The genius and character of the whole government seem to be that its action is to be applied to all external concerns of the nation, and to those internal concerns which affect the States generally, but not those which are completely within a particular State, which do not affect other States, and with which it is not necessary to interfere for the purpose of executing some of the general powers of the government.

The simplicity of the statement belies the difficulties inherent in erecting a federal union that attempts to divide sovereignty between a national government and its constituent states. Yet at the end of the opinion, the chief justice exhibited his annoyance both at the growing sentiment for a sharing of federal powers with state governments and at a political climate that fostered such a constitutional arrangement:

> Powerful and ingenious minds, taking as postulates that the powers expressly granted to the government of the Union are to be contracted by construction into the narrowest possible compass, and that the original powers of the states are retained if any possible construction will retain them may, by a course of well digested but refined and metaphysical reasoning, founded on these premises, explain away the Constitution of our country and leave it a magnificent structure indeed to look at, but totally unfit for use. They may so entangle and perplex the understanding as to obscure principles which were before thought quite plain, and induce doubts where, if the mind were to pursue its own course, none would be perceived. In such a case it is peculiarly necessary to recur to safe and fundamental principles to sustain those principles, and when sustained, to make them the tests of the arguments to be examined.

He thus called the nation to consider the entire opinion to be a summons to bring "safe and fundamental principles" to bear while engaging in construction of the federal Constitution, and second, to refrain from interpretations that would leave the Constitution "a magnificent structure indeed to look at, but totally unfit for use." Thus practicalities of administration and effective government must be combined with recourse to fundamental law to form a background against which constitutional issues must be resolved.

Turning to the second section's task of interpreting the commerce clause, the chief justice focused on the definition of commerce. At the same time, he tacitly rejected some of the major limitations that counsel for Ogden had placed on the term *commerce*. These were that commerce did not include the regulation of navigation but was limited to activity relating to the purchase or sale of goods. In addition, Oakley and Emmet had asserted that, assuming commerce did embrace navigation, it did not cover the conveyance of passengers. Although Marshall was willing to concede that commerce included trade, broadly construed, he insisted that the term as used in the Constitution covered much more. "Commerce, undoubtedly, is traffic, but it is something more: it is intercourse. It describes commercial intercourse between nations, and parts of nations, in all its branches, and is regulated by prescribing rules for carrying on that intercourse." It was inconceivable that such regulations should not deal with the admission of vessels of one nation into the ports of another. Historically, the United States had exerted power over navigation, specifying what vessels were to be classified as American, and requiring that they be navigated by American seamen. "All America understands, and has uniformly understood, the word 'commerce' to comprehend navigation." It was so understood when the Constitution was framed. Furthermore, the power over commerce was one of the primary objects for which the Constitution was adopted, and the Philadelphia convention used the term *commerce* as including the navigation of vessels.

Legal professionals are accustomed to examining the entire text of a document as a guide to the meaning of one of its particular words or phrases; today, the process is deemed to be an examination of the "four corners" of the document. Chief Justice Marshall was a master at applying this technique to the text of the Constitution. He pointed out that the Constitution makes specific exceptions to Congress's power over commerce, and that these limits help a judge in defining the term *commerce*. Section 9 of Article One, which follows after the commerce clause provision in Section 8, prohibits Congress from preferring the ports of one state over those of another, and it specifically refers to regulations of commerce as an area of concern. In addition, the exception provides that no vessels bound for one state may be required to "enter, clear, or pay duties" in the ports of another state. This language gives added weight to the point that the convention intended to include the navigation of vessels within the grant of commercial regulation to Congress.

Oakley and Emmet had mentioned the constitutional debate over the imposition of a trade embargo before the War of 1812, arguing that the legality of that prohibition on foreign trade rested on the federal government's war powers rather than the commerce clause. Marshall agreed that embargo might be used for military objectives, but he cited the historical fact that the Jefferson administration resorted to the measure to protect American trade and to preserve peace, not to wage war. Both supporters and opponents of the embargo treated those statutes as regulations of commerce, and the predominantly Federalist Party opposition was based not on the theory that the statutes were unconstitutional, but rather on the position that a perpetual embargo was the annihilation of trade, and not its regulation.

Turning to the forms of activity that were subject to commerce clause regulation, Marshall observed that commerce among the states was grouped in the same section as the grant of power to regulate foreign commerce and trade with the Indian tribes. Because of the inclusion of the interstate commerce provision in the same sentence of the Constitution, it was logical that the same construction should apply to all three forms of trade. Necessarily, conduct of international trade could not stop at the jurisdictional boundaries of a state, or the authority of the United States to regulate foreign commerce would be a "very useless power." Similarly, commercial activity between non-contiguous American states would necessarily pass through one or more interspersed states. The use of the term *among* in describing commerce within American territory thus further emphasized the fact that the regulation of interstate commerce involved supervision of commercial activity that was intermingled with one state as well as two or more states. Commerce *among* the states cannot stop at the external boundary of a single state but continues into, and perhaps through, its interior. Although he conceded that commercial activity that did not "extend to or affect other States" was beyond the reach of Congress's regulations, he insisted that to be effective, the commerce power of Congress must necessarily be exercised within state territorial jurisdiction. Indeed, this broad authority was "unequivocally manifested" by congressional statutes that provided for the carriage of goods on land between Baltimore and Providence, New York and Philadelphia, and Philadelphia and Baltimore.

Emphasizing that the commerce power was a broad and generous constitutional grant, Marshall observed that like all other powers vested in Congress, it was complete in itself and might be exercised to its utmost extent. Warming to his theme, he asserted that while the United States government was limited in its objects, in regard to those objects assigned to it by the Constitution, its power was "plenary," and he continued with the striking conclusion that "the power over commerce with foreign nations, and among the several States is vested in Congress as absolutely as it would be in a single government." Thus, in its exercise of the power granted by the commerce clause, Congress had the authority to pass the boundaries of New York State and to "act upon the very waters to which the prohibition [that is, the Livingston–Fulton monopoly's exclusion of Gibbons's vessels] now under consideration applies."

Undoubtedly, the third section of Marshall's opinion for the Court is at once the most exhaustive and the most perplexing portion of the adjudication. It was clearly designed to strongly reject arguments made by Oakley and Emmet, which urged the Court to interpret the commerce clause to permit concurrent and parallel legislation by both the federal government and the states. At the same time, it inadvertently exhibits one of the strongest points made by Ogden's attorneys: that the regulation and facilitation of interstate commerce rested heavily on governmental powers traditionally vested in the colonies and states, and that these state powers inevitably touched, and perhaps even encroached on, federal regulation of interstate and foreign commerce. Despite the chief justice's efforts, his opinion for the Court, as well as the subsequent evolution of commerce clause jurisprudence, fails to satisfactorily resolve this dilemma. In part, this may be because the dilemma has two horns: first, the need to create a federalism that can successfully and cleanly divide sovereignty between a central national government and its component states, which are far more than mere administrative subdivisions; and second, the desire to achieve national economic cohesion while reserving to states the capacity to wisely supplement national programs without falling into conflict with the supremacy clause and the overarching functions and powers assigned to the United States by constitutional mandate. Small wonder that in this decision and in its supporting opinion of the Court, John Marshall provides an outstanding American reproduction of the ambiguous Greek oracle at Delphi!

As we have noted, the arguments of Thomas J. Oakley and Thomas Addis Emmet were jammed with factual information and legal precedents that in the aggregate stressed the complexity of commercial activity and the difficulty of allotting regulatory activity between the states and the federal government. They also made much of the degree to which the states originated legal regulations of commerce-related activities that subsequently were either ratified by congressional action or supported by federal legislation that supplemented, and thus endorsed, prior state initiatives. This tactic demanded that Marshall give careful attention to the extensive body of economic regulation already on state statute books. In doing so, the chief justice was forced to concede, albeit reluctantly and usually by implication, that the states and their laws provided an essential and preexisting foundation on which interstate and foreign commerce was predicated. Arguments of counsel, and undoubtedly a continuance of their advocacy among the justices in their discussions and conferences, created a climate in which an exclusive construction of the commerce power came into conflict with the contemporary realities of law and economics. Marshall's long-standing position requiring that federal powers be construed to provide maximum efficiency and efficacy led him to give careful attention to drafting this critical third section of the Court's opinion. A construction that ignored either historical fact or business and economics would be unacceptable to him.

Summarizing Ogden's argument, the chief justice noted that the appellant and appellee agreed on all issues except what constituted an exclusive grant of power to the federal government. As he understood the appellee's point,

[A]n affirmative grant of power [to the Congress] is not exclusive unless in its own nature it be such that the continued exercise of it by the former possessor [that is, the states prior to ratification] is inconsistent with the grant.

On the contrary, the appellants insisted that a grant concerning a particular subject implies the grant of the whole power and leaves no residuum on which the Tenth Amendment can operate.

Marshall's summary of the central point at issue ignored the fact that Daniel Webster's argument ranged much more broadly than a simple insistence on the exclusive nature of the commerce clause. We recall that in addition to exclusivity, Webster submitted the proposition that although the "higher branches" of commercial regulation were reserved to Congress, the states could legislate on lesser matters without violating the Constitution and its supremacy clause. Black Dan had also modified his exclusivity position to maintain that state authority might be constitutionally exercised when harbor pilots, health regulations, and quarantine operations were involved.

Conversely, Oakley and Emmet had submitted a much more carefully nuanced view of exclusive and concurrent powers. Oakley provided the Court with a five-point menu by which it could be determined whether a given state action violated the Constitution. He did not deny the existence of exclusive powers in Congress, but he suggested that very few regulatory functions should be included within that category. He also argued that once concurrency was established, it became necessary to determine whether the existence of a federal power precluded the states from acting. Some authority, like the taxing power, might be exercised simultaneously by both state and federal governments. The same tolerance and concurrence applied to legislation that imposed criminal sanctions or established rules for the establishment and training of the militia. On the other hand, Oakley asserted that some regulatory activities assigned to Congress by their very nature were exclusive to Congress, and once those powers were acted on, state legislation would be unconstitutional. As examples, he cited the authority to fix weights and measures, to coin money, and to fix the value of foreign currency. Emmet pointedly rejected Webster's view that all major aspects of commercial regulation should be reserved for Congress. Quite the contrary, the historical record demonstrated that even though the Constitution accorded the paramount regulatory role to Congress, in a number of significant areas, the states had acted, and in some cases, congressional action was taken that ratified or was based on those state enactments.

Opening the third section of the Court opinion, Marshall considered the taxing power as a prime example of the two levels of government using the same means for different purposes. Presumably the nature of the taxing power, coupled with the fact that federal and state purposes necessarily are different, permitted a concurrent view of the taxing power. Subsequently, the chief justice touched on the constitutional origins of state or federal powers to resolve concurrency issues. The existence of an "immense mass of legislation which embraces everything within the territory of a state not surrendered to the General Government" might well allow a state to exercise its authority in the same way as the federal government. However, the legality of the state's action would not be based on the commerce clause, but rather on a separate and distinct power constitutionally possessed by the state authorities. Although the efforts of the state and general government might interfere with each other, he found no reason to conclude that one government was usurping powers conferred on the other.

Thus, John Marshall was willing to tolerate conflicts between the two levels of government when either the purpose of actions was different or the constitutional source of their respective authorities was distinguishable. To the reader, this emphasis on the nature or purpose of the action, and a similar resort to the source of a power, seem artificial. We may suspect that the chief justice was not comfortable with these standards by which sovereignty might be distributed within the American federal system. He wrote,

> All experience shows that the same measures, or measures scarcely distinguishable from each other, may flow from distinct powers, but this does not prove that the powers themselves are identical. Although the means used in their execution may sometimes approach each other so nearly as to be confounded, there are other situations in which they are sufficiently distinct to establish their individuality.
>
> In our complex system, presenting the rare and difficult scheme of one General Government whose action extends over the whole but which possesses only certain enumerated powers, and of numerous State governments which retain and exercise all powers not delegated to the Union, contests respecting power must arise. Were it even otherwise, the measures taken by the respective governments to execute their acknowledged powers would often be of the same description, and might sometimes interfere. This, however, does not prove that the one is exercising, or has a right to exercise, the powers of the other.

The complexity of the system and the resulting difficulty in analyzing powers granted to either level of government were amply demonstrated by the examples raised by counsel in arguing *Gibbons v. Ogden.*

Although Marshall was clear that the taxing power was concurrent in both federal and state governments, he also concurred in the view that states might impose import and export duties in the absence of the Constitution's provision that denied this power to the states. Observing that the Constitution includes duties within the same clause as the taxing power and does not include it in the commerce clause, he concluded that "[t]he power of imposing duties on imports is classified with the power to levy taxes, and that seems to be its natural place." Perhaps so, but did not history indicate that customs duties were a substantial part of trade regulation in both Britain and the American colonies and states during the Confederation period? Subsequently, in discussing a duty on tonnage, which the Constitution permits states to impose with the consent of Congress, the chief justice admitted that "duties may often be and in fact often are, imposed on tonnage with a view to the regulation of trade, but they also may be imposed with a view toward revenue." The confusion, of course, is that any given type of legislation may be justified on the basis of more than one power granted by the Constitution or reserved to the states by the Tenth Amendment. "Natural place" depends on the eye of the beholder, and classification is clouded with substantial ambiguity.

Finally, in concluding the third section of the opinion, Marshall dealt with situations in which federal commerce powers and state residual — that is, police — powers seem to have overlapped. Federal enforcement of a state's quarantine and health laws represented situations in which, in the interest of harmony and conciliation, Congress directed its officers to support and cooperate with the states. This cannot be claimed as a grant to regulate commercial activities. Rather, should state police power legislation clash with the commerce powers of the U.S. government, the laws of the states must be subordinated to federal authority. Similarly, the 1803 federal statute directing that federal officials comply with any state laws prohibiting the importation of slaves does not confer commerce power on the states. Another area in which federal and state regulation was involved dealt with harbor pilots. When the first Congress under the Constitution met in 1789, it found a system of state regulation of harbor pilots already in place. Consequently, an act of Congress in its first year of existence provided that until federal laws were enacted on the subject, the state acts were adopted on a temporary basis. Marshall acknowledged the right of a state to control pilots under its authority to regulate its police, its domestic trade, and its governance of its own citizens. The provision making the 1789 act temporary demonstrated conclusively that Congress considered itself entitled to control the entire subject of pilots whenever it decided to legislate on the matter. One of the least persuasive arguments advanced by Emmet was the fact that states and private individuals were permitted to erect lighthouses; Marshall dismissed this contention by observing that the states retained these powers, but that the exercise of the reserved powers did not imply that the states were entitled to regulate commerce along with Congress.

After this detailed consideration of the Livingston–Fulton monopoly's position, the chief justice returned to consider one significant contention made by Gibbons's attorneys — that the Constitution gave Congress

> full power over the thing to be regulated, it excludes necessarily the action of all others that would perform the same action on the same thing. That regulation is designed for the entire result, applying to those parts which remain as they were, as well as to those which are altered. It produces a uniform whole which is as much disturbed and deranged by changing what the regulating power designs to leave untouched as that on which it has operated. . . . There is great force in this argument, and this Court is not satisfied that it has been refuted.

Marshall's comment deals with at least four tentative propositions: (1) that the Constitution's grant of a given power to Congress "excludes necessarily" its exercise by all others; (2) that to determine a conflict between a congressional power and state action, it is necessary to examine whether the state has performed the same action on the same "thing"; (3) that it is not material whether states before the Constitution possessed a power granted by the Constitution; and (4) that the integrity of the constitutional power is violated as much by ignoring Congress's unwillingness to exercise the power as it is by operating on the same action and thing. Most lawyers of Marshall's generation were careful to avoid double pleading, or asserting two things within the same allegation, but here the chief justice provided what might be known as quadruple pleading! From its content, we are probably safe to assume that his intention was to leave open the question whether the mere existence of a power granted to Congress, absent any action by Congress under that power, precludes state legislation in the field. We may also suspect that he is hinting that in some future case, the Court might hold such a power to be exclusive, and that if a state acted concerning such an exclusive power that had not at that point been executed by congressional legislation, the state's action would be invalid under the supremacy clause in Article Six of the Constitution. The latter consideration is, of course, a suggestion that a dormant constitutional grant might prevent states from legislating in that field.

Clearly, in *Gibbons*, Marshall ruled that the 1793 federal Coasting Licensing Act was legislation that removed dormancy from the Court's consideration. Marshall's comment leaving open the issue of dormancy was dictum, but it was dictum that created confusion and doubt concerning the validity of state legislation in areas of federal–state overlapping authority. At the same time, this statement at the end of the third section strongly suggests that the Court was inclined to apply an exclusive construction in future cases, and that dormancy was not a license for states to legislate in areas reserved to Congress.

In the fourth section of the Court's opinion, Marshall considered the operation of the supremacy clause in Article Six of the Constitution; in doing so, he tacitly agreed that the commerce power was not exclusive. Had it been an exclusive power vested entirely in Congress, any state legislation, as he phrased it, dealing with the "same action on the same thing" would be invalid, independent of the existence of the supremacy clause. To begin his summary, he asserted that state legislation, enacted in the execution of its acknowledged powers, would be valid unless it was found to "interfere with, or [be] . . . contrary to the laws of Congress made pursuant to the Constitution." Should such interference or contrariness be demonstrated, the state law was required to yield to the federal legislation.

The first step was to examine the federal Coasting Licensing Act of 1793 on which the appellants relied. Contrary to the position taken by the Livingston–Fulton attorneys, he ruled that this act was a comprehensive provision dealing with the licensing and operation of American and foreign vessels in the coasting trade. As we have already noted, this statute and its 1792 predecessor were certainly relevant to the Washington administration's effort to avoid diplomatic or military conflict with belligerents during the Napoleonic wars. Although they did not purport to organize a commercial system or to implement a system of tariffs or other import duties, they might justly be viewed as an exercise of the interstate commerce authority granted to Congress by the Constitution.

Marshall observed that a license to do a certain thing confers on the recipient permission or authority to do that thing; and when a privilege is given to do something, or a when a release from an obligation to do something is issued, a right is granted to the recipient. Should a privilege be withheld from a grantee, a property right would be annihilated. A voyage from New Jersey to New York would be included within the American coasting trade, and the right to participate in that trade was granted to Thomas Gibbons on his receipt of a license under the federal act. The federal statute made no distinction between the carriage of passengers and the transport of cargo. Furthermore, the federal duty act, as well as legislation concerning the safety and comfort of passengers, demonstrated that the same federal regulations applied to ships that carried passengers as to those that transported freight. Significantly, the pleadings in the case did not complain that Gibbons's vessels carried either cargo or passengers; the main allegation of the complaint was that they were propelled by steam while in New York waters. Thus, the "real and sole question" was whether the state's prohibition on the use of steam in operating a vessel on its waters deprived a shipowner of the rights conferred on him by a coasting license. Congressional legislation specifically provided that steamboats might be licensed for the coastal trade. He concluded, "The act of a State inhibiting the use of either [steam or sail] to any vessel having a license under the act of Congress comes, we think, in direct collision with that act." Consequently, the New York statute granting the monopoly came into conflict with Gibbons's right to navigate in American coastal waters, and thus was unconstitutional.

As a final note, Marshall indicated that it was not necessary to consider the constitutionality of the New York monopoly grant in light of the Constitution's grant of patenting and copyright powers to Congress. The issue became moot because the dispute was determined by the commerce clause, supplemented by the supremacy clause in Article Six.

The fifth and final section of the chief justice's opinion for the Court, as we have earlier noted, contained an apology for the length of the opinion, explaining,

> The conclusion to which we have come depends on a chain of principles which it was necessary to preserve unbroken, and although some of them were thought nearly self-evident, the magnitude of the question, the weight of character belonging to those from whose judgment we dissent, and the argument at the bar demanded that we should assume nothing.

The concluding paragraph, quoted at length at the beginning of this chapter, contains a tacit criticism of concurrent construction positions taken by Oakley and Emmet on behalf of New York and Aaron Ogden. Had these submissions by "powerful and ingenious minds" been accepted, the Constitution would have been left a magnificent structure to look at, "but totally unfit for use." Yet viewed retrospectively in the cool light of nearly two centuries of commerce clause evolution, one wonders if perhaps the chief justice himself did not inadvertently "so entangle and perplex the understanding [of contemporaries and future generations] as to obscure principles" concerning the constitutional application of the commerce clause.

By way of contrast, Associate Justice William Johnson's concurring opinion is a model of judicial conciseness and systematic development; his biographer, Donald Morgan, rates it as "one of Johnson's best." Disagreements on the Court, evidenced either by dissenting or concurring opinions, always are valuable peepholes into the decision making process. The clarity of Justice Johnson's opinion leaves no doubt that Thomas Gibbons's attorneys had successfully presented a strong case for an exclusive construction of the Constitution, and there are passages throughout the Court's opinion that also seem to adopt that preference. However, it is equally true that Marshall's opinion for the Court took great pains to avoid an exclusive interpretation of the commerce clause. The complexity of commercial regulation persuaded the majority to avoid an exclusive construction, but it produced an opinion that leaned in the direction of endorsing a form of concurrent authority over commerce. Although Congress would play a leading role, states would supplement its legislation with action based on their police, or other reserved, powers. To the extent that this is true, Thomas J. Oakley and Thomas Addis Emmet shaped the jurisprudence of the commerce clause, even as they lost their clients' appeal.

Justice Johnson's opinion begins with what had become a standard apology for differing from the reasoning of the Court majority: because his views materially differed from those of his fellow justices, it was incumbent on him to exhibit those views. That determination was further implemented by his decision to issue an independent judgment and to publish his views in a personal opinion. More precisely, he was required to make an "effort to maintain [his] . . . opinion in [his] . . . own way." This latter expression closely paralleled the words used in an October 1822 letter he had received from former president Thomas Jefferson. It insisted that whenever possible, Johnson should write separate opinions that made his views readily available to the public. Although the advice was not followed in most situations, the justice clearly felt that *Gibbons v. Ogden* was of sufficient importance that his separate voice had to be heard, and that he was required to set before the public his differences from the reasoning of the Court's opinion. As a result, we have a concurring opinion that does four things: (1) it sets forth a nationalist construction of the commerce clause; (2) it adopts an exclusive construction of the commerce clause; (3) it partially explains the complexity and ambiguity of the Court's opinion; and (4) it suggests that Johnson's advocacy of Webster's exclusivity arguments was presented to the full Court during its deliberations and was rejected for the less clearly delineated position established in Marshall's Court opinion.

Tracing commercial arrangements under the colonial governments as well as intermittent efforts to centralize commercial regulation in the Confederation period, Johnson argued that the ratification of the Constitution transferred all commercial power to the federal government. The authority to govern foreign trade was clearly in the federal government, and the language that granted exclusive power to one form of commerce — that is, foreign trade — "grants it as to all." From the nature of the grant, and in the understanding of the framers and contemporary public opinion, the commerce clause conferred exclusive power on the federal government. Navigation was undoubtedly a part of commerce and thus included authority granted by the commerce clause; furthermore, the clause also covered the carriage of both goods and people.

He also accepted what would subsequently be deemed a "dormancy" construction of the commerce clause — that the Constitution itself granted Congress the power to regulate commerce, and the very grant, independent of any action of Congress, bestowed complete authority in the federal government and precluded the states from acting. Thus, if the federal Coasting Licensing Act were repealed tomorrow, it would have no significance for the appellant's rights to navigate New York waters with his steamboats. Looking closely at the statute, he concluded that it conferred certain privileges on registered and enrolled American vessels that were withheld from other ships, but that "the abstract right of commercial intercourse, stripped of those privileges, is open to all." Clearly, Justice Johnson rejected the majority opinion's view that the issuance of a coasting license conferred a property right to trade on Thomas Gibbons, and that New York's monopoly legislation conflicted with that right based on the federal statute. At the same time, the justice accepted Daniel Webster's first argument — that the very existence of the Constitution's provision precluded any state legislation that interfered with the constitutional grant. It will be recalled that the chief justice relied on the federal Coasting Licensing Act as removing the dormancy issue from the Court's consideration.

Having taken a strong position on the exclusive nature of the commerce power, Johnson turned his attention to the concept of limited federal government, noting that "as to all concessions of powers which previously existed in the states . . . [t]he practice of our government has been to occupy so much only of the field opened to them as they think the public interest requires." That solicitude was particularly demonstrated by the limited jurisdiction of federal courts, and it was also this concern for "aboriginal" powers (that is, powers exercised by the states before the Constitution's ratification) that made the federal

Coasting Licensing Act significant for the consideration of *Gibbons*. As far as the coasting trade was concerned, the 1793 statute "contains a full expression of Congress on the subject" and thus evidences an intention to exercise authority in that field of regulation.

Examining various state regulations touching on commercial activity, such as health and inspection laws, Johnson followed Marshall's position, which found their constitutional source in powers other than that of commerce: "Their different purposes mark the distinction between powers brought into action; and while frankly exercised, they can produce no evident collision." Constitutional provisions reserving to the states certain powers, such as inspection laws, presume coordinated action of the states and federal government:

> Inspection laws must combine municipal with commercial regulations, and, while the power over the subject is yielded to the states, for obvious reasons, an absolute power is given over state legislation over the subject, as far as that legislation may be exercised so as to affect the commerce of the country.

He conceded that clashes between state and federal laws were possible, although rare, and the line could not be drawn with sufficient distinction to separate municipal powers from commercial authority. Municipal and commerce powers might be exercised on the same object and yet be distinct; they might even use the same means without losing their origin in separate foundations of power. Although Justice Johnson carefully refrained from an express statement, his discussion strongly implies that clashes between municipal and commercial powers would be resolved on supremacy grounds by the U.S. Supreme Court.

William Johnson's concurring opinion illustrates the divergence of his constitutional views from those of Thomas Jefferson on one hand, and from states' rights advocates on the other. He was willing to concede an exclusive commerce power in Congress, which was based on his conviction that foreign and interstate commerce were aspects of a broad grant of constitutional power to the federal legislature. Necessarily, the power over foreign trade, being granted in the same clause of the Constitution, had to be construed in a similar fashion. And from *Elkison*, he well knew the embarrassments inherent in permitting state governments to interfere with foreign commercial activity. Unfortunately, the Court opinion does not explicitly touch on constitutional aspects of foreign trade, leaving us to speculate the degree to which that relationship shaped the Court's reasoning.

Johnson also accepted Marshall's point that when state actions were legitimated by their police powers, they might well touch on subjects and objects of federal commercial regulation as long as they did not conflict with Congress's acts. Basically, Johnson's opinion does not substantially differ from that of the Court except for its ready acceptance of an exclusive construction of the commerce clause, and his insistence on what would become a dormant interpretation of the Constitution's grant of commercial regulatory authority to Congress. Both opinions accord primacy to federal authority in the regulation of commerce while leaving ample room for state legislation that does not conflict with the Constitution or federal legislation enacted pursuant to the Constitution.

It is interesting to speculate that Justice Johnson's concurrence may well have expressed a position that would have been taken by Chief Justice Marshall individually if the Court had issued seriatim opinions. Speaking for the Court, Marshall was constrained to present the group's understanding of the commerce clause. This interpretation he would have gained through discussion with his colleagues, and his ultimate draft of the opinion represents an effort to reflect the various views held by his associate justices on the bench. Given the controversial nature of *Gibbons v. Ogden*, it is surprising that the chief justice was able to produce any opinion at all, much less one that began to lay the foundations for growing federal commercial regulation.

Justice Johnson's concurrence, undoubtedly profoundly influenced by his experiences in deciding the *Elkison* case in his federal circuit court, brings to the forefront the intimate relationship between interstate and foreign commerce. More pointedly, it goes directly to the basic question of how a nation may function internationally if it lacks the ability to direct its own internal commercial system. Both he and the chief justice were well aware of this international aspect of the *Gibbons* case, even though it was not a matter at issue. The Anglo-American peace treaty of 1783 contained a provision that the United States would endeavor to facilitate the collection of debts owed by American citizens to British mercantile firms. It also ceded the future Northwest Territory to the United States, opening to American settlement a vast tract of land north of the Ohio River and east of the Mississippi. After the exchange of ratifications, American states, including John Marshall's Virginia, enacted changes in their substantive and procedural laws that effectively blocked British merchants from collecting pre-Revolutionary debts from Americans. Citing this alleged breach of the treaty provisions, the British government refused to surrender the Northwest Territory to the United States. Ultimately, the collection of these debts was subjected to the deliberation of a joint claims commission established by the Jay treaty of 1794. Thus, by their unilateral actions, the states had seriously undermined American diplomatic efforts.

John Marshall's law practice in post-Revolutionary Richmond brought him into direct contact with these developments. A substantial part of his trial dockets after the opening of federal courts in 1790 included the defense of Virginia planters against the claims of British creditors. And his only appellate argument before the U.S. Supreme Court was his defense of Virginia debtors against claims asserted by their pre-Revolutionary British creditors in *Ware v. Hylton* (1796).

Admittedly the facts of *Gibbons* limited the Court's consideration to interstate relationships, yet the case's potentiality toward weakening of American diplomacy in commercial matters was certainly an important policy decision to be considered. Marshall, a former secretary of state, as well as his colleagues, must have been aware of these implications that would accompany their decision in *Gibbons v. Ogden*. In terms of federalism, such a consideration would strongly influence the Court in the direction of an exclusive regulatory power in Congress. At the very least, it might be expected to cause the Court to make a distinction that conferred primacy on the United States when foreign commerce was involved. This is another area in which *Gibbons* raises more questions than it answers. However, the choice to ignore the connection between domestic and foreign commerce in the text of the Court's opinion reinforces the conclusion that Marshall's opinion for the Court was the product of a hard-won compromise of divergent views within the majority. It also partially explains the unusually long delay between the end of oral argument and the announcement of the Court's disposition of the case.

Yet the length, ambiguity, and delayed appearance of Chief Justice Marshall's opinion for the Court may well reflect caution and concern for some of the political considerations we have considered in Chapter 4, particularly public outrage at what was considered Justice Story's abrupt dismissal of *Green v. Biddle*, the "occupying claimant" case. *Green* involved attempts by Kentucky to protect the interests of individuals who had occupied lands without having obtained Virginia land grants. The circumstances of the case were known to Chief Justice Marshall, who with family members had been involved in the acquisition and sale of Kentucky lands before 1792, when the district was admitted to the union. Because of his financial interest in the matter, Marshall refrained from participating in the consideration of the case, and the preparation of an opinion was assigned to Justice Story.

The federal Constitution required that the Commonwealth of Virginia consent to the admission of Kentucky as an independent state. In return for its agreement, Virginia insisted that Kentucky land grants issued by the Old Dominion be recognized by the new state of Kentucky, and suitable provisions were included in the Kentucky constitution and the federal enabling legislation. However, after the state's admission, the Kentucky legislature enacted a statute designed to protect squatters who had made improvements to the occupied land even though they lacked legal title. The holders of title secured from Virginia, most of whom were nonresidents of Kentucky, were awarded possession and ownership of the land by the state courts, but they refused to pay the squatters for improvements to the land. On appeal, the U.S. Supreme Court held that the Kentucky squatter legislation violated the contract clause of the federal Constitution and was invalid. Thus, the disposition of the improvements was controlled by the ancient common-law rule that squatters were not entitled to reimbursement for improvements made to the land they occupied. Understandably, the decision was not popular with the public and raised widespread criticism.

Justice Story's 1821 opinion was unusually brief, but the greater likelihood is that its failure to empathize with the sorry plight of the

Kentucky settlers was the cause of the public outcry. Another aggravating circumstance was the fact that the claimants, probably as a result of poverty, were not represented by counsel at the 1821 argument. In the 1823 term of Court, the Story opinion was withdrawn and a longer and more contemplative text was drawn by Justice Bushrod Washington and resubmitted as the Court's reasoning. Although the occupying claimants still lost the value of all improvements they had made, public opinion was mollified, and presumably the Court had learned a memorable lesson in public relations.

In *Green*, the Court felt compelled to apply the harsh common-law rule that improvements made by squatters on realty would be awarded to the holder of title on the eviction of the squatters. Given the uncertainty of many Kentucky land titles and the harsh result demanded by common law, national public opinion supported the palliative legislation passed by the Kentucky legislature. However, in *Gibbons*, the appellant, Thomas Gibbons, represented an entrepreneur trying to break a monopoly that interfered with popular steamboat transportation. Legislative and public support for the Livingston–Fulton syndicate had faded since the monopoly was granted in 1807, and a decision in favor of Gibbons would probably be widely acclaimed. On the other hand, the financial plight of Fulton's wife and child suggested that the opinion should be a carefully reasoned exposition of the law and constitutional principles that required this seemingly harsh result. In addition, *Gibbons* followed a series of cases, including *Green*, in which state legislation had been set aside by the Supreme Court. Supporting the appellant meant still another demonstration of federal judicial control over state action. Although the need to preserve Congress's paramount authority over foreign and interstate commerce dictated such a decision, due caution suggested that it be accomplished in an acceptable and exhaustively reasoned Court opinion.

Gibbons also witnesses a new leadership role emerging for Marshall as chief justice. The Steamboat Case presented a substantial challenge to John Marshall's newly emerging role as a mediator among his brother justices. Adjusting differing views on the numerous points raised by counsel would have taken time, patience, and diplomacy. Marshall could also call on the accumulated traditions and practice of the Court established during his twenty-three years as chief justice. Personality also played a critical role. The chief justice seems to have taken a leading part in making new colleagues welcome in the Court. He was considerate in his assignment of opinion-writing tasks and careful not to inflame personality clashes among the justices. When counsel complained that they had been treated badly in Court interchanges, it was Marshall who soothed ruffled feelings and protected the public image and professional reputation of the Court. It was also Marshall who was steadfast in the face of recurrent threats by Congress to alter the Supreme Court's appellate jurisdiction, or to eliminate entirely the Court's review of state court decisions that dealt with "federal questions." Although his age and the growing diversity of views on the Court may have diminished the chief justice's predominance in authoring opinions, he nevertheless continued to occupy the central leadership role on the Supreme Court.

Although we have stressed Jeffersonian influence on Justice Johnson, it is important to note that both Marshall and Justice Bushrod Washington once held the opinion that the commerce clause was exclusive. Is it possible that both urged Johnson to submit his views for publication? Although they and the rest of the Court were reluctant to express that position as clearly and as forcefully as did Johnson, there was increased emphasis on federal paramountcy because of Johnson's concurring opinion. In addition, the concurring opinion alerted the profession that the Court had given great thought to the concept of an exclusive commerce power, and to paraphrase Marshall, they were "not convinced that it had been refuted."

Most readers of Marshall's opinion for the Court would agree with Professor G. Edward White, who has characterized it as "highly inconclusive" and who has criticized the chief justice's exposition of the extent of the commerce clause as "odd." It is also true that congressional lack of substantial legislative action involving commerce had left the initiative in the hands of the states. White's analysis is perceptive when he points out that after *Gibbons*, the states were reassured that Congress would not use "its dominant regulatory powers as a means of keeping the states out of the area of commercial regulation." Nor, we might add, would the Supreme Court overlook the importance of state police powers as a complementary source of regulatory support in the area.

For better or worse, *Gibbons* is as important for what it did not decide as it is for what it did decide. It did not claim an exclusive scope for the federal commerce power, nor did it postulate a dormancy construction of the constitutional grant of power, which would have hamstrung the states in the field of economic regulation. It did not assert the sweeping nationalizing impulse for centralized control of commerce that triggered the gathering of the 1787 Philadelphia constitutional convention. Above all, except for a concession that commerce internal to a state was not subject to congressional regulation, it did not set forth the parameters or the limits of the commerce that might be regulated by Congress. The Court opinion also took an economic impact approach to defining the applicability of federal power to commercial regulation. Although the commerce power might be wide in scope and amorphic in its application, state legislation touching on economic subjects would be unconstitutional only if it affected interstate or foreign commerce.

Although slavery was only mentioned in passing in the *Gibbons* opinions, it was unquestionably a controversial issue that was much in the background as the justices deliberated. From 1818 through March 1820, Congress was actively engaged in considering Missouri statehood and whether the territory should be admitted as a slave state. Within that discussion, southern and northern legislators clashed over proposals to abolish the interstate slave trade, based on the Constitution's commerce clause. However, the domestic slave trade issue was not resolved at that time, and Missouri was admitted as a state in March 1820. Abolition of the domestic slave trade was never mentioned in the *Gibbons* opinion, leaving that hotly contested constitutional issue unresolved. For southern planters and politicians, who depended on the interstate slave trade to provide labor in the rapidly expanding agricultural areas of Georgia, Mississippi, Alabama, and Louisiana, the Court's silence provided little comfort. At the same time, judicial silence in the midst of political controversy proved to be the best course. Marshall's opinion did refer to the federal statute that prohibited the interstate transportation of slaves into a state whose law refused them entry. That legislation reinforced the impression that Congress would cooperate with the states in their efforts to either abolish or to accept the "peculiar institution" within their boundaries. At the same time, the 1820 Missouri Compromise demonstrated congressional willingness to admit territories as states only when the southern states maintained their equality of representation in the U.S. Senate. Thus, the likelihood of federal legislation abolishing the interstate slave trade was remote. *Gibbons* at the very least served as tacit reassurance that the Supreme Court was unlikely to upset this delicate political and constitutional balance.

Inadvertently, Marshall's opinion in *Gibbons* gave some semblance of support to abolitionist efforts to secure congressional action to restrict or end the interstate slave trade. Ogden's counsel had argued that the Constitution's conferral of the commerce power on Congress referred only to transportation of goods and not the conveyance of passengers. The Court rejected this distinction in its *Gibbons* opinion, facilitating federal abolition of the interstate slave trade, should Congress decide to limit or abolish carriage of slaves in interstate commerce. Common law in most American states was ambiguous concerning the legal status of slaves; for some purposes, slaves were treated as property, but for others, including apportionment of federal representation, they were considered persons. After *Gibbons*, it was clear that the Court, should it be required to resolve the constitutionality of federal abolition of the internal slave trade, would be bound by precedent to reject this distinction.

Gibbons can be best understood by separating holding from dictum, a skill learned only with difficulty in first-year law school — and a skill that thereafter has limited utility, for a judge's dictum today may well be his or her holding tomorrow. Chief Justice Marshall was careful to limit the holding of the Court by isolating the major issues: (1) Did the federal Coasting Licensing Act regulate commerce? (2) Did the New York monopoly granted to Livingston and Fulton conflict with the Licensing Act? And (3) was the New York legislation constitutional? All other considerations fell into the category of dictum — matter not necessary to resolve the controversy before the Court.

Ironically, dicta set the background against which the Marshall Court and its successors would shape the vast corpus of federal law and economic regulation that finds its constitutional foundation in the commerce clause. The chief justice rejected a strictly territorial or geographical understanding of state and federal authority, negating contrary views propounded by Chancellor James Kent and the New York court of impeachment and errors in the *Van Ingen* case and in *Ogden v. Gibbons*. Commerce among the states not only was trade that was intermingled within two or more states, but also involved federal paramountcy over state economic regulation that affected the conduct of interstate or foreign commercial activity. Both the qualitative and the quantitative aspects of state activity would be considered in determining whether there was an unacceptable trespass on Congress's regulatory power. Congress should regulate major aspects of commercial activity, leaving less significant matters to be covered by state laws enacted under police or other reserved powers. There was also a concern about the magnitude of a state's regulatory impact on interstate or foreign commercial activity. By implication, the fact that the Livingston–Fulton monopoly denied navigation to all unlicensed steam-powered vessels in New York waters created a situation in which there was a direct clash between the federal Coasting Licensing Act and the state statutes protecting the monopoly.

Even when state and federal power were concurrent, such as the taxing powers vested in both levels of government, the *Gibbons* majority was quick to point out that taxes and duties on imports and exports were subject to state exaction only if Congress gave its approval. Inspection laws might be enforced by the states, but fees charged were to be limited to sums necessary to reimburse the states for their enforcement expenditures. In the Constitution's text, and in Marshall's *Gibbons* opinion, there was a clearly expressed concern that the Founding Fathers' goal of a barrier-free national economic system within the American federal union should not be undermined by mercantilistic and protective state initiatives. And the degree of impermissible undermining depended on both the nature of what the state had done and the magnitude of its impact.

The perplexing task of creating an economic commercial union among a growing number of American states was vastly complicated by the need to define the purposes of the federal government. For the chief justice, and presumably for his supporting colleagues, the commerce power was among the most fundamental powers to be exercised by the central government. As such, it was plenary in nature, and as the chief justice phrased it, "the power over commerce with foreign nations and among the several States, is vested in Congress as absolutely as it would be in a single government." That authority was subject only to moral and electoral control:

> The wisdom and the discretion of Congress, their identity with the people, and the influence which their constituencies possess at elections, are in this as in many other instances, as that, for example of declaring war, the sole restraints on which they have relied, to secure them from its abuse. They are the restraints on which the people must often rely solely, in all representative governments.

The mention of the war powers of Congress raises the commerce power to be among "first tier" federal government powers. Presumably Marshall would also include the power of engaging in diplomacy as a mark of independent nationhood. Certainly, the regulation of foreign trade fits comfortably within this same category; did the chief justice, aware of state laws and actions that had the demonstrated capacity to embarrass American foreign relations, wish to elevate the interstate commerce power to the same level? This view is certainly supported by his linguistic analysis of the commerce clause, mentioned earlier: because both foreign and interstate commerce are granted in the same clause of Article One, Section 8, are they not to be accorded the same meaning, and perhaps the same status?

Offsetting this broad endorsement of federal commerce power in dictum is the chief justice's acknowledgment of the extensive police powers traditionally exercised by the states. By the Tenth Amendment, this residuary state regulatory power was raised to the status of constitutional principle. Marshall was willing to rationalize that because the source of these residuary powers was not a commercial authority either given to or retained by the states, there would not be an intrusion on Congress's authority under the Constitution's commerce clause. However, this did not resolve the question whether the state action interfered with, affected, or burdened federal commercial regulation; if it did, then the supremacy clause of the Constitution invalidated the state action.

Again, we need to remember that we are dealing with dictum. The decision of the case was that the grant of licenses under the federal

Coasting Licensing Act was in conflict with the Livingston–Fulton monopoly legislation of the New York legislature. Therefore, the New York law and the monopoly it created were both invalid because they violated the Constitution of the United States and a statute of the United States enacted pursuant to the Constitution.

Does the narrow basis for decision negate the influence of Marshall's dictum? Obviously not. The dictum in the Court opinion formed the basis, both in terminology and in conceptualization, on which future commerce clause judicial development would be predicated. The chief justice's wide-ranging discussion of the nature of the commerce clause and of the allocation of power between federal and state governments has come down in American constitutional law not as binding case law, but as a convenient and authoritative commentary on the intent of the framers of the federal Constitution. Its ambiguity is a by-product of the complexity raised by the need to allocate economic regulatory power between two levels of American government. That complexity necessarily generates difficult, and at times contradictory, constitutional and economic analysis.

At the constitutional level, federalism demands that sovereignty be divided between the state and federal governments, and the interplay of various types of commercial activity makes such an allocation not only difficult, but also subject to variation depending on the conditions in existence at any given time. If the process of regulation is complex, the economic nature of commercial activity is equally baffling. Ogden's counsel painted a detailed picture of the various legal and business relationships that supported economic activity in the early republic. It is clear that a vast field of state law supplied the economic basis on which commerce was conducted. State statutes provided for the construction of highways and their maintenance; state regulation of taverns, places of lodging, and wharves for berthing vessels made travel and trade possible. Local and state health and sanitary laws protected the public from disease transmitted by goods and passengers. The impact of state legislation and regulation on commerce was immense; it was left to future Supreme Courts to determine which state laws were obstructive to interstate and foreign commerce, and which were acceptable because they were complementary to and supportive of Congress's regulation of interstate and foreign trade.

CHAPTER 7

The Fallout from *Gibbons*

Delivered by a weak but rehabilitated chief justice on 2 March 1824, the Court opinion in *Gibbons* attracted prompt and generally favorable response. Legal historian Charles Warren provides us with a good cross section of professional and public reactions to their announcement. The *New York Evening Post* exulted over the destruction of the steamboat monopoly; it found the Court's opinion to be a "long and luminous view" as well as a "masterpiece of judicial reasoning." Across the Hudson River, a New Jersey newspaper breathed a sigh of relief that "the waters are now free," and a Missouri paper observed that the Supreme Court opinion was applauded in New York's sister states, "who can see no propriety in the claim of New York to domineer over the waters which form the means of intercourse between that State and others." South Carolina journalists sounded an antimonopoly note, approving the defeat of the navigation companies of New York, which had been "brought into existence and pampered by the unnatural and unconstitutional measures adopted" by the New York legislature.

Widespread acclaim with the general public was not shared by all. Chief Justice Marshall's distant kinsman and Virginia's gadfly congressman, John Randolph, cast a critical but not inaccurate eye on the Court's opinion. He found it both too long and cluttered with too much material that did not belong there; in short, he objected to the dicta that comprised a large proportion of Marshall's opinion for the Court. Randolph concluded, "since the case of *Cohens v. Virginia*, I am done with the Supreme Court." On both points he was perceptive. The actual holding in the case could have been set forth with greater brevity and simplicity; but it was the dicta that would shape future developments. And both in *Cohens* and *Gibbons*, the Court had, as Randolph complained, expanded the reach of federal judicial power at the expense of state independence.

A month after the opinions were read, another Virginian, Congressman Robert S. Garnett, rose in the House to warn about still another concern. Given the broad construction that Marshall had given to the commerce clause, Garnett asserted that such sweeping power might, combined with antislavery "political fanaticism," be used to regulate or prohibit the interstate slave trade. As we have discussed earlier, this was a growing sentiment in the slaveholding states, and a controversial topic that Chief Justice Marshall had avoided discussing directly in *Gibbons* and in an earlier case he decided in the U.S. circuit court for Virginia. Justice Johnson's experience in South Carolina with the *Elkison* case and the Negro Seamen's Act was more than adequate warning of southern sensitivity to the possibility of the federal interstate commerce power being exercised in regard to slavery.

Neither the Supreme Court nor the nation gained respite from commerce clause issues after the announcement of the opinions in *Gibbons v. Ogden*. The financial stakes were too high, and the state of constitutional law on the regulation of commerce remained uncertain. Consequently, there was probably little public surprise when a group of enterprising New York mariners challenged what remained of the Livingston–Fulton monopoly through a triangular voyage of their steamboat, the *Olive Branch*. On the first trip between New York City and Albany, they took the precaution of crossing the Hudson to Jersey City, landing there briefly, and then proceeding upriver to Albany. According to the Livingston–Fulton syndicate's amended complaint dated 28 June 1824, the *Olive Branch* had made more than fifty trips between the two New York cities without ever again touching on New Jersey's shores. The gravamen of the petition presented to New York chancellor Nathan Sanford was that the initial stopping was fraudulent in that it was not a bona fide voyage for commercial purposes. It was also claimed that the voyage was in defiance of New York law governing the operation of steamboats in New York waters. Chancellor Sanford denied the request for an injunction in the situation where the Livingston vessel docked briefly on the New Jersey shore. However, in regard to travel between two or more New York ports without any New Jersey stop, he granted an injunction to the North River Steamboat Company, thereby upholding the Livingston–Fulton monopoly's statutory rights. The case was then appealed to the New York court of impeachment and errors under the title *The North River Steam Boat Company v. Livingston*.

Because it was customary to reprint a lower court's opinion in the court of impeachment and errors report, we have a clear statement of Chancellor Sanford's reasoning. At the outset, he noted that the right of John R. Livingston to navigate was based on a law of the United States, whereas the claimant's rights were derived from New York state statutes that granted a monopoly to the Livingston–Fulton syndicate. In such circumstances, the state law would be "annihilated" to the extent it conflicted with the federal statute. The matter was determined by federal constitutional law and was not affected by equitable considerations of bona fides raised by the petitioners. Simply stopping in New Jersey, with nothing more, provided an adequate basis for bringing John Livingston's activity within the purview of interstate commerce regulation. Sanford decreed that

> [t]he supremacy of constitutional laws of the union, and the nullity of state laws inconsistent with such laws of the union, are principles of the constitution of the united states. Thus, this case is entirely different from any of those, in which various rights derived from one lawgiving source may exist together, and all may claim scope for their exercise.

Referring to *Gibbons*, he asserted that the defendant's rights under a federal coasting license were to engage in "free intercourse by navigation, from state to state," which included "a right to engage in every thing which constitutes the coasting trade." And if the consequence was that the defendants may circuitously do something that state law prohibited them from doing directly, that was just "one of the results of that complex [federal] system of government, which has no parallel, in its peculiar structure and the distribution of its powers."

Moving beyond the *Gibbons* opinion, Chancellor Sanford distinguished between travel on waters that are navigable from other states and sailing on internal waters of New York not so accessible. In other words, he was willing to entertain the view that vessels navigating entirely within New York State might nevertheless be engaged in the coasting trade and subject to Congress's regulation. In his view, that would follow from the accessibility of the body of water to ships from other states or foreign nations. However, Sanford stressed that navigability of New York waters to seagoing trade made them subject to congressional regulation only when interstate or foreign trade was involved; thus navigability alone did not open internal state commerce to federal regulation. It is apparent that the chancellor was well aware that New York bodies of water readily accessible to vessels from other states or foreign nations might, in various circumstances, be brought within regulation under the federal commerce power. Because the completion of the Erie Canal was then imminent, there was no question that interstate and foreign commerce would soon reach well into, and even through, the interior of New York State. The commercial and economic advantages of linking the Great Lakes to New York harbor far outweighed the limited and rapidly declining benefits, if any, attributable to the Livingston–Fulton monopoly. The chancellor noted that the state monopoly grant continued in effect, but that it did so "after the law of the union shall first have had its full operation," and that it remained in force "only when and where, the right to navigate from state to state, is not exercised."

Sanford's decree emphatically denied an injunction against New York–Albany voyages that touched on a wharf in Jersey City, and it rested solidly on the federal Constitution's supremacy clause and federal statutes enacted pursuant to the Constitution. It also upheld the authority of New York State to regulate internal navigation from New York City to Albany or Troy when no such extrastate contact was present. Thus his decree recognized that upriver navigation continued to enjoy the protection of the Livingston–Fulton monopoly; an injunction was issued restraining John Livingston from operating steamboats directly from New York City to Albany because he did not possess a license from the Livingston–Fulton syndicate. In effect, Chancellor Sanford provided partial relief to the complainants, but at the same time, he sanctioned an easy method for circumventing the impact of that portion of his decree that favored the steamboat monopoly. He had accepted the defendant's position that a mere formal touching on New Jersey territory, without exchanging goods or engaging in business, was a sufficient basis upon which to characterize an otherwise internal New York voyage into coasting trade activity. Technically, the North River Steamboat Company, as successor to the Livingston–Fulton monopoly interests, had won the battle, but John R. Livingston, the infringer, had won the war.

The Steamboat Company's appeal was taken to the court of impeachment and errors, which announced its decision in February 1825 affirming Chancellor Sanford's decision concerning voyages that touched in Jersey City before proceeding to Albany or Troy, New York. However, it reversed that part of Sanford's decree that enjoined John Livingston from operating steamboats on a direct trip between New York City and upriver destinations in New York State. As might be anticipated, the judicial nullification of all benefits under the monopoly legislation was far from unanimous. Twenty-one members joined with Chief Justice Nathan Savage and supported his majority opinion; eight members supported the dissenting opinion read by Supreme Court justice John Woodworth. The dissenting members of the Court agreed with the chancellor's upholding the Livingston–Fulton monopoly in regard to all voyages conducted entirely within New York State. They also rejected John Livingston's plea that a landing in Jersey City converted such a voyage into interstate activity subject to regulation under the federal Coasting Licensing Act. Presumably they agreed with North River Steamboat Company's argument that non-financial contact with New Jersey was insufficient to mark the voyage as a part of interstate commerce.

On the other hand, the majority adopted a generous interpretation of the *Gibbons* opinion, asserting that the federal Coasting Licensing Act conflicted with the Livingston–Fulton monopoly statute and thus invalidated the New York law, regardless of whether a stop was made in New Jersey. They pointed out that because John Livingston held a license under the federal Coasting Licensing Act, he might operate a steamboat from New York City either to Albany or Troy under the authority granted by that license; federal law protected him from injunctions issued to protect the Livingston–Fulton monopoly. A steamboat trip by a federally licensed vessel, even if entirely within New York waters, could not be restrained by the terms of the New York monopoly grant.

For the minority dissenters, Supreme Court justice John Woodworth had narrowly restricted *Gibbons v. Ogden* to the facts of the case, particularly noting that Thomas Gibbons's vessels were regularly engaged in navigation between a New Jersey port and New York City.

Woodworth asserted that *Gibbons* was clearly distinguishable from the matter before the court. The *North River Steam Boat Company* case raised the questions of purely internal commercial activity within New York State, and whether a single trip that touched briefly and without commercial significance in New Jersey thereby lost its internal character. Indeed, the issue of *intrastate* commercial activity had been merely speculative in *Gibbons,* and Chief Justice Marshall had taken pains to distinguish between trade internal to a state and commerce among two or more states. As to commerce internal to a state, "Ch. J. Marshall seems to admit that if the power exist, it is an incidental, not a direct power in Congress."

Woodworth conceded that Congress had plenary power over interstate commerce, and he even surmised that state legislation touching on the interstate commerce clause was invalid even though Congress had not acted. Thus he accepted what would be later termed a dormancy view of congressional power over commerce. Yet the focal point of his opinion was that Congress acted to regulate interstate coasting trade, and in this instance, no such trade had taken place in Jersey City. He noted that

> the touching at *New-Jersey* seems to have been for the purpose of fraudulently evading the laws of this state, and not for any *bona fide* purpose of commercial intercourse. . . . No principle is better settled than this: what cannot lawfully be done directly can not be done indirectly. The circuitous voyage was in evasion of the laws of this state; the touching at *New-Jersey* was colourable only.

Consequently, the minority voted to reverse the chancellor's decree, which held that noncommercial landings in New Jersey conferred federal coasting status upon voyages between two terminal points in New York State. It also viewed the direct route from New York City to upriver New York destinations to be strictly internal commerce, as that term was defined in Marshall's *Gibbons* opinion. Justice Woodworth's opinion thus represented the last enunciation of New York State's long-standing support for the Livingston–Fulton steamboat monopoly.

Chief Justice Nathan Savage, writing for the majority, lost no time in pointing out that New York courts had never decided whether navigation of the Hudson above the New Jersey–New York border was subject to regulation by Congress. He noted that Marshall's opinion in *Gibbons* specifically rejected the concept that interstate commerce began and ended with the crossing of a state boundary; quite the contrary, to be effective throughout the union, interstate commerce had to pass through two or more states. In addition, *Gibbons* enunciated the principle that the federal government's authority over commerce was operative in areas which generally concerned the nation, and also those matters "which affect the states generally; but not those which are *completely* within a particular state." From Marshall's statements, Savage concluded that there was a broad group of commercial matters entirely within a state over which Congress might exercise control in accordance with the *Gibbons* precedent. Savage also defined the coasting trade broadly: "The coasting trade is commercial intercourse carried on between different districts in different states, different districts in the same state, and different places in the same district, on the sea coast or on a navigable river." Thus a voyage of a suitable and licensed coasting trade vessel from New York to Albany was as much within the coasting trade as a trip from Boston to Plymouth or Bedford, even though in all cases, the terminal points of the voyage were in the same state.

Continuing, Sanford noted that although Marshall's opinion recognized extensive police powers with the states, he also insisted that under the interstate and foreign commerce powers, Congress might regulate commerce within a given state without usurping an authority to regulate the internal commerce of that state. Thus, "the navigation of the *Hudson*, a public navigable river, is not included in such internal commerce; but . . . composes a part of the coasting trade, and is, therefore, subject to the regulation and control of congress." As a ship involved in the coasting trade, John Livingston's vessel, the *Olive Branch*, was engaged in a lawful trade and had a perfect right to the navigation of the Hudson River. Furthermore, should the citizens of New York continue to be bound by the prohibitions of the Livingston–Fulton monopoly merely by virtue of their residence within the state, they would be at a disadvantage not applicable to commercial activity by citizens of sister states or foreign nations. It was only fair that in the future they would no longer be bound by the terms of the Livingston–Fulton monopoly grant.

In effect, the court of impeachment and errors had once and for all rejected New York's right to issue a monopoly license that was in conflict with statutes enacted under the federal commerce power. It had also accepted a broad construction of the commerce clause and adopted John Marshall's expansive enunciation of congressional power to regulate commerce-related matters even within the boundaries of a single state. Not only was the Livingston–Fulton monopoly dead as a matter of federal constitutional law, but it was also denied any legal significance or economic profitability by the decision of the highest appellate court of New York State.

The *North River Steam Boat Company* case, with its broad construction of the Constitution's interstate commerce clause, represents New York State's acquiescence in Chief Justice Marshall's opinion for the Court in *Gibbons*. However, it does more. It introduces the concept that navigable bodies of water situated entirely within a state may be subject to congressional regulation if they are accessible to vessels traveling from other states or foreign nations. This was new material not considered in *Gibbons*, and it lays a foundation on which future judicial opinions, at both federal and state levels, might expand the scope of commerce clause regulation. *North River Steam Boat Company* also enunciates the principle that common-law principles and equitable theories are not applicable to the allocation of constitutional authority between federal and state governments. Because of this, neither the motivation of John Livingston's peremptory touching the New Jersey shore nor the bona fides of his doing so had any impact on the legality of his navigation of the Hudson River to Troy or Albany. Nor did it influence the application of principles of federalism to the case. Finally, the court of impeachment and errors' decision delivered the death blow to the Livingston–Fulton monopoly and terminated New York State's efforts to protect what had become a virtually worthless grant of economic privilege.

While the *North River Steam Boat Company* case was working its way through the New York state court system, *Corfield v. Coryell*, the New Jersey oyster bed case pending in the U.S. circuit court for Pennsylvania, was under renewed consideration by Justice Bushrod Washington. It will be recalled that New Jersey authorities had prosecuted

Pennsylvania oystermen who had been caught taking oysters from beds near the New Jersey shore that were reserved by state statute for the use of New Jersey residents. Having paid their fine, the Pennsylvanians brought action in the Pennsylvania federal circuit court against the arresting officers, and the jury awarded damages in the sum of $500 for the seizure of their vessel and their arrest and detention. However, because *Gibbons v. Ogden* was then pending on the U.S. Supreme Court's docket, Justice Washington suspended judgment until the Court's opinion in the Steamboat Case was available. After the March 1824 announcement of the *Gibbons* opinions, the *Corfield* circuit court case began to move forward. The parties stipulated what points of law should be argued, and formal argument took place before Justice Washington in October 1824. Again the matter was taken under advisement, and Washington's opinion was not delivered until the April 1825 term of the Pennsylvania circuit court.

Corfield presented a number of new matters that had not been covered in any detail by the Supreme Court opinions in *Gibbons*. While *Gibbons* involved a state regulation of commercial activity and authority based on general police powers, *Corfield* touched on the traditional authority of a sovereign government to protect public resources and common lands for the benefit of its residents. *Corfield* also presented the assertion by the oystermen that they had been denied the privileges and immunities to which they were entitled under the federal Constitution's Article Four; and of course, they also claimed that the New Jersey restriction of oyster farming to New Jersey residents violated the interstate commerce clause and thus was unconstitutional.

Although Justice Washington was generally inclined to follow John Marshall's partiality toward strong national government, consideration of the issues in *Corfield* opened his eyes to the broad spectrum of state power that had been preserved to the states by the Tenth Amendment. Specifically, the case demonstrated that each of the several states was charged with common-law duties to manage the property held in trust for all of the people. That duty included the obligation to control access and use of such property, and if necessary, the authority to restrict access to residents of the state. New Jersey limited access to oyster beds, and in doing so, it had performed a duty that preserved a valuable economic asset for the use of its residents, who comprised the community of ownership. Washington recognized that when a state acted in this capacity, it exercised an ancient aspect of sovereignty that was part of the *ius privatum*. By way of contrast, the regulation of commercial activity was *ius publicum*, as were many other sovereignty functions reserved to the states by the Tenth Amendment. That distinction was important, for the delegation of constitutional powers to the federal government under the Constitution was an allocation of *ius publicum* authority that did not include the state's fiduciary duties to its residents. For Washington, quasi-governmental functions included within the *ius privatum* were by their very nature powers that were unaffected by the federal Constitution. And there might be other powers within the *ius publicum* that, despite the broad authority inherent in the commerce clause grant to the U.S. Congress, nevertheless remained properly within the control of the states.

Quoting *Gibbons v. Ogden*, Washington insisted that the state must be presumed to have exclusive power to regulate access to its oyster beds:

> No direct power over these objects is granted to congress, and consequently they remain subject to state legislation. If the legislative power of congress can reach them, it must be for national purposes; it must be when the power is expressly given for specific purposes, or is clearly incident to some power which is expressly given.

As he explained, the states could legislate "in such manner as in their wisdom may seem best, over the public property of the state . . . where such regulations do not interfere with the free navigation of the waters of the state for purposes of commercial intercourse." Because there had been no showing of any state interference with commerce or navigation — and indeed the Pennsylvanians were not engaged in trade but rather in harvesting oysters they did not own — there was no commerce clause ground upon which to invalidate the New Jersey statute.

Corfield also presented Washington with the need to construe the privileges and immunities provisions in Article Four of the Constitution. Counsel for the oystermen and owner had argued that this phrase of the Constitution required that nonresidents be accorded the rights of residents, and that discrimination in access to oyster beds violated their privileges and immunities as residents of Pennsylvania, a sister state. Because the Supreme Court in *Gibbons* declined to consider the inequalities inherent in New York's monopoly grant to Livingston–Fulton, the issue of privileges and immunities was not there touched on, and Washington's later opinion in *Corfield* addressed this point without guidance from his colleagues or the Supreme Court's opinion. But it becomes quite clear from his *Corfield* opinion that although he was willing to extend a broad interpretation to the equality of resident and nonresident rights in Article Four, he was also disinclined to favor an unlimited constitutional guarantee of equal rights under that constitutional provision. Quite the contrary, the privileges and immunities clause covered only those rights that "are clearly embraced by the general description of privileges deemed to be fundamental" and that are therefore necessary "the better to secure and perpetuate mutual friendship and intercourse among the people of the different states of the Union." The privileges and immunities clause did not open the private oyster-harvesting rights common to Jersey men to nonresidents, nor was the New Jersey legislature constitutionally bound to extend equal access to nonresident oyster farmers.

As a member of John Marshall's inner circle within the Supreme Court, Bushrod Washington had probably consulted his fellow justices, including the chief justice, concerning the constitutional issues raised by *Corfield* in light of the *Gibbons* opinion. It was not uncommon for the justices to consult with each other concerning difficult cases that were being tried before them, and so close on the heels of the *Gibbons* decision, it would have been unwise for Washington not to follow the usual practice. *Corfield* may well have given strong assurance that the Marshall Court would not interfere with traditional state functions unless a direct conflict with the federal commerce clause was involved. That was also true of the Article Four privileges and immunities clause as it applied to interstate dealings between private individuals or between a state and nonresidents of the state.

The first significant commerce clause case to reach the Supreme Court's docket after 1824 was that of *Brown v. Maryland*, which was decided by the justices during their tumultuous 1827 term. Chief Justice Marshall's opinion for the Court in *Brown* is important for two reasons: first, it expands on the meaning of *Gibbons*, clarifying some of the considerations that shaped the Court's opinion but that were left without elaboration in Marshall's final draft; and second, it emphasizes the relationship between interstate and foreign commerce, particularly the diplomatic implications of state action touching on foreign trade.

Maryland imposed a license tax on state residents who imported and sold foreign goods within the state. Several members of the Brown family were engaged in such transactions and sold goods without obtaining the required license. They demurred to a criminal indictment brought against them, and the denial of their demurrer was appealed to the court of appeals of Maryland, which sustained the validity of the complaint filed against them. The U.S. Supreme Court issued a writ of error, based on the Brown firm's assertion that the Maryland court of appeals refused to accept the plea that the licensing statute violated the federal Constitution's commerce clause as well as the clause denying states the power of imposing duties on imports to or exports from the state.

Although Chief Justice Marshall's opinion in *Gibbons* made passing references to foreign trade, it was in *Brown* that he took pains to emphasize the interconnection of foreign and interstate commerce, and to note the international necessity to have a centralized authority that dealt with foreign trade. Pointing to the history of commercial regulation during the Confederation period, he recalled once more the determination of the Philadelphia convention to provide for national and centralized direction of commercial activity. However, in regard to international commercial activity, he was able to highlight the inevitable diplomatic consequences if a state tax such as that enacted by Maryland was permitted to burden the sale of goods legally imported into the United States:

> What would be the language of a foreign government, which should be informed that its merchants, after importing according to law, were forbidden to sell the merchandise imported? What answer would the United States give to the complaints and just reproaches to which such extraordinary circumstances would expose them? No apology could be received, or even offered. Such a state of things would break up commerce.

To Marshall, it was clear that any state law that penalizes an importer for selling his goods in his character as an importer "must be in opposition to the act of Congress which authorizes importation." Strong and sweeping words from a former secretary of state! And perhaps also abandonment of the arguments he had in 1796 advanced before the Supreme Court in *Ware v. Hylton.* There he had unsuccessfully urged the Supreme Court to countenance Virginia's authority to erect judicial hindrances to the collection of British debts guaranteed collectible by U.S. treaties with Great Britain.

Effective federalism demanded that the states comprising the union should not be permitted to interfere with international affairs, including Congress's powers to regulate foreign commerce and to protect that trade even after its importation into the United States. Semantic quibbles in *Brown* could not shield the economic consequences of the Maryland licensing law from Supreme Court condemnation. Calling the exaction a licensing tax rather than an impost or duty did not protect the measure from being a duty on imports contrary to Article One, Section 10, of the Constitution. To allow such a construction would be "varying the form, without varying the substance." Similarly, taxing the occupation of an importer rather than the process of importation was indistinguishable in law. Either form of taxation, whatever its title, "must add to the price of the article, and must be paid by the consumer, or the importer himself." As such, it acted in the same manner as a direct duty and was contrary to the Constitution. Marshall also rejected Maryland's argument that imposts or duties referred to goods crossing a state's borders, while taxing an importer's occupation was a tax imposed once the goods were situated within the state. He observed that state taxes on imported goods within the state were as detrimental to foreign trade as those imposed when goods entered the state.

In addition, the chief justice insisted that there was a point at which state taxing authority might be asserted over foreign goods that had been previously imported into the state. Traditionally, duties were payable on items imported for purposes of sale; they were not assessed against sea stores, goods imported with the intention of reexporting, and cargos brought into port under the exigency of bad weather. There was thus a valid distinction based on the circumstances under which goods were carried across a state border. In the case of goods imported for purposes of reexport, there was, as Marshall noted, a practice that if the goods remained in their original package – the packaging at the time of importation — they were not subject to import duties. He observed,

> [W]hen the importer has so acted upon the thing imported, that it has become incorporated and mixed up with the mass of the property in the country, it has perhaps lost its distinctive character as an import, and has become subject to the taxing power of the State; but while remaining the property of the importer, in his warehouse, in the original form or package in which it was imported, a tax upon it is too plainly a duty upon imports to escape the prohibition in the constitution.

The first clause of this passage enunciates a general principle on which federal and state power might be applied to a transaction. But the second clause specifically cites the facts present in *Brown* that impelled the Court to hold the Maryland licensing tax unconstitutional. Both were to remain a significant part of commerce clause litigation in the centuries after the decision in *Brown v. Maryland*.

Counsel for Maryland had objected that although the federal government might grant the right to import goods on the payment of a duty, it did not thereby confer upon the importer the constitutional right to sell the goods. The Court's opinion rejects this distinction: "To what purpose should the power to allow importation be given unaccompanied with the power to authorize a sale of the thing imported? Sale is the object of the importation, and is an essential ingredient of the intercourse, of which importation constitutes a part." This holding was governed by Marshall's understanding of the proper construction of the commerce clause. After pointing to the power of the nation to enter into commercial treaties, he declared that the Constitution's draftsmen "perceived the necessity of giving control over this important subject to a single government," and they vested that power in Congress. Therefore, that "grant should be as extensive as the mischief, and should comprehend all foreign commerce, and all commerce among the states." Two points should be noted: first, Marshall's opinion treats foreign and interstate commerce as one unbroken chain in practice and one system of interpretation in constitutional adjudicatio; and second, the economic dynamics of both foreign and domestic trade play a critical role in the Court's construction of the commerce clause.

Perhaps the strongest argument favoring state regulation of imports was the suggestion that a broad construction of Congress's authority over foreign trade would deprive the states of the authority to regulate the importation and handling of gunpowder or materials detrimental to the public health. Marshall identified these state functions as part of traditional police powers vested in the states, and he also implied that they might fall within the category of inspections, which the Constitution specifically excepted from Congress's authority over foreign and interstate commerce. As for police powers, he freely conceded that these remained within the constitutional authority of state government.

On the other hand, *Brown v. Maryland* did not involve matters comprehended within the scope of police powers; quite the contrary, it involved the taxing powers of the states. More clearly than in *Gibbons*, Marshall's *Brown* decision evidences his inclination to view the regulation of commercial activity as an economic whole that embraced not only the importation event, but also the relationships and requirements that impacted the carriage and sale of goods virtually into the hands of the consumer. That broad construction caused the chief justice to refer to his discussion of taxing powers in *McCulloch*, and to assure the nation, and perhaps even his colleagues, that the *Brown* opinion did not represent an attack on constitutionally sound state tax enactments. Yet "the taxing power of the States must have some limits. It cannot reach and restrain the action of the national government within its proper sphere."

Justice Smith Thompson dissented from the Court's decision in *Brown*, asserting that the prohibition against states' imposing duties on imports was operative only prior to and during the actual importation of foreign goods into the United States. Once the imported property passed the border of the United States and Maryland, it became subject to the licensing and taxing laws of Maryland. Although the indictment identified the Brown firm as importers, it did so gratuitously; all residents of Maryland who sold foreign goods without a license were included within the group subject to penal sanctions. In this connection, Thompson seems to have been at pains to demonstrate that the Maryland law did not single out importers, but applied equally to all Marylanders similarly engaged. At the same time, he failed to recognize the fact that identifying foreign goods for special taxation carried with it the possibility that such a tax might interfere with foreign trade committed to Congress for regulation. Instead, he insisted that the Maryland statute taxed the individual who sold the foreign goods, or perhaps the consumer who bought it, but it did not tax the goods. Thus it was not an impost or duty on imports.

To a large degree, Justice Thompson's dissent parallels his earlier decision in *Livingston v. Van Ingen*, delivered while he was an associate justice of the supreme court of New York and a participant in the decision of the court of impeachment and errors. There, he had stressed that the Livingston–Fulton monopoly operated entirely within the territorial boundaries of the state of New York; thus it could have no impact on interstate commerce. This geographic determinism was also applied in Thompson's *Van Ingen* opinion when he briefly discussed the impact of the New York statute on interstate commerce. Had Thompson been present when the Supreme Court heard oral argument and decided *Gibbons*, it is quite likely that this boundary-crossing construction of interstate commerce would have been criticized more vigorously in John Marshall's opinion for the Court in the Steamboat Case, and there is also little doubt that Thompson would have filed a dissent not unlike his opinion in *Brown*. What is made clear by the two opinions filed in *Brown* is that Thompson — and presumably many other opponents of national commercial regulation — continued to apply geographic standards to interstate and foreign trade matters, while the chief justice's thought was shaped by the need to weigh the economic considerations of commercial activity.

In support of his vote in *Brown*, Justice Thompson cited the chief justice's opinion for the Court in *Gibbons* to the extent that Marshall recognized that internal trade within a state was not subject to congressional regulation. He was perhaps the first, but far from the last, to demonstrate that in an effort to be comprehensive, Marshall had provided a basis on which the commerce power could be narrowly construed. But Thompson's opinion, standing alone, suggests that there was a growing body of state-oriented constitutionalism that would in the future partially undermine the chief justice's sweeping analysis of federal power in *Gibbons*. Examining the history of commercial regulation before the Philadelphia convention, Justice

Thompson insisted that each state retained power to regulate commercial activity within its own borders; that authority could not be removed without a clear expression in the Constitution that each state was yielding that preexisting power to the central government. Pointing to *Federalist* No. 32, he agreed with the position there taken that with the exception of duties on imports and exports, the states after ratification retained all of their previous taxing authority, which he claimed included the ability to tax goods that had arrived within their territorial limits.

The dissenting opinion also referred to the discussion of taxation in *McCulloch v. Maryland*, where the chief justice noted that there was a difference between taxing the note issue of the Bank of the United States and taxing either the real property owned by that bank or the shares of its stock held by Maryland residents. Although the commerce clause was not involved in *McCulloch*, the distinction between a discriminatory, and perhaps direct, impact on loan operations of the bank, on the one hand, and the evenhanded application of realty taxes or income taxes on resident shareholders, on the other, may well have caused the *Brown* Court to pause. Clearly the economic impact on note issue was no more detrimental to the bank's activity and stability than would be the hypothetical taxes assessed against its real property holdings or excise taxes imposed on dividend income paid to shareholders. Justice Thompson may well have begun the process of undermining the chief justice's taxation position in *McCulloch*, and he also suggested that economic reasoning was an inherently ambiguous foundation for adjudicating commerce clause cases.

In the February 1829 term of the Supreme Court, the justices moved from international trade to what William Wirt for the defendants called a "sluggish reptile stream . . . that [does] . . . not run but creep[s]" through a Delaware marsh. This was the Black Bird Creek, which, according to Wirt, spread venom wherever it went and destroyed the health of those citizens imprudently resident on its banks. For these reasons, the Delaware general assembly incorporated the Black Bird Creek Marsh Company and authorized it to build a dam on the creek, which obstructed navigation of the waterway. Thompson Willson and his colleagues, owners of a sloop that navigated the creek, destroyed the dam, and the Black Bird Creek Marsh Company sued in trespass for damages to the dam. Willson demurred to the complaint, asserting that they had a common-law right to navigate the creek and that the enabling statute was invalid because it conflicted with the Constitution's commerce clause. The demurrer was overruled, and judgment was entered against Willson and his associates. On appeal, the Delaware high court of errors and appeals affirmed the trial court, and a writ of error brought the case to the Marshall Court under the title *Willson v. Black Bird Creek Marsh Company.*

The chief justice began his opinion for the Court by pointing out that, given the circumstances to which Wirt had referred, it was undoubtedly true that damming the creek enhanced the health and welfare of the Delaware citizens living near its banks. The state's authority to relieve such a threat was squarely within its reserved powers unless it conflicted with the federal Constitution or statutes of the United States enacted in accordance with the Constitution. Marshall agreed that if Congress had enacted a statute dealing with the navigation of tidal creeks, the Court would be required to invalidate the Delaware act authorizing the damming of the creek. "But Congress has passed no such act," and absent such legislation, Willson was forced to rely entirely on the Constitution's provision. He concluded,

> We do not think that the act empowering the Black Bird Creek Marsh Company can, under all the circumstances of the case, be considered as repugnant to the power to regulate commerce in its dormant state, or as being in conflict with any law passed on the subject.

With that terse explanation, he affirmed the decision of Delaware's highest appellate court, and denied Willson relief from the state judgment against him.

Willson brought Marshall face-to-face with the question of dormancy, a consideration he had deftly avoided in *Gibbons* by a broad reading of the consequences of the federal Coasting Licensing Act. If it were the case that the Coasting Licensing Act were not on the statute books, would the decision in *Gibbons* have read like that in *Will-*

son? We may surmise that Marshall might have held the Livingston–Fulton monopoly repugnant to the dormant commerce power granted to Congress by the Constitution. Although *Willson* and *Gibbons* are similar in regard to the issues presented, the factual background is clearly distinguishable. Black Bird Creek was far from a major corridor of commerce, and thus was distinguishable from the Hudson River in size alone. While the Hudson posed no health hazards to its riparian neighbors, the creek's sluggish progress fostered mosquito-borne disease, and its extended marsh rendered valueless lands that could otherwise be drained and cultivated for profit. Damming such a stream also promised the creation of a lake that could irrigate crops and perhaps provide drinking water for the population. Arguably, legislative intent was more culpable in the case of the New York monopoly than was the case of the Marsh Company charter. New York's statute regulated navigation not only on its waters, but also on the waters of New Jersey and Connecticut, and both states retaliated with their own statutory penalties and lawsuits. Delaware simply exercised its traditional police powers for the benefit of its own citizens, and the benefits conferred on the Marsh Company would not be exercised outside the state of Delaware.

However (and it is a big however!), none of these considerations was mentioned in John Marshall's opinion. We lack even a comment about the economic impact of the state's action on the Constitution's commerce clause. What would the decision have been if New York erected a dam across the Hudson at the northern boundary between New York and New Jersey? Should congressional inaction be allowed to sanction state obstruction of all navigable creeks or rivers on the eastern seaboard? Was it reasonable to expect that Congress would separately legislate concerning Black Bird Creek? Indeed, was navigation of marshy tidewater creeks a priority in the overall regulation of foreign and interstate commerce?

Willson reminds us that silence in U.S. Supreme Court opinions is far from golden. Most commentary on *Willson* suggests that the terseness of the opinion indicates a retreat from the principles set forth in *Gibbons* and thus evidences the declining influence of Chief Justice Marshall in the Court's deliberations. Unquestionably, Marshall's ability to mediate differing views among the justices had declined since 1819, and his dissent in *Ogden v. Saunders* (1827) stands as stark evidence of the degree to which the Court majority differed with him in regard to the construction and application of the contract clause of the Constitution. There is also abundant evidence that the Supreme Court's decisions since 1819 had generally raised a crescendo of protest over judicial nullification of popular state legislative initiatives. In this regard, *Willson v. Black Bird Creek Marsh Company* may justly be seen as a circumspect retreat from what had become a politically unwise, and indeed highly vulnerable, position of the Supreme Court in American life and public opinion.

Yet even if all of these influences were operative, the Court's brief opinion probably obscures from modern readers some extensive judicial discussion of public policy before the decision was announced. May we not suspect that the justices were troubled by the relatively minor function Black Bird Creek would play in either interstate or foreign commerce? On the other hand, Delaware's initiative of incorporating the Marsh Company and authorizing that body to dam the creek was a long-established and ostensibly wise application of state police powers.

The state legislation stood a slight probability that it would enmesh the United States government in international difficulties. Even if all other states would follow Delaware's example and authorize dam construction on all small tidal creeks in their territory, would trade among the states be adversely affected? *Willson* for the first time introduced some new and serious questions of federalism; it probed the hitherto indistinct line that divided Congress's commerce power from the reserved police powers of the states. Rather than clearly delineating that dividing line, it suggested that matters of scale and economic impact were valid considerations in deciding such a case. Counsel had suggested these considerations in oral argument. The Court, speaking through Marshall's opinion, simply declined to introduce them in its formal explanation of its reasoning.

Doctrinally, Thompson Willson and his colleagues justly expected to be within the protection of the dormant commerce clause. In practical terms, a decision in their favor would have further extended the scope of the commerce clause. Poised on the horns of a stare decisis dilemma, Marshall and his colleagues chose to deny the preemptive effect of the dormant commerce clause. Interestingly, Justice Smith Thompson did not dissent. But he had an opportunity to register his thoughts in the U.S. circuit court for New York in *Miln v. New York* (1834). The case, which was later appealed to the Supreme Court in 1836 after Marshall's death, involved a New York statute requiring ship captains to report the names and residences of their passengers. Justice Thompson referred to *Willson* as providing a "full answer" to the issues raised in *Miln.* He first stated the dormancy reasoning in *Willson* to be that "until that power is exercised it does not conflict with the state legislation." Not content to leave his decision based on dormancy alone, Thompson proceeded to point out that obtaining information concerning new arrivals and controlling immigrant access to its territory

> relates entirely to the internal police of the state, and falls within that class of subjects which the supreme court says in *Gibbons v. Ogden*, 9 Wheat 203, forms a portion of that immense mass of legislation, which embraces everything within a state not surrendered to the general government.

His second point formed the basis for the Taney Court's decision on appeal in *Mayor of the City of New York v. Miln* (1836).

The alignment of justices in deciding the *Miln* case in Chief Justice Roger B. Taney's first term would suggest that the *Willson* Court six years earlier was sharply divided in its views concerning the *Black Bird Creek Marsh Company* case, but that it avoided making that division public by its official holding based on dormancy. Issues of federalism — applying the commerce clause in tandem with respect for state police powers — continued to dominate the Court's consideration of congressional action well beyond John Marshall's death. These were situations in which stare decisis, the rule-of-law position, was vastly complicated by a clear and practical need to harmonize commercial regulation with a state's authority to provide for the health and welfare of its citizens. The passage of years would not make this judicial task any easier.

CHAPTER 8

The Extraordinarily Long Half-Life
of *Gibbons v. Ogden*

Shortly after the Supreme Court's decision in *Gibbons v. Ogden*, steamboats were made obsolete by the introduction of a reliable steam locomotive for railroads. Thereafter, commerce was no longer limited to locations that had ready access to navigable waterways, and inland towns and cities joined in the competition for a role in the expanding American transportation and communication network. Of course, steamboats did survive as recreational facilities, and when bulky cargoes were involved, water transportation powered by steam remained more economical. So too did cargo and passenger traffic in coastal areas and on the great river systems of the Mississippi, Ohio, and Missouri. For the most part, however, the promise of steamboating, so bright in 1807, had become tarnished by obsolescence and ruinous litigation by 1850. Yet *Gibbons* lives on in constitutional legend as a critically important analysis of the constitutional framework within which American business has grown and through which a continental common market has flourished for nearly two hundred years.

As we head into the second decade of the twenty-first century, *Gibbons* continues to be cited as a fundamental case in American constitutional law. Although antiquity has virtually eliminated any precedential value it might have as ruling case law, the Court's opinion continues to shape discussion of the interstate and foreign commerce clauses of the Constitution. This is because its comprehensive discussion of the interplay of federal and state constitutional power ensures its status as a classic case in the lawyers' lexicon. That preeminence remains despite widespread acknowledgment that virtually all of its lasting material was merely dictum, well beyond relevance to the narrow ruling of the case.

The Steamboat Case also continues to assist judges and legislators in resolving critical points of law concerning the nature of the federal union. It is basic to defining the nature of the American common market established by the federal Constitution and thereafter elaborated primarily through decisions by the U.S. Supreme Court. Professors John Nowak and Ronald Rotunda, in their Hornbook Series treatise on constitutional law, assess *Gibbons* as "one of the most important [opinions] in history." They are quite correct, for the case is undoubtedly the first of a long series of opinions that have shaped federal power in the area of commercial regulation both before and after the American Civil War. Indeed, *Gibbons v. Ogden* has retained landmark case status through two major shifts in American constitutionalism. The first was the dramatic alteration in federal rights and enhanced national power triggered by the ratification of the Thirteenth, Fourteenth, and Fifteenth Amendments (1865–1870). The second was the New Deal constitutional revolution (1937–1941) that ultimately established what was a nearly plenary federal commerce power. Even today, *Gibbons* continues to be the starting point for academic study of the structure of federalism as well as a guide for analyzing the sharing of commercial and economic regulation between the states and the government in Washington.

After John Marshall's death on 6 July 1835, the Court under Chief Justice Roger B. Taney found itself occupied with developing a rationale for the decision of cases involving the commerce power of Congress, on one hand, and the residual police powers of the several states, on the other. Because federal legislation regulating commerce was limited in scope and ambiguous in purpose before the enactment of the Interstate Commerce Act in 1887, the Taney Court for the most part dealt with the dormancy question. Although Marshall had adroitly avoided consideration of dormancy in *Gibbons*, he there suggested that the Court had been impressed by the argument that the constitutional grant of the commerce power to Congress, standing alone and without legislative action, provided a limit to state legislation in the area. And of course, in *Willson v. Black Bird Creek Marsh Company*, the Marshall Court subsequently considered the dormant commerce clause but declined to invalidate a Delaware statute on the basis of dormancy. However, Chief Justice Taney adamantly opposed giving any effect to the Constitution's commerce clause unless there was express congressional legislation implementing the constitutional provision. His colleagues were not inclined to adopt the chief justice's views in this regard, and the Court began to work out a rationale for dealing with federal–state conflicts in the commerce area.

Justice Benjamin Curtis's opinion for the Court, in *Cooley v. Board of Wardens* (1851), held that in regulatory situations where uniformity was not a matter of national concern and diversity in local regulation was desirable, state and local measures touching on foreign and interstate commerce were constitutionally acceptable. Current theory holds that state legislation cannot be patently discriminatory against out-of-state competition, nor may a state regulate beyond its jurisdictional boundaries. In addition, even if constitutionally valid, state legislation may not impose an undue burden on interstate or foreign commerce.

Beginning with the enactment of the Interstate Commerce Act of 1887, the Supreme Court had a broader congressional statement of the scope of the commerce clause. However, the justices also drew on Chief Justice Marshall's recognition that the states possessed authority to regulate aspects of commerce because of police powers reserved to them by the Tenth Amendment. At the same time, it was patently unconstitutional, in Marshall's view, for the states to legislate regulations of interstate or foreign commerce without the existence of an independent state constitutional power justifying their statutes. During this period, the Supreme Court was engaged in applying the difficult test of whether state actions directly or indirectly impacted interstate or foreign commerce. In the case of direct impacts, the Court invalidated state actions; however, the standards for applying this test only became more ambiguous, bringing the Court into popular distrust.

Before 1937 the Court's jurisprudence evolved into two distinct tracks. In many situations, it held to the *Gibbons* view that except in regard to strictly internal trade, states might not take actions that had an economic impact on the conduct of out-of-state commercial activity. Thus the purchase of cattle at a Chicago market that served a significant portion of the national "current of commerce" in meat and meat products was subject to federal regulation even though the market was located entirely in one state (*Swift & Co. v. U.S.*, 1905), and monopolization of corporate stock was subject to federal antitrust prosecution even though the situs of the holding company was in one state (*Northern Securities Company v. U.S.*, 1905). When federal railroad rates were undermined by intrastate rates between the same terminal points, the state rates were held unconstitutional (*The Shreveport Rate Cases*, 1914).

On the other hand, the Supreme Court also developed a focus on the nature of the activity, holding in *U.S. v. E.C. Knight Company* (1895) that manufacturing activities were not commercial and thus not subject to federal antitrust laws. It was the *E.C. Knight* case's "manufacturing" distinction that defeated Congress's attempt to deny interstate markets to furniture produced by child labor (*Hammer v. Dagenhart*, 1918). Yet the Court was willing to sanction federal legislation that assisted state law enforcement (*Champion v. Ames*, lottery ticket sales, 1903; *Hoke v. U.S.*, prostitution, 1913; and *U.S. v. Caminetti*, white slave traffic, 1917). In the face of an increasingly integrated national economy and Progressive-era reforms attempting to deal with growing areas of national economic and social concern, the Supreme Court found itself vacillating between a territorial construction of the commerce clause and Marshall's position in *Gibbons*, which stressed the economic impact of state actions on the conduct of interstate and foreign trade.

This doctrinal dilemma set the stage for a direct clash between the Supreme Court and the two political branches of the federal government — Congress and the president. During the Great Depression, launched by the 1929 crash of the stock markets, Congress attempted to strengthen financial institutions and encourage cooperation among government, capital, and labor. With the 1932 election of President Franklin D. Roosevelt, the stage was set for a New Deal that emphasized the use of federal legislative power — especially that granted by the commerce clause — to reduce unemployment, to alleviate uneven distribution of vital commodities and services, and to stabilize erratic securities and credit markets. Much of the remedial federal legislation was founded on the commerce clause, but the Supreme Court found more than adequate precedents to declare key New Deal statutes unconstitutional. Frequently, the Court held that Congress's enactments were beyond the reach of the commerce clause because the activity was entirely within one state. Other federal statutes were found unconstitutional because they were found to be in excess of the authority granted in the Constitution's enumerated powers.

One of the major New Deal initiatives was the enactment of a nationwide labor law designed to minimize the frequency of strikes and other work stoppages. Key portions of this National Labor Relations Act were declared unconstitutional in *A.L.A. Schechter Poultry Company v. U.S.* (1935). Essentially, the Court found that the flow of commerce ended when a live chicken arrived at the shop of a kosher butcher, there to be killed according to Jewish religious requirements and sold shortly thereafter to a consumer. The Court applied a strictly territorial construction of the commerce clause, declared the federal legislation unconstitutional, and precipitated a direct clash with the president and his party, which held a majority of the seats in both the House of Representatives and the Senate. After his reelection in November 1936, President Roosevelt requested legislation that would increase the number of justices on the Supreme Court and thus empower him to appoint an additional justice for every member of the Court over the age of seventy. The stage was set for a major revolution in constitutional law.

While the so-called court-packing bill legislation was pending in Congress, the Supreme Court reversed itself in *National Labor Relations Board v. Jones & Laughlin Steel* (1937), holding that labor conflict created a burden on the interstate and foreign commerce of the United States. Hence, conditions of labor were a valid subject for federal regulation under the commerce clause. In effect, the Court majority had returned to John Marshall's expansive view of the commerce power as well as his economic understanding of the scope of activities that fell within the regulatory power of Congress. Labor relations "affected" the conduct of commercial activity, even though the employment might be within one state, and even though manufacturing was the nature of the economic activity.

Although historians continue to disagree about how and when the Court, under the leadership of Chief Justice Charles Evans Hughes, changed its construction of the commerce clause and chose to adopt the broader economic interpretation of what constituted commerce, it is accepted virtually without dissent that a shift in judicial philosophy eventually resulted in the establishment of a plenary congressional authority over all aspects of American trade and commerce. Emblematic of this sweeping federal domination of national economic life is the landmark case of *Wickard v. Filburn*, a 1941 decision upholding a fine assessed against a farmer who raised wheat that he did not sell on the open market, but simply fed to his own livestock. The Agricultural Adjustment Act of 1938 established a system of administratively assigned quotas designed to limit the amount of wheat that might be raised by a farmer. Filburn had exceeded his quota. Although the Supreme Court conceded that Filburn's harvest of fewer than five hundred bushels was minimal in its impact on the national market price, the justices reasoned that, had all farmers exceeded their quotas by feeding the surplus to their livestock, there would be a substantial impact on the stability of the wheat market. As a consequence, farmer Filburn paid his $117 fine, and John Marshall's comment on things that "affected" interstate commerce gained a new and broader meaning. Suffice it to say that after 1941, this new principle of aggregation made it possible to invoke federal authority under the commerce clause in virtually every economic relationship or activity.

Before the decision of *U.S. v. Lopez* in 1995, it was axiomatic that there was nothing so small or so remote from interstate commerce that it could not fall within Congress's legislative power under the commerce clause. Chief Justice Marshall's concern that internal economic activities should remain within state control seemed to have been forgotten amid the Court's enthusiastic revival of his broad and economically based construction of the federal commerce power. Yet to the great surprise of veteran Court watchers, *Lopez* called a halt to what had become an almost routine judicial assignment of sweeping economic power to Congress. The case involved a federal statute providing criminal sanctions for persons who knowingly possessed a firearm within a school zone. For the Court, Chief Justice William H. Rehnquist noted that the *Jones & Laughlin Steel* case, along with *Wickard v. Filburn*, introduced changes in commerce clause doctrine that reflected the expansion of economic activity into a matter of national, rather than merely local, concern. Those and other cases also showed that commerce clause decisions before the New Deal revolution of 1937 "artificially had constrained the authority of Congress to regulate interstate commerce." But even these cases accepted the fact that the commerce power had its limits. In the view of the *Lopez* majority, that limit had been reached in the federal gun-free school zone legislation. Rehnquist went on to define three areas of activity that Congress might regulate under the commerce clause: (1) the regulation of use of the channels of interstate commerce; (2) the protection and regulation of the instruments of interstate commerce, or persons or things in interstate commerce, even though the threat may come only from intrastate activities; and (3) the regulation of those activities having a substantial relation to interstate commerce. However, the chief justice focused on the nature of the activity that Congress attempted to make criminal. It was the simple possession of a firearm on school premises, without any clear connection of that offense to economic activity, that could be regulated by the federal government. That type of regulation was traditionally vested within the states, as a "prime element of the States' police power." Furthermore, Rehnquist quickly pointed out that a majority of states had already passed statutes outlawing the unauthorized possession of a firearm on school property. Not only had Congress exceeded its powers, but the evil addressed had already been dealt with by the exercise of state police powers.

Three years later, in *U.S. v. Morrison* (2000), Chief Justice Rehnquist returned to the issue of congressional authority under the commerce clause. The statute in question was the federal Violence Against Women Act of 1994, which provided a civil remedy for victims of gender-related violence. A female student at Virginia Polytechnic Institute brought an accusation under the university's disciplinary system charging two football players with rape. Frustrated by the moderate punishments imposed, she brought a federal civil action under the 1994 statute, and the defendants challenged the constitutionality of the Violence Against Women Act, which had been enacted by Congress pursuant to the commerce clause.

Unlike the gun-free school zone statute considered in *Lopez*, the statute in *Morrison* was predicated on what the four dissenting Supreme Court justices termed "a mountain of data assembled by Congress . . . showing the effects of violence against women in interstate commerce." The dissenters also pointedly argued that at any time between *Wickard* in 1942 and *Lopez* in 1995, the Violence Against Women Act would have passed constitutional muster; that was a time, they opined, when the law "enjoyed a stable understanding that congressional power under the Commerce Clause, complemented by the authority of the Necessary and Proper Clause . . . extended to all activity that, when aggregated, has a substantial effect on interstate commerce." They cautioned that upsetting that stability was unwise because

> [w]e live in a Nation knit together by two centuries of scientific, technological, commercial, and environmental change.
>
> Those changes, taken together, mean that virtually every kind of activity, no matter how local, genuinely can affect commerce, or its conditions, outside the State – at least when considered in the aggregate.

Despite this strong plea for stability in the Court's construction of the commerce clause, the majority remained unpersuaded. For the Court, Chief Justice Rehnquist repeated the *Lopez* construction that because there was no economic activity involved in the subject matter of the case or in the operation of the statute, the Violence Against Women Act was improperly predicated on the commerce clause. An opposite conclusion would lead to a blanket permission to Congress, permitting federal regulation of or prohibition of noneconomic and violent criminal conduct. Without citing Marshall, Rehnquist referred to one of Marshall's salient dicta in *Gibbons*: "The Constitution requires a distinction between what is truly national and what is truly local."

In 2005 the Supreme Court returned to commerce clause issues in its consideration of the Comprehensive Drug Abuse Prevention and Control Act of 1970, commonly known as the Controlled Substances Act (CSA). This encyclopedic statute was designed to develop a closed regulatory system that incorporated all essential prior federal legislation, including regulation of the manufacture, distribution, dispensing, or possession of marijuana. The appeal involved a request for injunctive relief and a declaratory judgment against the federal Drug Enforcement Agency and the U.S. attorney general. The petitioners were individuals who, in accordance with California's Compassionate Use Act of 1996, raised marijuana for their personal medicinal treatment. Denied relief by the U.S. district court, the petitioners appealed to the Ninth Circuit's court of appeals, which reversed the district court and ordered the entry of an injunction. In *Gonzalez v. Raich*, the U.S. Supreme Court granted certiorari because of the "obvious importance of the case" but vacated the judgment of the court of appeals, commenting that "well-settled law controls our answer. The CSA is a valid exercise of federal power, even as applied to the troubling facts of this case." The circumstances of the appeal definitely made *Raich* a case of "troubling facts." In support of their request for injunctive relief, the petitioners had shown the severity of their afflictions, their inability to obtain relief from conventional medications, and the opinions of their doctors that they needed to use marijuana. A six-to-three vote among the Supreme Court justices demonstrated that the law was far from settled.

For the majority, Justice John Paul Stevens observed that in enacting the CSA, Congress had been especially concerned with the need to prevent the divergence of narcotics and other illegal substances to illicit channels. Its investigations determined that local distribution and possession of controlled substances contributed to the increase of illegal interstate traffic in those drugs. In addition, federal control of intrastate incidents of the drug traffic was essential to effective control of interstate transactions. Justice Stevens also noted that in 1913, California had been among the first states to prohibit the sale and possession of marijuana, and in 1996, it was again a pioneer when it enacted the Compassionate Use Act, giving seriously ill residents access to the drug for medicinal purposes.

Turning to the contention that the commerce clause did not authorize regulation of intrastate growing and in-state private consumption of marijuana, Stevens pointed out that Congress is permitted to regulate local activities that may have a substantial effect on interstate commerce. That was the case even if the specific incident under consideration was of minimal impact on national commerce; here, he specifically cited *Wickard v. Filburn*.

Recognizing the need to distinguish *Lopez* and *Morrison*, Justice Stevens asserted that in neither case was economic activity involved, but in *Raich*, the CSA performed a "quintessentially economic" function by denying controlled drugs access to an illegal but thriving interstate market. Furthermore, the provisions of the CSA prohibiting local possession or manufacturing were "a rational (and commonly utilized) means of regulating commerce in that product." Referring to the Constitution's supremacy clause, he concluded that the CSA, as a federal statute enacted pursuant to the commerce clause, invalidated California's compassionate use statute.

Concurring in the Court opinion, Justice Antonin Scalia took pains to assert that under the commerce clause, in accordance with *Lopez* and *Morrison*, local economic activity that had a substantial effect on interstate commerce might be regulated. However, under the necessary and proper clause, noneconomic local activity also may be regulated if the means selected are reasonably adapted to attain a legitimate end under the commerce clause. In other words, the operation of the necessary and proper clause, although tied to the effectuation of an enumerated power, is not necessarily restricted by the limits imposed on the enumerated power. Use of the necessary and proper clause authorization is limited by the rule that it be "appropriate" and "plainly adapted" to achieve a constitutional end, that it not be prohibited, and that it be consistent with the letter and spirit of the Constitution.

For the dissenting justices, Justice Sandra Day O'Connor pointed out that the Court's decision overlooked the role of states as laboratories for the examination of novel approaches to national as well as local problems. She asserted that the majority opinion condemned the California effort without providing any proof that local marijuana use for medicinal purposes has a substantial effect on interstate commerce. Furthermore, *Lopez* and *Morrison* were substantially identical to *Raich*, except that in *Raich*, Congress legislated comprehensively, whereas it acted piecemeal and without careful investigation in *Lopez*. Justice O'Connor dismissed this difference in legislative procedure as not being significant. Constitutionality should not depend on such "superficial and formalistic distinctions." She concluded that the majority's definition of economic activity in *Raich* was "breathtaking." And if the Court's deference to Congress continued, little would be left of the concept of enumerated powers in the Constitution.

These recent developments in commerce clause construction suggest three things. First and foremost, nearly two centuries after their delivery, the opinions in *Gibbons v. Ogden* continue to shape judicial consideration of this critical provision of the federal Constitution. Second, the Court's approach to cases in this area continues to have as great an impact on federalism as it does on national economic regulation. And third, judges and legislators who deal with the regulation of commerce, and more broadly economic activity, are confronted with a very complicated task of defining the nature and scope of interstate and foreign commerce. The parameters in which Supreme Court decisions are made has not changed since 1824.

There is also much to be learned about the dynamics of American constitutional government from the evolution of commerce clause jurisprudence. Ostensibly, the Constitution anticipates that Congress will take the initiative in implementing commercial regulation. But the first major legislative step (enactment of the 1887 Commerce Act) was taken no less than a century after the federal Constitution was drafted in Philadelphia. To make up for lost time, Congress since 1937 has legislated, at times comprehensively but more frequently peri-patetically and unadvisedly, to exert federal dominance in fields remote from commercial regulation. These well-intentioned but misguided intrusions into areas traditionally reserved for the exercise of state police powers today continue to strain federal–state relationships.

From 1824 to the present day, the U.S. Supreme Court has expended much time and energy in deciding commerce clause cases, acting in many situations without any direction or assistance from congressional legislation. After the New Deal Court's confrontation with the political branches of the federal government, the justices have perhaps been too deferential in judging the constitutionality of con-gressional initiatives. The past fifteen years have evidenced a resur-gence of critical attention to John Marshall's concern that there must continue to be areas of economic activities internal to the individual states, and the Supreme Court has been engaged in a struggle to resolve this Gordian knot of American federalism. Although that judi-cial process originated well before the economic downturn of 2008, we may well expect that the need for centralized federal action will ultimately bring new and challenging economic regulatory issues before the Court.

The multifaceted process of regulating commercial activity within a federal union has become a difficulty in world federal systems as well as within the United States. This federalism problem has been condi-tioned, in no small degree, by recurrent American attempts to fine-tune a smoothly running common market system within the United States. The American experience, summarized briefly above, has been followed by several nations that achieved self-government well after John Marshall decided *Gibbons*. It is appropriate that three federal systems and their approach to interstate and foreign commerce should be briefly summarized, simply to demonstrate the widespread impact of *Gibbons* throughout the world.

One of the first foreign efforts at implementing and fine-tuning the American federal system occurred in the dominion of Canada. The various North American provinces of the British empire had reached the point of forming a federal union just at the time the United States had completed an exhausting and costly civil war. Canadians were conscious of the dangers of disunion and were determined to avoid the constitutional mistakes that contributed to the outbreak of war between the American states. The 1867 British North America Act (BNA), now renamed the Constitution Act of 1867, established the structure of the Canadian federal system. Initially drafted by a dominionwide convention but enacted, with modifications, by the British Parliament, the BNA was designed to create a strong central government. This was attempted by the careful enumeration of powers assigned to the dominion Parliament, and an equally detailed enumeration of powers retained by the provinces. Unlike the U.S. Constitution, the BNA reserved powers to the federal government rather than to the component provinces. However, the judicial committee of the Privy Council — which served as the highest court of appeal until 1875, and as a parallel court of appeal with the supreme court of Canada until 1949 — followed the interpretive practice of reserving powers to the provinces.

It was also the case that the general trade and commerce provision of the BNA, vesting power in the dominion government, was linked to the dominion's reserved powers, encompassed in the "peace, order and good government clause" (sec. 91). Since 1989 the Canadian supreme court has gradually expanded the trade and commerce provision when nationwide economic regulation is needed. However, currently, the provincial legislatures retain much more authority to regulate local economic activity than do the legislatures of the U.S. states. This is due to their enumerated power to make laws concerning property and civil rights in their province (sec. 92 [13]) and to legislate concerning "local works and undertakings" (sec. 92 [10]). Thus, the unique Canadian constitutional institution of "double enumeration" — of assigning specific authority to both the dominion government and the provincial legislatures — has slowed the tendency toward federal domination that manifested itself in the United States from 1937 to the 1995 decision in *Lopez*.

Just as the United States was on the verge of embarking on the so-called Progressive period of American political reform, and shortly after its emergence as a world power after 1898, the Australian states began to experiment with the task of forming a federal union. These discussions resulted in the creation of a commonwealth in 1900. Again, the status of the American union provided both a model and a warning to the founders of their commonwealth. Not without significance were the experiences of Canada after 1867. Although Australia's statesmen made the attempt, they were unsuccessful in preventing appellate judicial supervision by the judicial committee of the British Privy Council.

The Commonwealth Act of 1900 (also called the Constitution Act), which establishes the basis for the Australian federal constitution, has striking parallels to the U.S. federal Constitution. The Commonwealth Parliament has enumerated powers, and the residuum of governmental functions is reserved to the states. Section 51(i) of the Constitution Act of 1900 confers broad authority on the commonwealth Parliament to regulate "trade and commerce with other nations and among the states." The high court of Australia has construed this grant of power liberally; it includes the preparation of goods and commodities for ultimate inclusion in international or interstate trade, and it also allows regulation of goods after shipment from foreign nations, or after carriage among the Australian states. At the same time, the high court has been alert to the need to distinguish between this type of trade and commerce that is internal to the individual states. In part, this is because the Constitution Act reserves nonenumerated governmental powers to the states, but also provides that state legislation that is inconsistent with commonwealth enactments shall be invalid to the extent of the inconsistency (secs. 106–109).

Given the parallel structure of the U.S. and Australian federal constitutions, it is not surprising that judges in the two nations have struggled with similar interpretive issues. The reservation of unenumerated powers to the states has posed difficulties in both federal systems. Although Australia's Constitution Act lacks a necessary and proper clause, it does authorize the Commonwealth Parliament to exercise those powers that are "incidental" to implementation of enumerated powers. This has given the commonwealth broad authority to regulate commercial activity that takes place within a single state, but that has consequences for international or interstate trade. However, it has been insisted that there is a constitutional mandate that a distinction be made between intrastate commerce subject to regulation by the state parliaments, and international and interstate activity assigned to the commonwealth for regulation and control. As the United States moved toward a plenary federal commerce power after 1937, Australia's judiciary continued to exhibit marked sensitivity to the reserved governmental powers in the states. That continues despite frequently expressed judicial views pointing out that the distinction has become anachronistic in modern economic conditions.

The three federal systems — the United States, Canada, and Australia — despite variations within their forms of federalism, have been remarkably consistent in dealing with the commerce question. They have all tended to expand the application of federal and unifying legislation, particularly in times of economic crisis, and more generally as trade and commercial activities became more national and international in scope. All three systems have relied heavily on their courts to make vital distinctions between interstate and international trade, on one hand, and localized state trade, on the other. However, it is important to remember that both the Canadian and Australian systems work within a tradition of parliamentary supremacy, causing judicial bodies to be more cautious in exercising what in the U.S. system is termed "judicial review." In addition, even a rudimentary comparison of the three systems gives rise to the impression that American cultural preferences for local government initiatives and limited federal government have exerted a stronger brake on the evolution of the U.S. interstate and foreign commerce clause than is the case in Canada or Australia. American preference for state government regulation and pressure for local control of economic activity may well reflect the historical baggage of colonial commercial competition before the Declaration of Independence; another source may be a strong and persistent emphasis on protectionism in state economic activity, dating to the Confederation period. Finally, Americans have traditionally valued the greater control they have over state and local governments, even as they distrust the programs and decisions originating in a distant and seemingly insensitive central authority centered in Washington.

By way of contrast, in Canada and Australia, there have been numerous cooperative governmental initiatives, launched through joint federal and provincial/state legislative action. In Australia's case, this includes a centralized income tax system, coupled with commonwealth allocation of revenues in proportion to needs of the various states. In addition, in Canada and Australia, the constitutional and legal foundation for authority rests with the British crown, facilitating cooperative enterprises by two or more governments who share common allegiance to the queen. Although both nations are self-governing, this shared tie to the monarchy represented by the federal governor-general and state or provincial lieutenant governors is more than an empty formalism.

In Europe since the end of World War II, there has been a gradual evolution of a common market based on multilateral treaties among member states. Today, the resulting European Union has become a vigorously administered political and economic system that probably exceeds U.S. federal commercial regulation, both in complexity and sophistication. The European court of justice has played a major role in the evolution of a free market for goods within the nations of the union. Although taxation measures that discriminate on the basis of national origin are clearly contrary to the treaties establishing the union, the European court also has been active in rejecting subsidies that favor local products or commodities. It examines the economic impact, or even the possibility of such an impact, when it reviews national measures restricting free access to national markets. Similarly, quotas on the exportation or importation of goods are illegal per se, but other measures that the Court deems equivalent to quota limitations are also impermissible. They include national requirements dealing with size, shape, or mode in which the goods are presented. Marking goods as to national origin may also be unacceptable, even if the practice is only remotely likely to induce a consumer to "buy local."

Like the Marshall Court and its successors, the European court of justice has been required to examine the impact of quarantine and other health measures, and to determine whether they are bona fide exercises of national police powers or represent efforts to discriminate against foreign goods. Again, the focus is on the degree to which these measures restrict the flow of commercial activity throughout the union.

The 1999 Amsterdam treaty established citizenship in the European Union. It confers on all citizens of member nations the right to travel freely throughout the European Union. In addition, although the treaty recognizes the continuance of national citizenship, it expressly empowers citizens of the EU to vote in elections held in the nation in which they reside, and also to hold political office within that nation. Furthermore, the component nations within the European Union are required to extend political and economic privileges to European Community citizens resident within their territories.

Finally, the European court of justice has ruled that EU law — treaty provisions, directives, regulations, and judicial decisions — is supreme over national enactments and decisions. The consequence is a vast body of supranational economic and social law that supersedes national rules of law. Within that context, a broad supervisory jurisdiction is vested in the European court of justice. Unlike the U.S. Supreme Court, which exercises only limited constitutional and statutory authority, the European court is readily available to all individuals and institutions claiming rights under the EU, and cases pending in national courts may be suspended until the European court decides and refers back answers to questions involving EU law. In these jurisdictional areas, as well as in its approach to establishing a free and open common market, the EU may well be the outstanding example of an improved mousetrap that has evolved from Marshall's opinion for the Court in *Gibbons*.

Historically and geographically, John Marshall's opinion for the Supreme Court has indeed had a very long and formative impact on American law. It shows no promise of declining in importance as a vital area for the interpretation of federalism in the union, and as an instrument for implementing national programs both within the nation and in the international world. Yet *Gibbons* deserves its lasting reputation as much for what it left unsaid as for what it decided. In its broad and catholic discussion of interstate commerce, it laid down general principles of law and economic regulation that have lasting validity. And its balanced approach to federal and state authority, taking care that neither governmental system should improperly usurp the functions of the other, provided a primer for constitutional thought in the vital areas of business and economics. For these reasons, the passage of time has not diminished the impact of what undoubtedly is one of John Marshall's greatest achievements in shaping future constitutional jurisprudence in the United States of America.

CHRONOLOGY

1793, 18 February	Federal Coasting Licensing Act becomes law
1798, March	New York legislature transfers John Fitch's conditional monopoly grant to former chancellor Robert R. Livingston of Clermont
1802, 10 October	Livingston enters into a partnership with Robert Fulton, agreeing to use their efforts to fulfill the condition of the New York legislative grant; this requires the establishment of regular steamboat service between New York City and Albany
1806, December	Robert Fulton arrives in New York City to begin work on a steamboat
1807, 17–18 August	The *North River Steamboat* sails from New York City to Albany in thirty-two hours
1808, 11 April	New York legislature extends the Livingston–Fulton monopoly for a maximum of 30 years
1809, February	A federal patent is issued to Robert Fulton for the invention of a steamboat
1811, 1 May	James Van Ingen and associates begin steamboat service between Albany and New York City; the Livingston–Fulton syndicate seeks a temporary injunction from the New York chancery court
1811, 18 November	Chancellor John Lansing denies Livingston and Fulton an injunction in *Livingston v. Van Ingen*
1812, 12 March	New York court of impeachment and errors reverses Chancellor Lansing's ruling and grants an injunction to the Livingston–Fulton syndicate in *Livingston v. Van Ingen*
1813, 13 February	Robert R. Livingston dies
1815, 23 February	Robert Fulton dies
1815, 5 May	John R. Livingston, on behalf of the Livingston–Fulton syndicate, licenses Aaron Ogden to navigate by steam from Elizabethtown, New Jersey, to New York City
1818, October	Thomas Gibbons begins steamship service between Elizabethtown, New Jersey, and New York City

1818, 20 October	Aaron Ogden, as licensee of the Livingston–Fulton syndicate, files bill in chancery, requesting injunctive relief against Thomas Gibbons
1818, 21 October	Chancellor James Kent issues a temporary injunction against Thomas Gibbons's navigation of the Hudson River
1818, 18 December	Gibbons's attorneys appear in case
1819, 1 August (?)	Gibbons's attorneys file an answer on his behalf
1819, 10 September	Gibbons's attorneys move to dissolve injunction and dismiss the case for failure to prosecute
1819, 6 October	Chancellor Kent denies motion to dismiss, and because the case was at issue, submits an opinion denying that the federal Coasting Licensing Act conferred any rights on Gibbons
1820, January	Court of impeachment and errors affirms Chancellor Kent's decree
1821, 15 March	U.S. Supreme Court declines to hear Thomas Gibbons's appeal from the decision of the New York court of impeachment and errors, reasoning that Chancellor Kent's decree was not a final order, and thus not appealable
1822, 22 January	On formal hearing before Chancellor Kent and its affirmation by the New York court of impeachment and errors, the case of *Gibbons v. Ogden* is appealed to the U.S. Supreme Court
1824, 4 February	Arguments begin with presentation by Daniel Webster, counsel for Thomas Gibbons
1824, 4–5 February	Thomas J. Oakley argues on behalf of Aaron Ogden and the Livingston–Fulton monopoly
1824, 7–9 February	Thomas Addis Emmet continues argument on behalf of Aaron Ogden and the Livingston–Fulton monopoly
1824, 9 February	William Wirt closes argument on behalf of the appellant, Thomas Gibbons
1824, 19 February	Chief Justice Marshall falls on ice and dislocates his shoulder
1824, 2 March	Marshall announces the Court's opinion; Associate Justice William Johnson files a concurring opinion.

BIBLIOGRAPHICAL ESSAY

Note from the Series Editors: The following bibliographical essay contains the major primary and secondary sources the author consulted for this volume. We have asked all authors in the series to omit formal citations in order to make our volumes more readable, inexpensive, and appealing for students and general readers. In adopting this format, Landmark Law Cases and American Society follows the precedent of a number of highly regarded and widely consulted series.

This essay is intended to serve as a guide to the source materials used in the preparation of this volume, and as an introduction to some particularly valuable material available concerning the background, litigation, and subsequent importance of *Gibbons v. Ogden* in American law and life.

Maurice G. Baxter, *The Steamboat Monopoly:* Gibbons v. Ogden, *1824* (New York: Alfred A. Knopf, 1972), continues to provide an outstanding discussion of the background of *Gibbons* and a reliable chronology of the progress of litigation. Unfortunately, and as discussed in the Introduction, it did not benefit from the newer discoveries that have been made concerning decision making in the U.S. Supreme Court and personal relationships among the justices. Last year, legal history was fortunate to have this void filled with the publication of the exhaustive research on *Gibbons* conducted by Thomas H. Cox: Gibbons v. Ogden, *Law, and Society in the Early Republic* (Athens: Ohio University Press, 2009). As its title suggests, this volume brings a new law and society perspective to bear on the Steamboat Case, and it also explores in detail the complex set of business, economic, and personal relationships that affected the litigation in New York courts and continued to influence its appeals to the Supreme Court of the United States.

Two other sources are essential to understanding modern scholarly analysis of the case critical to the author's interpretation of the *Gibbons* story. They are G. Edward White, *The Marshall Court and Cultural Change, 1815–1835*, volumes 3 and 4 in one volume of *The Oliver Wendell Holmes Devise History of the Supreme Court of the United States*, edited by Paul A. Freund and Stanley N. Katz (New York: Macmillan, 1988); and David P. Currie, *The Constitution in the Supreme Court: The First Hundred Years, 1789–1888* (Chicago: University of Chicago Press, 1985). Both have been mined deeply for historical details as well as for a wealth of interpretive insights, and their contributions are obvious throughout all of the chapters of this volume. However, readers are cautioned that in some vital respects, my conclusions are contrary to the interpretations of these distinguished scholars, certainly at my own risk.

More than four decades of work on the career of John Marshall, focused largely on his role as chief justice of the United States Supreme Court, has affected my interpretation of *Gibbons v. Ogden* and the materials in this volume. Research on Marshall Court decision making, Court administration, and relationships between the justices has been earlier detailed in George L. Haskins and Herbert A. Johnson, *Foundations of Power—John Marshall, 1801–1815*, volume 2, *The Oliver Wendell Holmes Devise History of the Supreme Court of the United States*, edited by Paul A. Freund (New York: Macmillan, 1981), and *The Chief Justiceship of John Marshall, 1801–35* (Columbia: University of South Carolina Press, 1997). Consideration of *Gibbons v. Ogden* as a turning point in Marshall's style of Court leadership appears in "John Marshall," *Milestone Documents of American Leaders*, edited by Paul L. Finkelman (Dallas: Schlager Group, 2009), 3:1462–1483; the shift to a mediatorial role is also touched on in "Federal Union, Property, and the Contract Clause: John Marshall's Thought in Light of *Sturges v. Crowninshield* and *Ogden v. Saunders*," in *John Marshall's Achievement: Law, Politics and Constitutional Interpretations*, edited by Thomas C. Shevory (Westport, Conn.: Greenwood Press, 1989), 33–55.

Writing on the broad sweep of political and constitutional history, one relies heavily on the precise work of biographers. Careful studies provide invaluable insight into the personalities of individuals and become a strong basis on which it is possible to build a more accurate picture of group dynamics and decision making that is so important in Supreme Court history. That is always the case, but it was particularly true of the eventful and formative era under the leadership of Chief Justice John Marshall.

On Marshall, Francis N. Stites provides a brief and reliable introduction in *John Marshall: Defender of the Constitution* (Boston: Little, Brown, 1981), but the definitive biography of Chief Justice Marshall is now R. Kent Newmyer, *John Marshall and the Heroic Age of the Supreme Court* (Baton Rouge: Louisiana State University Press, 2001), with the *Gibbons* discussion at 302–315. It replaces Albert J. Beveridge, *The Life of John Marshall*, 4 volumes (Boston: Houghton Mifflin, 1916–1919); the still-useful *Gibbons* discussion is at 4:397–461. Senator Beveridge's text reflects a strong pro-nationalist bias that has not survived the work of more recent scholars, and this monograph forms part of a much larger body of work that challenges Beveridge's adulatory view of Chief Justice Marshall. It also questions the degree to which Marshall was able to dominate his colleagues on the Court. However, Beveridge continues to provide useful details and a comprehensive grasp of legendary and anecdotal material on the chief justice that tends to be ignored by later writers. There are also two careful modern biographies of Marshall: Leonard Baker, *John Marshall: A Life in Law* (New York: Macmillan, 1974), and Jean Edward Smith, *John Marshall: Definer of a Nation* (New York: Henry Holt, 1996).

The text of the chief justice's opinion, with a careful editorial introduction, appears in *The Papers of John Marshall*, edited by Charles F. Hobson, 12 volumes (Chapel Hill: University of North Carolina Press, 1974–2006), 10:7–34. An extremely valuable study of Marshall's thought and jurisprudence, based on Hobson's editorial work on the Marshall Papers project, is Charles F. Hobson, *The Great Chief Justice: John Marshall and the Rule of Law* (Lawrence: University Press of Kansas, 1996); an earlier study also devoted to Marshall's political and legal theory is Robert K. Faulkner, *The Jurisprudence of John Marshall* (Princeton: Princeton University Press, 1968).

Two summaries of Marshall's life and views on the commerce clause provide useful contrasting interpretations. They are George L. Haskins, "John Marshall and the Commerce Clause of the Constitution," *University of Pennsylvania Law Review* 104 (1955): 23–37, and William W. Crosskey, "John Marshall and the Constitution," *University of Chicago Law Review* 23 (1956): 377–397, which takes an interesting revisionist view.

On Justice Joseph Story, R. Kent Newmyer, *Supreme Court Justice Joseph Story: Statesman of the Old Republic* (Chapel Hill: University of North Carolina Press, 1985); Gerald T. Dunne, *Justice Joseph Story and the Rise of the Supreme Court* (New York: Simon and Schuster, 1970); and James McClellan, *Joseph Story and the American Constitution: A Study in Political and Legal Thought with Selected Writings* (Norman: University of Oklahoma Press, 1971), are valuable analyses of the life and judicial contributions of the justice who undoubtedly stood closest to Marshall during their time together on the Court.

Justice William Johnson has long been known to us through the path-breaking monograph of Donald G. Morgan, *Justice William Johnson, the First Dissenter: The Career and Constitutional Philosophy of a Jeffersonian Judge* (Columbia: University of South Carolina Press, 1954). This volume is a classic in the field of constitutional history, providing for the first time a comprehensive understanding of a justice who frequently found himself in opposition to his colleagues, but who nevertheless withstood the importunities of former president Thomas Jefferson, who appointed him to the Supreme Court. Unfortunately, no modern biographer has undertaken a book-length study of a man who played a crucial, although at times disruptive, role on the Marshall Court. My analysis of secondary materials on Johnson, with citations to the article-length literature, appears in Herbert A. Johnson, "The Constitutional Thought of William Johnson," *South Carolina Historical Magazine* 89 (1988): 132–145; also of value is Sandra F. VanBurkleo, "In Defense of 'Public Reason': Supreme Court Justice William Johnson," *Journal of Supreme Court History* 32 (2007): 115–132.

A second associate justice who deserves careful attention is Bushrod Washington, a close supporter of Marshall while both were on the Supreme Court bench, and also the chief justice's collaborator in his five-volume *Life of George Washington*. Justice Washington has benefitted from careful scholarly attention in James R. Stoner Jr., "Heir Apparent: Bushrod Washington and Federal Justice in the Early Republic," in *Seriatum: The Supreme Court before John Marshall*, edited by Scott D. Gerber (New York: New York University Press, 1998). For a closer consideration of Justice Washington's work on the Court and his association with the chief justice, see Herbert A. Johnson, "Bushrod Washington," *Vanderbilt Law Review* 62 (2009): 447–490.

Arguably, commercial activity is as old as the recorded history of the human race, but certainly it predates the ratification of the federal Constitution in 1787–1788. Some background treatment is necessary, not merely to provide a solid foundation for the discussion that follows, but also to identify those patterns of thought and experience that shaped contemporary public opinion concerning the regulation of foreign and interstate commerce and its relationship to federalism and the national union. In the interest of brevity, the discussion has been limited to the colonial period of American history, the commercial problems that beset the United States under the Articles of Confederation, and the drafting and ratification process of the federal Constitution.

Richard B. Morris, *The Forging of the Union, 1781–1789* (New York: Harper and Row, 1982), provides a good summary of the political and legal developments from the end of the Revolution through the adoption of the federal Constitution. For commercial regulation in the British empire in the American colonial period, see Lawrence A. Harper, *English Navigation Acts: A Seventeenth-Century Experiment in Social Engineering* (New York: Columbia University Press, 1939; reprint, New York: Octagon Books, 1964). Still indispensable for an understanding of the law and commercial relations in the period 1776 to 1789 are Merrill Jensen's two monographs, *The Articles of Confederation: An Interpretation of the Social-Constitutional History of the American Revolution, 1774–1781* (Madison: University of Wisconsin Press, 1940), and *The New Nation: A History of the United States during the Confederation, 1781–1789* (New York: Alfred A. Knopf, 1950). There is a good discussion of economic issues during the Confederation period in Janet A. Riesman, "Money, Credit and Federalist Political Economy," in *Beyond Confederation: Origins of the Constitution and American National Identity*, edited by Richard Beeman et al. (Chapel Hill: University of North Carolina Press, 1987), 128–161.

When dealing with the political and constitutional antecedents of the federal Constitution, I have placed reliance on Edward S. Corwin, "The Progress of Constitutional Theory between the Declaration of Independence and the Meeting of the Philadelphia Convention," *American Historical Review* 30 (1925): 511–536, conveniently reprinted in *The Formation and Ratification of the Constitution: Major Historical Interpretations*, edited by Kermit L. Hall (New York: Garland, 1987), 113–138. Forrest McDonald's *Novus Ordo Seclorum: The Intel-*

lectual Origins of the Constitution (Lawrence: University Press of Kansas, 1985), neatly combines political and economic history with a summary of early American political theory.

Among the vast body of writing concerning the Philadelphia convention and subsequent debates and ratifying conventions, I have found Carol Berkin, *A Brilliant Solution: Inventing the American Constitution* (New York: Harcourt, 2002), and David O. Stewart, *The Summer of 1787: The Men Who Invented the Constitution* (New York: Simon and Schuster, 2007), to be valuable quick reads for familiarization, as is the shorter treatment in Leonard W. Levy's introduction to *Essays on the Making of the Constitution*, edited by Leonard W. Levy (New York: Oxford University Press, 1969). The standard scholarly accounts are Charles Warren, *The Making of the Constitution* (Cambridge, Mass.: Harvard University Press, 1937; reprint, New York: Barnes & Noble, 1967); Max Farrand, *The Framing of the Constitution of the United States* (New Haven, Conn.: Yale University Press, 1962; originally published in 1913); and Carl Van Doren, *The Story of the Making and Ratification of the Constitution of the United States* (New York: Viking Press, 1948). Because there was no commerce clause consideration on the floor of the convention, views of the delegates have been drawn from *The Founders' Constitution*, edited by Philip B. Kurland and Ralph Lerner, 5 volumes (Chicago: University of Chicago Press, 1987), especially 2:477–528. Also of value is *The Constitution and the States: The Role of the Original Thirteen in the Framing and Adoption of the Federal Constitution*, edited by Patrick T. Conley and John P. Kaminski (Madison, Wis.: Madison House, 1988). A printed edition of sources dealing with drafting and ratifying the Constitution is available in volume 1 of the *Documentary History of the Ratification of the Constitution* (Madison: State Historical Society of Wisconsin, 1976). There are numerous editions of the *Federalist Papers*. One of the best is *The Federalist*, edited by Jacob E. Cooke (Middleton, Conn.: Wesleyan University Press, 1961).

The history of technology, invention, and governmental support through monopolies and patents is a fascinating but relatively little-studied area. Driven as much by a quest for fame as by a search for financial rewards, the path to success in invention has been a rocky route to either goal. In part this is due to the nature of the American patent system and the resulting litigation in federal courts; but it is also attributable to the relatively short term of federal patent protection and the need not only to design a practical application for the invention, but also to assemble adequate capital to finance widespread production and marketing. In regard to steamboat navigation, this already difficult task was complicated by two factors: the emergence of state-originated monopolies to reward successful inventors, and the prior existence of federal provisions making patent protection available to inventors as well as rules and regulations issued concerning foreign and interstate commerce.

There is a good summary of the importance of the steamboat for river transportation in Robert C. Post, *Technology, Transport, and Travel in American History* (Washington, D.C.: American Historical Association and Society for the History of Technology, 2003), 33–41. On the Fulton–Livingston relationship, George Dangerfield, *Chancellor Robert R. Livingston of New York, 1746–1813* (New York: Harcourt, Brace, 1960), is valuable, as is Cynthia Owen Phillip, *Robert Fulton: A Biography* (New York: Franklin Watts, 1985). Andrea Sutcliffe, *Steam: The Untold Story of America's First Great Invention* (New York: Palgrave Macmillan, 2004), provides an excellent summary of the competition among inventors, replacing an earlier book by Alice Sutcliffe, *Robert Fulton* (New York: Macmillan, 1929).

For an exhaustive discussion of steamboat navigation in western waters, Louis C. Hunter, *Steamboats on the Western Rivers: An Economic and Technological History* (Cambridge, Mass.: Harvard University Press, 1949; reprint, New York: Octagon Books, 1969), is indispensable. It provides a thorough explanation of the business and legal ventures and misadventures of the Livingston–Fulton syndicate on the Mississippi River and its tributaries. George Rogers Taylor, *The Transportation Revolution, 1815–1860* (New York: Holt, Rinehart and Winston, 1962, originally published in 1951), remains the classic study of transportation theory and practice for the *Gibbons* era. James W. Ely Jr., *Railroads and American Law* (Lawrence: University Press of Kansas, 2001), carefully details the process by which railroads replaced the steamboat as the primary American transportation system.

A succinct and, for the mathematically unsophisticated reader, readable survey of American economic development is Douglass C. North, *The Economic Growth of the United States, 1790–1860* (New York: W. W. Norton, 1966), 66–121. It stresses the "take off" of American economic development in the wake of the War of 1812 and the shift of American investment emphasis from transoceanic shipping into transcontinental trade and industrialization.

The critically important New York court of impeachment and errors decision in *Livingston v. Van Ingen* is published at 9 Johnson's Reports 507 (N.Y. Court of Impeachment and Errors, 1812). There is an old but still-useful biography of Chancellor James Kent: John T. Horton, *James Kent: A Study in Conservatism, 1763–1847* (New York: D. Appleton Century, 1939; reprint, New York: DaCapo Press, 1969).

Although *Gibbons v. Ogden* was the first commerce clause case to be presented to the U.S. Supreme Court, the circuit courts of the United States had already dealt with these matters. Because the justices of the Supreme Court were required to preside over the trials held in the U.S. circuit courts, many of them were already familiar with many of the issues that would arise in the Court's consideration of *Gibbons*. The text of the various cases, arranged alphabetically, is available in *Federal Cases . . . 1789–1880*, 30 volumes (St. Paul, Minn.: West Publishing, 1894–1898); it is also available on Westlaw in the database for older U.S. district court cases.

The jurisdiction of the lower federal courts and their procedures is treated in George L. Haskins and Herbert A. Johnson, *Foundations of Power: John Marshall, 1801–35*, volume 2 of *The Oliver Wendell Holmes Devise History of the Supreme Court of the United States*, edited by Paul L. Freund (New York: Macmillan, 1981), 373–406, 612–646; many of those conclusions are included in this volume. The *Elkison* case and Justice Johnson are discussed in Morgan, *Justice William Johnson*, 192–202. Justice Bushrod Washington's work on circuit, including a discussion of *Corfield v. Coryell*, is summarized in Herbert A. Johnson, "Bushrod Washington," *Vanderbilt Law Review* 62 (2009): 474–490. Private law litigation supportive of federal commercial regulation is touched on in Herbert A. Johnson, *The Chief Justiceship of John Marshall, 1801–1835* (Columbia: University of South Carolina Press, 1997), 205–216.

Early litigation in *Ogden v. Gibbons* is summarized in Herbert A. Johnson, "*Gibbons v. Ogden* before John Marshall," in *Courts and Law in Early New York: Selected Essays*, edited by Leo Hershkowitz and Milton M. Klein (Port Washington, N.Y.: Kennikat Press, 1978), 105–113, 147–148. A more detailed discussion, including related cases in both New York and other state courts, is available in Thomas H. Cox, Gibbons v. Ogden, *Law, and Society*, 44–132. Cases in the *Gibbons v. Ogden* chain are *Gibbons v. Ogden*, 17 Johnson's Reports 488 (Court of Impeachment and Errors, 1820), which embodies Chancellor Kent's decree in the chancery court below; *Gibbons v. Ogden*, 19 U.S. (6 Wheaton) 449–450 (1821); and *Gibbons v. Ogden*, 22 U.S. (9 Wheaton) 1–240 (1824).

Cohens v. Virginia is reported at 19 U.S. (6 Wheaton) 264–448 (1821).

Cox, Gibbons v. Ogden, *Law, and Society*, 251–269, provides a careful description of the oral arguments of all attorneys, expanding on the cursory discussion by Beveridge, *Life of John Marshall*, 4:424–428. White's discussion of oral argument, in *The Marshall Court and Cultural Change*, 285–289, is balanced and excellent. Counsels' arguments are reported in detail at 22 U.S. (9 Wheaton) 1, 3–186 (1824); because the printed reports are the only evidence we have of these presentations, they may raise questions concerning their accuracy and their impact on the justices.

Supporting documentation is available in *The Papers of Daniel Webster, Legal Papers*, volume 3, *The Federal Practice*, part 1, edited by Andrew J. King (Hanover, N.H.: University Press of New England, 1989), 255–291. Maurice G. Baxter, *Daniel Webster and the Supreme Court* (Amherst: University of Massachusetts Press, 1966), provides a good, but perhaps overly laudatory, discussion of Webster's argument at 195–226. Galen V. Thorp, "William Wirt," *Journal of Supreme Court History* 33 (2008): 223–303, provides the best analysis to date of William Wirt's practice and his participation in *Gibbons*. Unfortunately, neither Thomas J. Oakley nor Thomas Addis Emmet has received similar coverage.

Chief Justice Marshall's opinion is reported at 22 U.S. (9 Wheaton) 1, 186–222 (1824); it is followed by the concurring opinion of Justice Johnson at 222–240. Felix Frankfurter's essay on Marshall's opinion for the Court still deserves attention; see Felix Frankfurter, *The Commerce Clause under Marshall, Taney and Waite* (Chicago: Quadrangle Paperbacks, 1964; reprint, Chapel Hill: University of North Carolina Press, 1937), 11–45. Thomas P. Campbell Jr., "Chancellor Kent, Chief Justice Marshall, and the Steamboat Cases," *Syracuse Law Review* 25 (1974): 497–534, provides a careful comparison of the views of Kent and Marshall. On Smith Thompson, the justice who missed taking part in *Gibbons* but who might have influenced the result, see Donald M. Roper, *Justice Smith Thompson* (New York: Garland, 1987), and Gerald T. Dunne, "Smith Thompson," in *The Justices of the United States Supreme Court, 1789–1969: Their Lives and Major Opinions*, edited by Leon Friedman and Fred L. Israel, 5 volumes (New York: Chelsea House, 1969), 1:475–492.

Secondary material on *Gibbons* is immense. Norman R. Williams, "Gibbons," *New York University Law Review* 79 (2004): 1398–1472, is excellent, as is Randy E. Barnett, "The Original Meaning of the Commerce Clause," *University of Chicago Law Review* 68 (2001): 101–147, which provides a classical liberal view and advocates a narrower construction of the term *commerce* than that used by Marshall in *Gibbons*.

There is a growing body of literature on the internal dynamics of the Supreme Court in the Marshall era and the functions of the chief justice. Of particular value are Robert G. Seddig, "John Marshall and the Origins of Supreme Court Leadership," *University of Pittsburgh Law Review* 36 (1975): 785–833; G. Edward White, "The Internal Powers of the Chief Justice: The Nineteenth-Century Legacy," *University of Pennsylvania Law Review* 154 (2006): 1463–1510; and Charles F. Hobson, "Defining the Office: John Marshall as Chief Justice," *University of Pennsylvania Law Review* 154 (2006): 1421–1461.

The implications of *Gibbons* for the internal slave trade debate are exhaustively covered in David L. Lightner, *Slavery and the Commerce Power: How the Struggle against the Interstate Slave Trade Led to the Civil War* (New Haven, Conn.: Yale University Press, 2006). Lightner, a historian, successfully contests the assertions of Walter Berns, a political scientist, who asserted that the commerce clause, coupled with the language of the clause permitting abolition of the international slave trade in 1808, authorized Congress to abolish the interstate slave trade. Also useful in regard to *Gibbons* and the interstate slave trade is Earl M. Maltz, *Slavery and the Supreme Court, 1825–1861* (Lawrence: University Press of Kansas, 2009), which correctly points out that the Marshall Court and its successors before the 1857 decision of the *Dred Scott* case approached slavery decisions, including matters involving the interstate slave trade, on the basis of constitutional doctrine rather than political considerations. It is unfortunate that Maltz's treatment of *Gibbons* was not more exhaustive.

The *North River Steam Boat Company* case is reported at 3 Cowen's Reports 713–729 (Court of Impeachment and Errors, 1825); *Brown v. Maryland* is reported at 25 U.S. (12 Wheaton) 419–461 (1827); *Willson v. Black Bird Creek Marsh Company* is reported at 27 U.S. (2 Peters) 245–252 (1829).

Robert L. Clinton gives us a good description of the continuing impact of *Gibbons* while discussing differing approaches to judicial review in the Marshall Court and its successors in "Judicial Review, Nationalism, and the Commerce Clause: Contrasting Antebellum and Post Bellum Supreme Court Decision Making," *Political Research Quarterly* 47 (1994): 857–876. Old and elusive articles that are illuminating are Robert E. Cushman, "National Police Power under the Commerce Clause of the Constitution," *Minnesota Law Review* 3 (1919): 289–319, 381–412, and Clyde B. Aitchison, "The Evolution of the Interstate Commerce Act," *George Washington Law Review* 6 (1937): 289–403. The overall role of the Supreme Court in economic regulation is well covered in Arthur S. Miller, *The Supreme Court in American Capitalism* (New York: Free Press, 1968).

The literature on the century between Marshall's death in 1835 and the 1935–1937 confrontation between the Franklin D. Roosevelt administration and the Hughes Court is extensive. John E. Nowak and Ronald D. Rotunda provide a brief description in *Constitutional Law*, 6th edition (St. Paul, Minn.: West Publishing, 2000), 312–316, as does Laurence H. Tribe, *American Constitutional Law*, 3rd edition (New York: Foundation Press, 2000), 1:807–811. Contemporary scholarly criticism of the Supreme Court's pre-1937 stance was led by Princeton professor Edward S. Corwin in *The Commerce Power versus States' Rights: "Back to the Constitution"* (Princeton: Princeton University Press, 1936; reprint, Gloucester: Peter Smith, 1962), and in his subsequent appreciation of the "Revolution of 1937" entitled *Court over Constitution: A Study of Judicial Review as an Instrument of Popular Government* (Princeton: Princeton University Press, 1938). Scholarly historical treatments of the crisis include William E. Leuchtenburg, *The Supreme Court Reborn: The Constitutional Revolution in the Age of Roosevelt* (New York: Oxford University Press, 1995), especially 82–179, 213–237; Barry Cushman, *Rethinking the New Deal Court: The Structure of a Constitutional Revolution* (New York: Oxford University Press, 1998); and William G. Ross, *The Chief Justiceship of Charles Evans Hughes, 1930–1941* (Columbia: University of South Carolina Press, 2007).

Debate over the Rehnquist Court's limitation of commerce clause application is also extensive. Two good examples are John T. Valauri, "The Clothes Have No Emperor, or Cabining the Commerce Clause," *San Diego Law Review* 41 (2004): 405–440; admitting to the status of an "Old Federalist," Valauri argues that in the wake of *Lopez* and *Morrison*, the Court should return to Marshallian basics; perhaps his wish was granted in *Raich*. By way of contrast, see Ashley Dean, "The Untimely Death of the Commerce Clause: *Gonzalez v. Raich*'s Threat to Federalism, the Democratic Process and Individual Rights and Liberties," *Temple Politics and Civil Rights Law Review* 18 (2008): 213–252.

Cases cited in the last two chapters but not identified above are as follows:

Champion v. Ames, 188 U.S. 321 (1903)
Cooley v. Board of Wardens, 53 U.S. (12 Howard) 299 (1851)
Gonzalez v. Raich, 545 U.S. 1 (2005)
Hammer v. Dagenhart, 247 U.S. 251 (1918)
Hoke v. U.S., 227 U.S. 308 (1913)
Houston E. & W. Texas Ry Co. v. U.S., 234 U.S. 342 (1914)
Northern Securities Co. v. U.S., 193 U.S. 197 (1904)
Schechter Poultry Co. v. U.S., 285 U.S. 495 (1935)
Shreveport Rate Cases, see *Houston E. & W. Texas Ry Co. v. U.S.*, above
Swift & Co. v. U.S., 196 U.S. 375 (1905)
U.S. v. Caminetti, 242 U.S. 470 (1917)
U.S. v. E.C. Knight Co., 156 U.S. 1 (1895)
U.S. v. Lopez, 514 U.S. 549 (1995)
U.S. v. Morrison, 529 U.S. 598 (2000)
Wickhard v. Filburn, 317 U.S. 111 (1942)

INDEX

aboriginal powers. *See* residual
   powers
Active (boat), 47. *See also* embargo
   acts
aggregation, 163–64, 167
Agricultural Adjustment Act, 164
A.L.A. Schechter v. U.S. See
   Schechter v. U.S.
appellate advocacy, 74, 85–87, 92,
   101
   reading the court, 88, 102
Articles of Confederation
   boundary disputes, 15
   foreign commerce, 51
   interstate cooperation, 14, 15–16
   limited federal powers, 15
   privileges and immunities, 50, 77
   state initiatives, 14, 15–17
Australia, Commonwealth of,
   171–72

bankruptcy clause, 4, 108–10
Bellona (steamboat), 67
Black Bird Creek, 154, 156
boundary disputes, 15
British debts, 128–29, 150
British Parliament and trade
      balances
   hat act (1732), 11
   iron act (1750 and 1757), 11
Brown v. Maryland, 81, 148–54
   clarifying *Gibbons*, 148–49
Burr, Aaron, 56–57

California's Compassionate Use
      Act, 166
Canada, Dominion of, 170–71
Champion v. Ames, 162
chancery, court of (N.Y.), 1
   appearances in, 57–58
   injunctive relief in, 30
   practice, 57–58

property rights in, 31
transfer to federal courts, 57–58
child labor, 162
Coasting Licensing Act, federal
      (1793), 1, 47, 56, 58–59, 70, 75,
      77, 78, 80, 84, 122, 126–27, 134,
      142
   congressional intent, 127
   foreign relations and, 123, 125–26
   insignificance of, 122–23, 126
   legislative history, 90
   licensing under, 110, 112, 136–37
   Livingston–Fulton monopoly
      and, 135
   property rights and, 77–78, 90,
      126, 140, 142
   taxation, 90
   war powers and, 123
coasting trade, 144
Cohens v. Virginia, 61–65, 70, 138
Coke, Sir Edward, 6
commerce, 97, 143, 144, 161
   chain of, 151, 163
   defined, 114, 145
   Federalist Papers and, 22, 24
   foreign relations and, 24, 51–52,
      128
   higher branches, 72, 117–18
   history of, 10–14, 66
   interstate and foreign, 46–47,
      50–51, 115–16, 149
   laissez faire approach to, 18
   local advantages and burdens, 13,
      17, 20–21, 24–25
   manufacturing and, 162
   navigation as, 46–47, 48–49, 114
   passenger, distinction from cargo,
      123, 134
   Philadelphia convention and,
      19–22, 135
   slave trade and, 20–21, 49
   territorial expansion and, 16, 39

commerce clause, 151
  "among," significance of, 115, 135
  Coasting Licensing Act (1793)
    and, 35
  Cohens v. Virginia and, 62–63
  construction of, 33–34, 150–51,
    160–62
  domestic and foreign aspects,
    115–16
  economic analysis, 67, 150–51,
    163–64
  embargo acts, 44–46
  exceptions from, 33, 114
  exclusive construction, 92–93,
    94–95, 112, 132
  general policy applications, 46,
    131–32
  geographical construction of, 34,
    67–68, 133–34, 135, 142–44, 162,
    163
  internal trade excluded, 83–84,
    116, 133, 153, 163, 168, 169
  legislative history of, 87–88,
    89–90
  licensing importers, 148–50
  necessary and proper clause
    application to, 168
  New Deal and, 162–64
  non-intercourse acts, 44–45
  territorial construction, 162–63
  uniformity of interpretation, 62,
    63, 66–67
commerce power, 74, 165
  augmentation by state law, 33–34,
    74, 87–88, 116–17, 135
  channels of, 99, 151, 163
  complexity of regulation, 90–91,
    93, 100, 116–18, 135–36
  concurrent, 32–34, 74–76, 78,
    100–101, 109–10, 122, 124, 125
  dormancy, 109–10, 121–22, 125–26,
    133, 143, 155–56, 160
  economic impact, 133–34, 156, 162
  exclusive, 48, 51, 56, 73, 76, 80,
    125
  "first tier" importance, 136

  fundamental, 135–36
  goods, distinction from
    passenger, 84, 113–14
  reserved state powers, 121, 156,
    161
  residual state powers, 120–21, 161
  state and federal
    interconnections, 99, 100,
    115–16, 120–21, 132–33, 135–36,
    146–47, 156
  substantial impact on, 164, 165,
    166, 167
commercial chaos, 76. *See also*
  Confederation period
commercial regulation
  balancing in, 156
  complexity, 100, 103, 116–17, 119,
    125, 137, 158
  dilemma of, 116
  federalism and, 45, 87, 99–100
  historical, 10–18
  sources of power, 118–19, 127–28
  uniformity of, 110
common market, 24–25, 135, 159,
  169–73
Compassionate Use Act
  (California), 166
Comprehensive Drug Abuse
  Prevention and Control Act
  (1970), 166, 167
  concurring opinions and, 124,
    167–68
  decision making and, 124
  See also Controlled Substances
    Act (CSA)
Confederation congress, 26–27
Confederation period, 34, 75, 83,
  128–29, 149. *See also* "critical
  period" *under* United States
Congress (U.S.)
  authority over foreign trade,
    152
  investigations, 164, 167–68
  judicial deference, 169
  plenary commerce power, 163
  restraints on, 136

federal court jurisdiction, 53–54
    certificate of division, 53, 108
    certiorari, 52
    choice of, 53–54
    diversity of citizenship, 30, 53, 56
    party to action, 62
    patents and, 30
    procedure, 52–53, 57
    transfer to federal courts, 56–58
federalism
    Articles of Confederation and, 12–13
    balance in, 49, 157
    Gibbons and, 138–39, 174–75
    sovereignty allocation, 137
    state commercial competition, 97
    U.S. Constitution and, 18–19, 168–69
Federalist papers
    commerce and, 22, 23–24, 90, 154
    constitutional construction, 90–91
    residual powers, 154
    supremacy and, 83
federal powers
    concurrent, 33, 80–82, 84–85, 118, 119
    electoral limits on, 136
    express, 80, 147
    implied, 80
    incidental, 143, 147
    national, 80
    state boundaries and, 80
    strict construction of, 81, 82
    See also preemption
Fifteenth Amendment, 5
Fitch, John, 26–28
Fletcher v. Peck, 93
foreign affairs, state interference with, 44–46, 128–29, 149–50
Fourteenth Amendment, 5
Franklin, Benjamin, 26
free market adjustments, 17–18
Fulton, Robert, 1, 27–30, 35

Gibbons, Thomas, 1, 8, 28–29, 35, 39, 42, 52, 55–58, 59, 75, 91, 92, 105, 112, 123, 126, 131
Gibbons v. Ogden
    economic impact, 39–42
    guide for commercial regulation, 5, 159–60
    historiography of, 1–5
    international application of, 169–74
    litigation strategy, 55–57
    precedent value, 159, 162
    shaping federalism discussion, 159
    subsequent history, 5–6
Gibbons vs. Ogden, opinion of the Court in, 124, 125
    ambiguity of, 104, 124, 132
    authorship, 105
    compromise, 129
    consensus driven, 128
    delayed, 104–05
    double pleading in, 121–22
    foreign trade, 104
    Johnson's concurring opinion, 124–28
    political considerations, 130–31
    state commercial initiatives in, 133
    structure, 111–12
    supremacy and Johnson opinion, 125–28
Gonzalez v. Raich, 166–68
Green v. Biddle, 93, 98, 130–31

Hall, Dominick Augustus, 38
Hamilton, Alexander, 17, 18, 23, 24, 33
Hammer v. Dagenhart, 162
harbor pilots, 120–21
high court of errors and appeals (Del.), 155
historiography (historical interpretation), 1–5
A History of the Colonies Planted by the English on the Continent of North America . . ., 66
copyright protection, 81

Hoffman, Josiah Ogden, 68
Hoke v. U.S., 162
Houston v. Moore, 89
Hughes, Charles Evans, 163

inspection laws, 135, 152
international affairs, 5, 62, 104,
    125–26
ius privatum, 145, 147
ius publicum, 145, 147

Jay treaty (1794), 15, 129, 150
Jefferson, Thomas, 125, 127
Johnson, William, 4, 63, 107
    concurring opinion in *Gibbons*,
        106, 124–28
    dormancy, 106
    exclusivity, 125, 126
    foreign trade, 125–26
    health and inspection laws, 127
    Jefferson, Thomas, and, 125, 127
    nationalism, 125
    police powers, 128
    states' rights, 127
    supremacy in Court opinion,
        125–28
    See also *Elkison v. Deliesseline*
Jones, Samuel, Jr., 68
judicial review, 6, 46–47, 131, 172
justiciability, 95

Kent, James
    becomes chancellor, 55
    Coasting Licensing Act, 70
    dormancy, 32, 35
    exclusive federal powers, 33, 34–35
    federalism, 32–33
    injunctive relief, 31
    partiality to Livingston–Fulton,
        56
    reputation of, 31–32
Kentucky statehood, 130–31

laissez faire regulation, 18
Lansing, John, 30–31
"law and society" approach, 2

legislative history, 89–90
limited government, 136
litigation, 39, 42–43
Livingston, Brockholst, 30, 61
Livingston, John R., 140, 142
Livingston, Robert R., 1, 27, 28, 29,
    35, 37, 61
Livingston–Fulton partnership
    contract clause and, 93
    Fitch rights received, 27–28
    formation of, 27
    monopoly, 36, 139
    patent rights, 69
    state safety incentives and, 82
    See also mootness
Livingston v. Van Ingen, 30–35
    commerce clause and, 55
    economic consequences, 36–37
    precedent in *Gibbons*, 55–56,
        68–69, 79–80
    state sovereignty, 52
    Thompson, Smith, and, 60, 75,
        151–52

Madison, James, 17, 24
Marbury v. Madison, 6
Marshall, John
    British debt cases, 128–29
    commerce power, 49
    direct collision, 88–89
    as dissenter, 6, 110
    dormancy, 35, 110, 122, 126, 128,
        155–56, 157–58, 160
    efficacy of government, 113, 117,
        124
    and health and inspection laws,
        127
    Kentucky land speculations, 130
    leadership roles, 4–5, 105–07,
        131–32, 156–57
    shoulder injury of, 105
    states' rights, 49
    use of words and definitions, 92,
        105
    writing characteristics, 105
Marshall, The Papers of John, 3

Martin v. Hunter's Lessee, 62
Massachusetts, 15
Mayor of the City of New York v.
  Miln, 157–58
McCulloch v. Maryland, 51, 52, 64,
  98, 107, 111, 152, 154
mercantilism, 10–12, 69, 97
militia, 118
Miln v. New York, 158
Mississippi River, 37–38, 40, 84
monopoly
  economically dangerous, 76
  Gibbons and, 138
  Jacksonian democracy and, 42
  Livingston–Fulton, 1, 37, 38, 93
  Orleans territorial grant, 36,
    38
  patents contrasted with, 33–34
  Philadelphia convention, 26
  political issue, 35–36
  repeal petitions, 29, 40
  state boundaries and, 40
  steamboat navigation, 55
  western opposition to, 36
Monroe, James, 27
mootness
  Livingston–Fulton patent, 91,
    95–96
  patents and state monopolies,
    123–24

Napoleonic wars, 44
National Labor Relations Board v.
  Jones & Laughlin Steel
  Corporation, 163, 164
natural law
  ius commune and commerce, 84
  navigational rights, 68
  property rights in, 31
navigation
  common law right of, 155
  passenger transport as, 113–14
navigation acts, 11
necessary and proper clause, 108,
  165, 168
negotiable instruments, 100

New Deal constitutional revolution,
  160, 162–64
New Jersey, retaliatory laws, 29, 34,
  75
New Orleans, battle of, 38
non-intercourse acts, 44
Northern Securities Company v. U.S.,
  161
North River Steamboat Company,
  35–39, 139
North River Steamboat Company v.
  Livingston, 139–45

Oakley, Thomas J., 72–73
  argument, 78–85
  catalog, constitutional powers,
    78–79, 81
Oakley–Emmet team
  research and preparation by,
    102–03
  strategy of, 78–79
  underestimated, 101
O'Connor, Sandra Day, 168
Ogden, Aaron, 1, 28–29, 42, 52, 54,
  55, 56, 58, 60, 78, 124
Ogden v. Saunders, 109–10, 156–57
Olive Branch (steamboat), 139, 144
opinion of the court, 6–7
originalism
  Federalist and, 33, 90–91, 154
  Gibbons and, 137
  ratifying convention debates and,
    33, 90
original package doctrine, 17, 150–51
Orleans territory monopoly
  Livingston–Fulton grant, 36, 38,
    40
  Mississippi River navigation free,
    38
  Ohio towns protest, 40

patent clause, 26, 56
  concurrency, 79–80
  exclusivity of, 81
  ignored, 123–24
  limited scope, 91–92

194

pre-existing rights and, 91
reserved powers and, 79
state patenting power, 81–82
patents (U.S.)
English practice contrasted, 92
federal cause of action, 92
narrow limits, 33–34, 82
property rights, 91, 92
short term, 95
state monopolies and, 31–32, 81–82
use of, 67–68, 82–83
value of, 29–30
See also mootness
peace treaty, 13, 127–28, 150
Pennsylvania
boundary disputes, 15
retaliatory legislation, 34
Philadelphia convention, 114
commerce and, 19, 75–76, 89–90,
133
committee on detail, 19–20
economic cooperation, 20–21,
133–34
heat wave, 19–20
steamboat exhibition, 26
Pinkney, William, 60–61
Platt, Jonas, 59, 68–70, 78
Potomac River, 16–17
powers, concurrent, 80–81
taxes and, 81, 135
precedent
Gibbons as, 159
Livingston v. Van Ingen, as, 31,
79–80
preemption
actual and practical collision, 81,
123, 140
nature of federal power, 81,
116–17
permissible state initiatives, 117
sources of power, differing,
118–19
privileges and immunities clause,
50, 77
fundamental privileges, 146–47
limited application, 147–48

property rights, 18
Coasting Licensing Act and, 78,
126
distinctive character of, 150–51
equitable remedies, 31
license as, 123
Livingston–Fulton monopoly
and, 78
natural law and, 31
public health and welfare, 154–56
public opinion
federal and state balance, 65
Gibbons v. Ogden and, 138–39
judicial review, 157
Livingston–Fulton monopoly, 131
monopolies, 35, 36–38, 40
slavery in, 65
states' rights, 98, 156–57
Supreme Court and, 98
transportation, 38, 40
*Willson v. Black Bird Creek Marsh
Company*, 157

railroads, 41–42, 159
Randolph, John, 137
real property
improvements, 130
occupying claimants, 130
regionalism, 50–51
Rehnquist, William H., 164, 165
repugnancy
collision as, 33, 88
direct collision, 88
immediate and inevitable conflict,
81, 91
reserved powers, federal–state
coordination and, 127, 156–57
residual powers
limited government and, 126–27,
146–47, 155
preferences for, 126
retaliatory laws, 34
threat to union, 75
Revolutionary War
transportation during, 13
unifying impact of, 12–13

Webster, Daniel, 8, 72
  argument, 73–78
  confidence of, 100–101
  dormancy, 126
  "higher branches" argument, 74,
    117–18
  self-assessment, 100–101
  Story, Joseph, and, 105, 106
Webster–Wirt team
  confidence of, 100–101, 106
  preparation, 73, 101–02, 106
  strategy, 72
western river navigation, 37–38
Wheaton, Henry, 98
Wickard v. Filburn, 163–64, 167

William (vessel), 45–47
*Willson v. Black Bird Creek Marsh
  Company*, 154–58
  Gibbons distinguished, 155–56
Wilson v. U.S., 48–49, 50–51
Wirt, William, 8, 60–61, 72, 73
  argument, 94–98
  editing of argument, 98
  heavy caseload of, 102
  Marshall's opinion and, 101
Woodworth, John, 142–43
word definitions, 91, 150

Yates, Joseph, 31